THE ENTREPRENEUR'S INFORMATION SOURCEBOOK

THE ENTREPRENEUR'S INFORMATION SOURCEBOOK

CHARTING THE PATH TO SMALL BUSINESS SUCCESS

Susan C. Awe

LIBRARIES
UNLIMITED
A Member of the Greenwood Publishing Group

Westport, Connecticut • London

Library of Congress Cataloging-in-Publication Data

Awe, Susan C., 1948–
    The entrepreneur's information sourcebook : charting the path to small
business success/by Susan C. Awe.
        p. cm.
    Includes bibliographical references and index.
    ISBN 1–59158–242–3 (pbk.: alk. paper)
1. New business enterprises. 2. Entrepreneurship. I. Title.
HD62.5.A96   2006
658.02′2—dc22   2005036162

British Library Cataloguing in Publication Data is available.

Library of Congress Catalog Card Number: 2005036162
ISBN: 1-59158-242-3

First published in 2006

Libraries Unlimited, 88 Post Road West, Westport, CT 06881
A Member of the Greenwood Publishing Group, Inc.
www.lu.com

Printed in the United States of America

The paper used in this book complies with the
Permanent Paper Standard issued by the National
Information Standards Organization (Z39.48–1984).

10   9   8   7   6   5   4   3   2

62593622

CONTENTS

CONTENTS

ILLUSTRATIONS

ACKNOWLEDGMENTS

I'd like to thank the University of New Mexico University Libraries for giving me the time to research and write this book. And, of course, I thank the staff of UNM's Parish Memorial Library for Business and Economics and Johann van Reenen, all of whom filled in for me while I was on sabbatical.

I want to thank my husband, Steven Maddock, for all his love and support throughout my library career and while working on the book! Chaco, Gretta, and Poudre, my feline assistants, also provided moral support and companionship.

And I am grateful for the help and assistance of Barbara Ittner, Acquisitions Editor at Libraries Unlimited, who has been so enthusiastic about the book from the day she read the first version of the proposal.

INTRODUCTION

"Hitch your wagon to a star."
—Ralph Waldo Emerson

Small business, defined generally by the U.S. Small Business Administration (SBA) as firms with fewer than 500 employees, represent over 99% of all employer firms, create three out of every four new jobs, and employ 51% of all private workers (U.S. SBA Office of Advocacy, *Small Business Economic Indicators for 2003*, published August 2004). Small businesses, i.e., entrepreneurs, through the creation of new companies or expansion, generate virtually all new jobs in the U.S. economy. They also fill niche markets, innovate, increase competition, and provide individuals with a chance to succeed. Small businesses play a vital role in our free-market society.

According to the U.S. Department of Commerce, gross domestic investment for private companies was nearly $1.6 trillion in 2002. In 2005, there are nearly 6 million small businesses with fewer than 100 employees in the United States per the SBA statistics. Small businesses represent 97% of all U.S. exporters. Also, 35% of federal contracts go to small businesses each year, amounting to $53 billion worth of federal contracts in fiscal year 2002.

Now with all this good news about small businesses and how they're thriving, you dream of working for yourself and being your own boss. You should have and probably do have hundreds of questions. Where and how to begin? This book will inform you on what you don't know and why you need to know it to prevent your new enterprise from collapsing before it has a chance for success. You will also learn that you need professional, expert help to effectively and successfully start and run a small business; learn when and how best to ask and receive that assistance.

WHY ANOTHER BOOK ON ENTREPRENEURSHIP?

First remember, many small businesses fail every year. Starting a successful business is not a simple task. Thorough research and planning, resourceful management, and the necessary financial resources are required. Thomas Edison said, "Many of life's failures are people who did not realize how close they were to success when they gave up." Entrepreneurs are often technical experts, but often fail due to a lack of formal training or experience in management practices and principles. A good product or service fails because the owner could not manage people and things or make the change from technical expert to strategic thinker and did not get the assistance he or she needed. Sometimes entrepreneurs are said to be different from business owners because they create a new product, service, or process and a small business owner merely manages, but this book will use the terms interchangeably because all small business owners must innovate daily in the way they run, market, manage, and improve their operations.

This guide will direct you, as an entrepreneur, to the print and Internet resources needed to discover what type of business to open, where to locate it, whether to buy a franchise or not, how to raise capital, how to market and manage, how to work with government agencies, how to analyze the competition, when to get professional assistance, when and how to expand your business, and how to get out.

ORGANIZATION

Chapters are organized by functional areas such as start-up, business planning, marketing, management, franchising, raising capital, and competitive analysis that take you step-by-step through the process of starting, running, and growing a business; the book is designed to get you to the information you need quickly and easily. Subheadings in each chapter highlight important concepts. Each chapter discusses important concepts and resources that are particularly appropriate or useful for that subject area, and resources are described thoroughly. Following the narrative of each chapter is a long list of print and online resources that will provide you with advice, guidance, and information to accomplish the tasks described in the chapter. Often resources are listed in more than one chapter if they can help readers accomplish the tasks involved with several different functions. Both the print and online resources are listed in alphabetical, not priority, order. You the reader determine which resources are best for your particular situation and mindset. The table of contents and index can also help get readers to the information they want or need. A glossary is included to explain some of the jargon of the business world and also to act as an acronym dictionary.

Besides lack of management skills, one of the top reasons that new enterprises fail is inadequate planning; poor planning results in undercapitalization and poor cash flow. *The Entrepreneur's Information Sourcebook* gathers together in one source a vast amount of information to help new small businesses locate and use data from a wide range of resources to plan every step of their new business. It is imperative that as an entrepreneur you understand the concepts covered and use current, accurate information for your plans. Small business is vitally important to our nation and helping small businesses succeed helps us all.

We begin with what an entrepreneur is and end with growing or expanding your business and different exit strategies. Because individuals think and work differently, many different resources have been included as all the issues in starting a small business are covered. Resources are frequently listed in more than one chapter because they provide outstanding information on a variety of small business topics. When looking for a resource to use for some phase of your business, try several before determining which ones work best for you. Check the print resources out at a library if possible; some, if not owned by a local library, may be obtained through a library system called interlibrary loan. Libraries lend each other different resources for their patrons. Buy some of the books if you can. Purchase information is provided; and although prices change, these prices are current as of spring 2005 and were taken from *Books in Print* online. The books and websites included have been selected for their quality and because they represent different approaches to the various aspects of starting a new business. Books were selected for their unique approach, relevancy, authority, organization, and clarity. Websites selected provide practical information and/or research data rather than just expressing opinions or selling products. All sites have been evaluated for authority, currency, objectivity, stability, and usefulness. Many of the websites may be familiar to readers but new uses and additional important aspects are often identified.

ASK AND PAY FOR HELP!

As you begin to plan, don't be afraid to ask for experienced help. There are many free or reduced fee services available from the SBA, the Service Corp of Retired Executives (SCORE), and the Small Business Development Centers (SBDCs), as well as experienced business owners willing to act as mentors. Several of these resources can be located and accessed through websites mentioned in this book. Although this book does not focus on e-commerce or home-based businesses, these business types have not been totally ignored. All of the major websites listed will contain some articles and information on e-commerce because it is such a rising star in the small business world. Additionally, in Chapter 10, Legal/Taxes, several resources designed to help start up a home-based or e-commerce business are listed to help navigate the legal world. Check the index to find specific resources.

One important concept that it is hoped you will take away from this book is that before any contracts or agreements are signed, you should contact a lawyer and understand all the fine print and points. A small business needs an accountant to help with financial paperwork as well. Interview these professionals just as you would any employee, and hire one who works well for you and with you.

Now, where and how to begin? Look through the table of contents, and find a chapter that interests you or that you know something about. Start reading and learning about starting a small business. After working your way through this book, it is hoped you will have realized your dream of self-employment! Good luck in all your small business adventures.

ARE YOU AN ENTREPRENEUR?

1

CHAPTER HIGHLIGHTS:

- What Is an Entrepreneur?
- What Are the Characteristics Needed?
- A Note of Caution
- Self-Assessment
- First Resources to Explore
- Talk About It!

So, you're considering a small business. Do you have what it takes? At this point in the process, you might ask yourself, "What is an entrepreneur? What are the qualities needed to become a successful entrepreneur? Am I an entrepreneur?"

WHAT IS AN ENTREPRENEUR?

Webster defines an entrepreneur as "one who organizes, manages, and assumes the risks of a business or enterprise." The *Entrepreneur's Desk Reference* gives this definition, "A businessperson who perceives and fulfills a need in the market for profit; vitality is created by the entrepreneur's dual role." An entrepreneur is often described as creative and innovative, while a small business person is expert at running and growing a business. Both must be dedicated, innovative, and willing to spend long hours making their business a success.

WHAT ARE THE CHARACTERISTICS NEEDED?

Required entrepreneurial skills include a compelling vision, a driving passion, versatility or flexibility in planning and changing plans, and confident execution. Learn from your mistakes and move on. Additionally, curiosity is another necessary attribute, since curious people are creative or innovative—and questioning of current practices, procedures, and methods triggers innovation. See every obstacle as an opportunity and turn it into an advantage.

Lastly, but perhaps most importantly, entrepreneurs are high-energy, ambitious individuals who persevere. A small business revolves around a key person, and that person needs energy, enthusiasm, and drive. And though successful entrepreneurs have a positive attitude towards their business and life in general, entrepreneurship and small businesses involve risk. As an entrepreneur, you will be the engine of a new venture and its success or failure depends in large measure on you.

A NOTE OF CAUTION

A cautionary note should be added here: if you want to start your own business because you are unhappy with your current job, profession, or personal life, remember that starting, running, and succeeding in your own business takes a lot of work, involves wearing lots of hats, and keeping lots of balls in the air at once. "Don't quit your day job" is a hackneyed expression, but testing the waters by starting a business in your spare time is a time-tested proven method of discovering if you have what it takes and if you might succeed. If you do decide to quit your job to devote yourself full-time to the new enterprise, it's prudent to set aside enough savings to cover your living costs for a year as it may be at least that long before you can pay yourself a salary.

SELF-ASSESSMENT

To start asking the right questions to find out if you are or can be an entrepreneur, on the web consult the *Entrepreneur's Guidebook Series* at www.patsula.com/ businessplanguides/. In guidebook #1 entitled *Personal Planning*, you'll have the opportunity to assess your entrepreneurial talent. This guide discusses what an entrepreneur is and why people become entrepreneurs. It also asks 29 questions to help discover if you have what it takes. Finally, common traits of successful entrepreneurs are succinctly summarized.

FIRST RESOURCES TO EXPLORE

If your curiosity has been piqued or if you want to read and investigate more aspects of entrepreneurship and starting a business, several good books are available. Lisa Rogak's first chapter in *The Smart Guide to Starting a Small Business* contains a short, 10-question quiz to help you discover why you want to become an entrepreneur. Similar to a job interview, it asks you questions about your goals, weaknesses, how you approach challenges, and it prompts you to honestly think about why you want to start a business and helps you focus your energy and motivation.

Tom Ehrenfeld's *The Start-up Garden: How Growing a Business Grows You* is a terrific guide to helping you understand yourself and walks you through the process of determining what type of business best fits your experiences, talents, and aspirations. Each chapter identifies a skill you need to be successful in business and includes interviews with successful entrepreneurs to illustrate how they used their strong points and developed weak ones. Worksheets help you take an honest look at yourself.

The Smart Woman's Guide to Starting a Business by Vickie L. Montgomery is not for women only. In Chapter Three of her book, Montgomery helps readers identify personal characteristics and experiences that will help them succeed in business, such as fundraising or marketing experience, management or supervisory skills, and communication and listening skills. Also it helps you analyze what skills you need to learn or improve such as accounting. Although outsourcing works, owners still must understand the basics to ask questions and ensure correct procedures. Personal computers or PCs have become time- and money-savers and wasters, but they are essentials in today's business life. Computer skills are necessary. And leadership and management skills are essential, because you are the key person to the business's success or failure. You need high-level skills in organization, delegation, and coordination to marshal resources and people. Montgomery's exercise on choosing a business will also help focus the reader's thoughts on preferences, knowledge, and desires for her or his small business. Finally, her Entrepreneurial Test requires readers to take a further journey into self-discovery by writing an essay on 10 areas that can help identify potential problems or weaknesses in the new entrepreneur. Detailing what you are willing to lose, how you react to change and/or chaos, and how much you enjoy selling, servicing, managing, and networking is the first of many challenges entrepreneurs face. Listed in the resource list at the end of the chapter are several more books that can help you test the strength of your entrepreneurial characteristics.

TALK ABOUT IT!

One last piece of advice in determining if you're entrepreneurial is to discuss your idea with others, i.e., coworkers, family, friends, and neighbors. Networking should begin early. Find a role model, someone who is higher up the ladder in the business world such as an established business owner, and find a mentor, someone who will let you bounce ideas off of him or her, give you pointers, and help you learn the ropes. Learn from others' mistakes or setbacks even as you make your own. Observe them in action and ask questions.

Besides tapping your local community, look for a community of like-minded individuals on the Internet. The "Entrepreneurs" website from About.com at http://entrepreneurs.about.com has forums, chat groups, and other resources useful to new entrepreneurs. Talking through your ideas and interacting with a similar group of folks will help you make good decisions and take fewer missteps.

Figure 1.1 Screenshot of About: Entrepreneurs & Entrepreneurship (entrepreneurs.about.com)

If you're a people-person, or an extrovert who needs to verbalize your ideas, you may want to start your own local group of entrepreneurs or find one at a community college or university in your area. A small business can be a lonely enterprise, and if that is a drawback for you, find a way to interact in a productive way. Trade shows and conferences of like-minded business owners or entrepreneurs are other social and beneficial outlets. Listed next are various resources that will help you determine your entrepreneurial tendencies and what you need to learn to be successful in your own small business.

REFERENCES

(Starred titles discussed in the chapter)

■ Print Resources

Allen, Kathleen. *Entrepreneurship for Dummies*. For Dummies, 2000. 384p. ISBN 0-764-55262-7. $19.99.

This step-by-step guide to getting started in business is well organized and simply written, like all the books in the For Dummies series. From identifying a concept to organizing a start-up team, and conducting a marketing campaign, new entrepreneurs will find they refer to this resource again and again.

**Applegate, Jane. *Entrepreneur's Desk Reference*. Bloomberg Press, 2003. 399p. ISBN 1-5766-0086-6.

This easy-to-use guide is an alphabetical compilation of answers, solutions, advice, and ideas for small business owners/managers, covering over 300 topics from the basics, such as accounting, taxes, marketing, and networking to more advanced concepts, such as buy-out contracts, joint ventures, and employees' benefits and problems. Applegate, one of the United States' top small business experts, provides a comprehensive guide that entrepreneurs will refer to often.

Beech, Wendy. *Black Enterprise Guide to Starting Your Own Business*. John Wiley & Sons, Inc., 1999. 465p. ISBN 0-471-32454-X. $19.95.

Beech offers essential tips on all aspects of entrepreneurship, including 10 qualities you must possess to be a successful entrepreneur, researching the industry and competition, choosing the best location you can afford, establishing a web presence, and more. A multitude of checklists, sample forms, and lists of resources enhance the book's continuing usefulness. One highlight is the testimonials of black entrepreneurs who have persevered again the odds. Written clearly and organized logically, new entrepreneurs and small business owners will benefit from the guidance and practical knowledge presented here. Readers will also be motivated and inspired.

Bygrave, William D. and Zacharakis, Andrew (eds.). *The Portable MBA in Entrepreneurship*. 3rd ed. John Wiley & Sons, Inc., 2003. 398p. ISBN 0-471-27154-3. $34.95.

Using case studies and examples, this usable volume provides practical guidance on the basics of starting and running an entrepreneurial venture effectively. This new edition explores the changing legal, tax, and regulatory climates for small businesses. Written in a clear, scholarly style, it is a reference book that you can refer to when faced with a small business decision or problem.

**Ehrenfeld, Tom. *The Start-up Garden: How Growing a Business Grows You*. McGraw-Hill, 2001. 288p. ISBN 0-07-136824-8. $18.95.

This unique guide helps entrepreneurs understand themselves. Learn what type of business matches your talents, personality, and experiences. See how other entrepreneurs have become successful when they chose the best business for themselves. Identify what skills are needed to turn your dream business into a reality.

**Montgomery, Vickie L. *The Smart Woman's Guide to Starting a Business*. Career Press, 1998. 287p. ISBN 1-56414-368-6. $15.99.

With practical advice, insight, and encouragement, this revised edition is not for women only and covers a variety of basic concepts and start-up issues and challenges such as startup options, business plans, marketing, accounting, technology, and employees. Chapters are filled with practical advice and resources to help you make decisions about your business and move it forward. Sample forms, checklists, and referrals to associations and websites will help the new entrepreneur find his or her way through the process of starting a new business. Chapter 2 is a collection of success stories that are sure to inspire budding entrepreneurs. Approximately 300 helpful websites are also included.

Parks, Ronald K. and Parks, Judith Stolz. *Manager's Mentor: A Guide for Small Business*. Prairie Sky Publishing Co., 2003. 256p. ISBN 0-9729165-0-4. $19.95.

This complete guide to starting and running your small business emphasizes the importance of management principles and their practical applications. However, this is an entrepreneur's story and after you work through the section on "Should You Be in Business?," you will want to read the rest of this entrepreneur's saga and learn more from him. An entire chapter is devoted to "Efficiency" and finding and developing ways to work more efficiently. Discover how to develop a company culture, develop good communication skills, manage capital assets, manage customers, vendors, and consultants, and find ways to improve your management skills. As the title says, if you need a mentor to help in starting and managing your small business, the Parks can help you.

Reiss, Bob. *Low Risk, High Reward: Starting and Growing a Business with Minimal Risk*. Simon & Schuster, 2000. 336p. ISBN 0-684-84962-3. $27.50.

Reiss starts out with a carefully compiled list of 10 personal attributes entrepreneurs should possess and explains why each personal attribute contributes to the likelihood of success. Reiss' chapter on "Numeracy" discusses cash flow and the importance of updating cash flow statements as well as including an example of a cash flow statement in the appendix. His chapter on "Getting the Money" thoroughly covers the best sources of startup capital. Full of practical suggestions and insights, this guide will help all entrepreneurs but especially those with little experience and little money.

**Rogak, Lisa. *Smart Guide to Starting a Small Business*. John Wiley & Sons, Inc., 1999. 176p. ISBN 0-471-31885-X. $10.95.

Using "Self-Assessment Quizzes" to help potential entrepreneurs to start facing the realities of small business ownership, Rogak helps readers focus on determining the kinds of businesses that fit different personalities, identifying likes and dislikes plus identifying strengths and weaknesses, assessing the competition, and identifying customers or markets. Also covering the very basics of starting and running a business, this guide will especially assist readers who like a well-organized, quick-reading style with lots of sidebars, tables, and a comprehensive index. Use this resource to get your new business off to a quick, productive start.

The Ultimate Small Business Guide: A Resource for Startups and Growing Businesses. Basic Books, 2004. 501p. ISBN 0-7382-0913-9. $19.95.

Besides helping you answer the question "Do I have what it takes to run a business?," this large reference work has sections on "Refining and Protecting Your Idea," "Finding

Premises," "Working and Communicating with Customers," and "Working and Selling Online." A large section on calculating ratios and creating financial statements is also very useful for the new business owner. The directories in the back present a collection of print and online resources in a wide variety of business areas. This well-organized resource is a bargain.

Online Resources

**About.com Entrepreneur's site: entrepreneurs.about.com (Accessed Fall 2005).

This site contains a wealth of information such as articles on what states are the most supportive of entrepreneurs, best links for entrepreneurs, ethics, intrapreneurship, professional associations, rural entrepreneurs, and more. Continually updated and easy to navigate, new and old entrepreneurs will visit this site often.

**Entrepreneur's Guidebook Series: www.smbtn.com/businessplanguides/ (Accessed Fall 2005).

Defining real entrepreneurs as managers who adopt key behaviors developed by understanding key market concepts and theories and who are successful because of their planning and researching skills, this site discusses why people become entrepreneurs and the type of life entrepreneurs generally lead. Here you will discover what your entrepreneurial talents are and common traits of successful entrepreneurs. Explore this website for more good ideas.

Small Business Administration: www.sba.gov (Accessed Fall 2005).

This official government site offers a wealth of resources and programs for starting and growing a small business. Under Startup Basics, users will find an Entrepreneurial Test of 25 questions, which will help them in doing a personal evaluation of their possible success in their own business. Other major sections cover business planning, financing, managing, marketing, employees, taxes, legal aspects, and business opportunities. Find here online forms, business plans, loan information, and many publications. Some contents available in Spanish.

Wall Street Journal **Center for Entrepreneurs:** www.startupjournal.com/ (Accessed Fall 2005).

WSJ's Startup Journal is an authoritative site that has a section entitled How-To, and entrepreneurs will find there a great deal of help deciding if they are entrepreneurs and how to get started in business. Collected here are many articles about different aspects of starting a business such as legal structure, finding a name, business plan tools, and more. The sample business plans are very thorough and will really help new business owners fill in the gaps in their own plans. Articles on important issues such as "Should You Hire an Accountant?" will also get entrepreneurs off on the right foot. Continually updated and well-written, this site is useful to all entrepreneurs.

RESEARCH, STATISTICS, AND INFORMATION GATHERING

2

CHAPTER HIGHLIGHTS:

- Federal Government Statistics
- The U.S. Census Bureau
- The North American Industry Classification System (NAICS)
- FEDSTATS
- State Government Agencies
- Commercial Publishers
- Statistical Concepts

When starting a new business, it's impossible to have too much information. Statistics, the classification, tabulation, and study of numerical data, are vital to making good decisions. Statistics concern both the systematic collection of numerical data and its interpretation. You'll need details on customers, competition, the industry, industry trends, location, vendors, markets and potential markets, the local and national economy, trends in the economy, and more. You will need to find out income information for your area to see if there are enough customers to buy your product or service. If you have a business affected by the sale of new homes, you will want to find statistics to see how many are being built in your city, county, or state. All these types of statistics can be found through government resources, many online, listed later in this chapter. Market research can help you successfully launch a new venture and weed out ideas that are not feasible. Decision making based on intuition and expertise with a thorough (statistical) understanding of the facts available can help you gain and maintain a competitive edge.

Because the cost of collecting and analyzing primary statistical data is great, most businesses depend on secondary statistical data generated by a variety of sources including government agencies, trade associations, commercial publishers, and less often on private research firms. Generally, the online and print resources listed here you will be able to find at local libraries or use free on the Internet. Some of the sites, although they provide free information, are commercial enterprises, and will try to sell you their products. Please note that this guide does not endorse any of these products.

FEDERAL GOVERNMENT STATISTICS

The U.S. government is probably the largest single compiler and publisher of statistics pertaining to U.S. businesses. More than 70 agencies produce statistics of interest to the public, and many of these are useful to entrepreneurs and small business people. Many of the agencies have websites with statistics free to all Internet users, and the various search engines such as Google, Yahoo!, and AltaVista crawl these sites and index some of the data. If you search for "small business statistics," you will find a wealth of sites, free government ones and of course many dot-com sites wanting to sell you a variety of things. In this chapter, useful fee and free sites will be included for you to use in your research. Although the information and sites are presented in as linear a fashion as possible, there is a lot of interconnectivity and crossover. URLs are included whenever confusion seems possible.

One place to start is the U.S. government's official web portal called "FirstGov.gov" (www.firstgov.gov). Users will see a long list of "Information by Topic," many of which will interest and amaze first-timers. The Federal Government collects and publishes a great deal of data and information. If at any time you decide you'd like to see what paper publications the government has produced, visit a Regional Government Depository at your State Library or a large university library in your state. On FirstGov.gov, under the Reference Center, clicking on "Data and Statistics" brings up an alphabetical list of links to resources chock full of statistics. "Economic Indicators" is the website of the Economics and Statistics Administration, part of the U.S. Department of Commerce (www.economicindicators.gov), and it provides timely access to the daily releases of key economic indicators from the Bureau of Economic Analysis (BEA) and the Census Bureau.

The BEA's website (www.bea.gov) produces a wealth of statistical information on the U.S. economy. The mission of the BEA is to produce and circulate accurate, timely, relevant, and cost-effective statistics and to provide a comprehensive, up-to-date description of U.S. economic activity. The ups and downs of the U.S. economy and regional economic development affect every small business in some way. The cost of a barrel of oil goes up and it costs more to get supplies to your door; consumers pay more for gas and have less to spend on clothes, food, whatever. As a small business person, you want to keep a close eye on what's happening in the economy. The BEA's "Overview of the Economy" section will help you do just that.

The BEA also produces the *Survey of Current Business*, a monthly publication that provides data on personal income, state and regional economic statistics, and more.

The U.S. Department of Labor's Bureau of Labor Statistics (www.bls.gov) presents the latest numbers on areas including "Inflation and Consumer Spending," "Wages, Earnings, and Benefits," and "Demographics" in general. Explore their site to find the Inflation Calculator; understanding inflation and how it affects business and prices is essential for an entrepreneur. When you hire employees to help you in your business, you will want to visit this site for information on compensation and working conditions and to review publications like the *Occupational Outlook Handbook* (www.bls.gov/oco/) for help with job titles and descriptions, training needed, and pay/earnings.

THE U.S. CENSUS BUREAU

The largest statistical agency of the government is the Bureau of the Census (www.census.gov), and it collects, compiles, and publishes, as mentioned above, economic as well as population statistics. On the home page of the Census Bureau, you will find listed the "American Factfinder." This site has a huge online collection of data on the people, housing, geography, and business of the United States. At the bottom of the page, you will find a link to the "Economic Census." The Economic Census profiles the U.S. economy every five years. Here you can find statistics on the state you live in by Metropolitan Statistical Areas (MSAs), counties, and even by zip code. When completely finished, over 1600 publications will be part of the 2002 Economic Census. It contains 651 Industry Series reports, entitled *Census of Wholesale Trade*, for example, and covers manufacturing, retail, construction, finance and insurance, information, health care and social assistance, service, and many more. Before 2002, only goods-producing industries were covered, but the Industry Series reports now are published for all industries. Statistics on number of establishments, sales, receipts, revenues, expenses, product, payroll, and more are presented in tables.

Another part of the U.S. Census Bureau's data is the *Current Industrial Reports* (CIR). Since 1904, the CIR program has provided monthly, quarterly, and annual measures of industrial activity. The program's surveys measure manufacturing activity in commodities like textiles and apparel, computer and electronic components, consumer goods, and more. Reports can be accessed by subject or NAICS subsectors.

New measures of the way America does business are always being added. In the 2002 reports, information on the e-commerce sales for most industries is included. Data for e-commerce sales and Electronic Data Interchange (EDI) is found at http://www.census.gov/estats.

Another publication of the Economic Census is called *County Business Patterns*; this is a collection of data by county for every state similar to the Industry Series including number of establishments, payrolls, employment by industry, etc. Zip Code Business Patterns (includes 40,000 5-digit zip code areas) and Metro Business Patterns present the same type of data for those areas. See Chapter 7, Marketing and Advertising, for a specific example of how to use this data for your small business. Some other examples of how the data in the Economic Census is used include calculating market share, identifying new site locations, and showing or finding new markets for products or services.

THE NORTH AMERICAN INDUSTRY CLASSIFICATION SYSTEM (NAICS)

Many of the U.S. government's statistics are gathered and presented by the North American Industry Classification System or NAICS. Each business when it files its taxes will have to identify itself by a NAICS number. NAICS has replaced the U.S. Standard Industrial Classification (SIC) system. NAICS was developed jointly with the United States, Canada, and Mexico to provide new comparability in statistics on business activities throughout North America. The NAICS also introduced a number of new industries including residential remodelers, electronic shopping and auctions, Internet publishing and broadcasting, and web search portals. On the Census Bureau site you will find a link to NAICS where you can look up the code for your industry. Many statistical sources present industry ratios and trends by NAICS code.

Another great statistical resource, often called "the nation's databook," is produced by the Census Bureau, the *Statistical Abstract of the United States*. It provides statistics such as number of cell phones in the United States, average cost of a home in different areas of the United States, educational level in various parts of the country, fastest growing jobs, where population growth is happening, and more in over 1,400 tables and charts.

Also from the Census Bureau, the State Data Center (SDC) program is a cooperative program between the states and the Census Bureau created in 1978 (www.census.gov/sdc/www/). The Business and Industry Data Center Program (BIDC) was added to the State Data Center in 1988 to help meet the needs of local business communities for economic data. The SDC's mission is to provide easy and efficient access to U.S. Census Bureau data through a wide network of state agencies including lead, coordinating, and affiliate agencies. At this main website, you can click on your state and see a list of "Census State Data Centers," where you will find people to help you access and use your state's data. The SDCs are the Census Bureau's official sources of demographic, economic, and social statistics. The SDCs provide training and technical assistance in accessing and using Census Bureau data for research, planning, administration, and decision making by local governments, the business community, and researchers.

FEDSTATS

FEDSTATS (http://www.fedstats.gov) is the official website of the Federal Interagency Council on Statistical Policy. This gateway to statistics from over 100 U.S. federal agencies includes the large departments such as Agriculture, Commerce, and Health and Human Services as well as specific small agencies such as the Bureau of Labor Statistics, Economic Research Services, Federal Deposit Insurance Corporation, and International Trade Administration, for example, and is well organized and easy to use. Important statistical resources such as the *Statistical Abstract of the United States* (www.census.gov/prod/www/statistical abstract-03.html), for instance, can be accessed here.

Users can find statistics and information under "Links to Statistics," "Topic Links A–Z," "MapStats," and "Statistics by Geography from U.S. Agencies." The "Statistical Reference Shelf" a bit further down on the home page lists a large collection of online reference sources such as the *Statistical Abstract of the United States*, which we've already discussed. You will find a variety of other sources such as the *State and Metropolitan Area Data Book* and *Digest of Education Statistics*, which provide statistics on many topics of interest to small businesses. On the other half of the page, "Links to Statistical Agencies," under "Agencies by Subject," click Economic on the drop-down arrow to lead you to a list of "Periodic Economic Censuses."

The links and descriptions included here lead you to the U.S. Census Bureau, Bureau of Economic Analysis (BEA), Customs Service, Directorate for Information

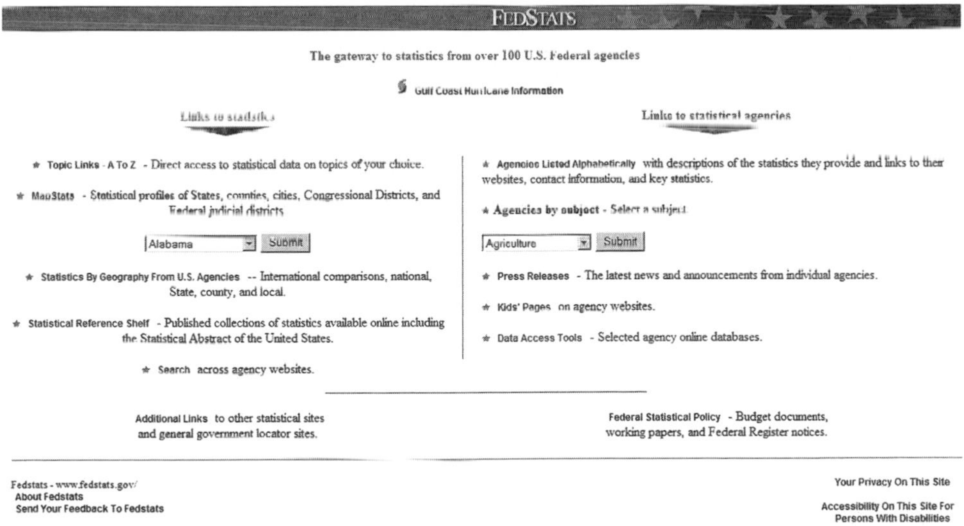

Figure 2.1 Screenshot of FedStats: Home page (www.fedstats.gov)

THE ENTREPRENEUR'S INFORMATION SOURCEBOOK

Back To Fedstats Home Page | **Topic Links - A To Z** | **Information Quality**

Periodic Economic Censuses

U.S. Census Bureau conducts several periodic censuses every five years, covering the years ending in 2 and 7. The Economic Censuses include censuses of manufacturing, mineral industries, construction industries, retail and wholesale trade, service industries, and transportation and other businesses. They also provide statistics on businesses owned by minorities and women and companies operating at multiple locations. The Census of Governments collects state and local data on public finance; public employment; and governmental organization, powers, and activities.	• Contact Information • Key Statistics

Current Economic Statistics

Bureau Of Economic Analysis measures, presents, and interprets Gross Domestic Product (GDP), personal income, corporate profits, and related items in the context of the National Income and Product Accounts. BEA also maintains personal income and related measures for States and localities, the U.S. balance of payments accounts, and the foreign direct investment accounts.	• Contact Information • Key Statistics
U.S. Census Bureau provides information on retail and wholesale trade and selected service industries; construction activity, such as housing permits and starts, the value of new construction, residential alterations and repairs, and quarterly price indexes for single-family houses; quantity and value of industrial output-e.g., manufacturing activities; shipments, inventories, and orders; capital expenditure information; foreign trade-including imports, exports, and trade monitoring; and state and local government activities. The Census Bureau also maintains the Standard Statistical Establishment List that is used for statistical frames and the production of aggregate data on County Business Patterns.	• Contact Information • Key Statistics
U.S. Customs & Border Protection collects and verifies tariff and trade data, which are tabulated, analyzed, and disseminated by the Census Bureau.	• Contact Information
Directorate For Information Operations And Reports (DIOR) in the Department of Defense (DOD) collects DOD contract information in support of national economic indictors and the Small Business Competitiveness Demonstration Program. DIOR also produces statistics on DOD purchases from educational and nonprofit institutions, and state and local governments.	• Contact Information • Key Statistics
Economics And Statistics Administration (ESA) in the Department of Commerce carries out Congressionally-mandated studies, such as the annual assessment of foreign direct investment in the United States. ESA disseminates current economic statistics through an electronic system known as STAT-USA.	• Contact Information
International Trade Administration (ITA) in the Department of Commerce, involve data on imports, exports, production, prices, foreign direct investment in the United States, and other economic data to analyze domestic and foreign market situations. ITA also tracks data on international travel to and from the United States for many private sector firms.	• Contact Information • Key Statistics
Small Business Administration (SBA) maintains a small business data base and conducts economic and statistical research into matters affecting small businesses	• Contact Information

Figure 2.2 Screenshot of FedStats: Economic Statistics (www.fedstats.gov/programs/economic.html)

Operations and Reports (DIOR), Economics and Statistics Administration (ESA), International Trade Administration (ITA), Small Business Administration (SBA), and Statistics of Income (SOI). The Statistics of Income (SOI) provides market researchers with statistics on annual personal and corporate income.

Part of the Economics and Statistics Administration is known as STAT-USA; this subscription service is available through many university and depository libraries throughout the United States. The State of the Nation section of STAT-USA covers current and historical economic and financial releases and economic data. Look at "Today's Hot Releases" or "Daily Releases" for up-to-date economic data. On the lower left of the home page, you'll find the most recently added State of the Nation (SOTN) files. Find here interest rates and new State and Regional tables. Check out the "State of the Nation Library" (SOTN Library button at top of page) for a collection of over 3,000 files of U.S. economic information, including Industry Statistics, Economic Indicators, and the Survey of Current Business. Another part of STAT-USA is the GLOBUS & National Trade Data Base (NTDB); the NTDB is chock full of useful trade statistics.

Learning to use the many and varied statistical resources of our federal government is no easy task. The Internet has certainly improved their visibility and searchability, but the enormity of available information is still daunting. When you start your search, have a clear idea of what you need, but be flexible in the vocabulary you use to describe it. Also, ask a librarian to help you get started in your search. Remember that you will probably have to use the data you find to extrapolate, which means you will estimate by projecting from known information or data.

STATE GOVERNMENT AGENCIES

Statistical sources for state data vary greatly state-to-state. Many state and local government organizations simply collect the data and then submit it to the federal government for compilation and publication such as the Census Bureau's State Data Centers. However, most states publish some information on the state's economy, economic or industrial development, and employment and unemployment statistics. Once again, you can easily find a state website by searching Google, Yahoo!, AltaVista, or other search engines. Another resource for state data is the State and Local Government on the Net website at http://www.statelocal gov.net/, a site that provides convenient access to all state and local government sites by listing the states alphabetically. Frequently updated, this directory of official state, county, and city government websites also provides a list of topics to choose from plus listings of government grants, with applications.

COMMERCIAL PUBLISHERS

Staying with the statistics theme, many commercial publishers produce detailed and high-quality statistical sources. Industry research and averages are an important component of a business plan. Three key resources for operating and financial ratios for many industries are Leo Troy's *Almanac of Business and Industrial Financial Ratios*, Dun and Bradstreet's *Industry Norms and Key Business Ratios*, and Robert Morris and Associates' *RMA Annual Statement Studies*; check your local library to see if they have these resources. Although available through subscription on the web, the costs for these services can be substantial.

RMA Universe at http://www.rmahq.com, allows users to purchase single industry data online for a reasonable price. *Standard and Poor's Industry Surveys* only cover about 50 industries in a three-volume set but the overview, ratios, and trends data are invaluable. Specific company ratio and balance sheet comparisons are provided under the Basic Analysis section. The financial ratios in the resources listed above are organized by either Standard Industrial Code (SIC) or the new North American Industrial Code System (NAICS). *Value Line Investment Survey Standard Edition* (Value Line, weekly) is another place to check for industry analysis and company data. Organized by industry, each of the 93 industry reviews contains current and future business environment descriptions and is followed by pages describing and evaluating individual companies. With the financial ratios in these resources, you can compare your projections with companies that are already established in your industry. Find out more about financial ratios and how to figure them for your business in the "Accounting and Bookkeeping" section of Chapter 8, Management.

BizStats.com

Due to the growth in small and franchised businesses in the United States, the market for popular statistics continues to grow and develop. An outstanding website for financial ratios, business statistics, and benchmarks is called BizStats.com, at http://www.bizstats.com/. Here you can find Profitability and Operating Ratios for S corporations, partnerships, and sole proprietorships for industries such as furniture stores, electronics, gas stations, and sporting goods. You can find Retail Industry Benchmarks like sales per foot (SPF), average sales per foot in malls, and SPF for a three-year trend. Look at the table of Safest and Riskiest Small Businesses to see if your research agrees with this site. You can find lists of the Most Popular Small Businesses, Current Ratios and Balance Sheet Ratios by Industry, and Industry Profitability for Sole Proprietorships, for example. This site has financial and operating ratios for 30,000 industry segments. Even if you cannot find your industry here, this site will show you how to do a financial and industry analysis using the figures you have gathered. CPA Patrick O'Rourke has produced the data on this terrific site for small business statistics.

A wide range of industry directories can provide you with information on industries and specific companies, i.e., your competitors. You can also use existing firms' actual performance to validate your projections in your business plan. Listed below are two helpful websites to check for industry information.

About.com: www.about.com/business (Accessed Fall 2005)

This large site has many different parts and is at times a bit difficult to navigate. Use the search feature if you have trouble. On the left side of this main page, you will find "Industry." This site covers the Biotech/Biomedical, Composites/Plastics, Metal, Insurance, and Retail industries. The Retail Industry (www.retailindustry. about.com/od/retail), which is notoriously difficult to locate information about, is especially well done; articles provide information on current retail trends, retail statistics, retail industry profile, apparel trends, consumer trends, and more. Here users will also find articles on, for example, retail strategy, store operations, store design and atmosphere, and branding.

Market Research, Industry Research, Business Research: www.virtualpet.com/industry (Accessed Fall 2005)

This major portal for researching companies and industries presents a step-by-step process to begin researching an industry. Here you can find sources to help you learn about legal issues, regulatory issues, competition, markets, and even the history of the industry for your new business. Additional links to Industry Portals are also available. Three other linked sites offer help on "How to Learn about a Company by Examining Its Products," "How to Review, Evaluate, Critique a Web Site," and "How to Conduct a Patent Search."

STATISTICAL CONCEPTS

Every business person needs to be familiar with some key statistical concepts and to be able to use them in business planning and projections. Above you have seen that the government and commercial publishers present you with both "descriptive statistics," which utilize numerical and graphical methods to look for patterns, and summarize and present that information in a set of data, and "inferential statistics," which utilize sample data to make estimates or predictions about a larger set of data as an aid to decision making. Below you'll find brief definitions of some of the concepts relevant to business statistics in general.

■ Sampling and Probability

Sampling is the process of selecting units (e.g., people, organizations) from a population of interest so that by studying the sample we may fairly generalize our results back to the population from which they were chosen. A sample is anything less than a survey of the full population. Population statistics are important to business owners and researchers, and while it would be best to collect information from each person in the population being studied, surveying each individual is usually not practical or even possible. Therefore, sampling is used to select a small but representative sample and make inferences or conclusions about the entire population. A good source to learn more about sampling, especially in relation to market research, is Paul Hague's *Market Research: A Guide to Planning, Methodology, and Evaluation.* A descriptive citation follows:

> Hague, Paul. *Market Research: A Guide to Planning, Methodology, and Evaluation.* 3rd ed. Kogan Page, 2002. 278p. ISBN 0-7494-3730-8. $37.50 (with CD-ROM)
>
> Hague presents clear, concise advice with real-life case studies on the topic of market research. Slightly distracting is the very British slant. Tools and techniques used by market researchers are described and explained. Learn how to use a sample to see trends in your business and your local area.

Sampling is based on the theory of probability and can only be understood in those terms. Probability is the basis of sampling; it shows the likelihood or chances for each of various potential outcomes based on a set of assumptions about how the world works generally. Using the data from a random sample, you can infer knowledge or probability about the population from which the sample was drawn. The objective of sampling is to select a part that is representative of the entire population. For example, the television rating service Nielsen tracks television-watching behavior of a sample of viewers and makes inferences about the popularity of shows to the majority of television viewers.

Earlier in this chapter we looked at statistical sources produced by the Census Bureau. The Census Bureau uses sampling extensively to produce many of its publications. To be aware of when and how sampling is used to produce statistics, careful readers always check the introductory matter and/or the footnotes to ascertain what methods were used for the statistics presented. When checking the source of statistics also ask yourself two important questions:

1. Are the statistics self-serving?

2. Is the source biased?

Obviously, the government does not have any vested interest in presenting the population statistics, but when you use other sources for statistics, forecasts, or ratios, remember to keep the above questions in mind. Statistics works best when you combine them with your own expert judgment and common sense.

Forecasts, Projections, and Estimates

Forecasting is the use of known measurements to predict the value of unknown measurements that will occur at a later date generally no more than two years into the future. Forecasting always applies to the future, but is based on information about the ways in which variables have behaved in the past. In forecasting it is assumed that the behavioral patterns traced in the past will continue in the future. Business forecasting is a process that seeks to answer a variety of forward-looking questions about the operations of a company and the demands that will be placed upon it. Business forecasting cannot deliver absolutely accurate, error-free forecasts, but it can have a reasonably small margin of error and will reduce your future uncertainty to a manageable level.

Statistical projections don't always yield accurate forecasts, because any analysis of trends depends on the assumption of stable political, economic, and social conditions. Projections are predictions made about the distant future, so they are more speculative and prone to error than forecasts. Projections cannot always take into account the effect of technological advances and man-made and natural disasters. Small business owners need to understand forecasting and projections as they are important elements in planning and control in any business. Management decisions must often be based on what is likely to happen in the future, which may be tomorrow, next week, or next year. To arrive at a sales forecast, the owner may start with an economic forecast, which considers trends in the whole economy.

An estimate is an approximation of an unknown value based on an extrapolation from a known value. Estimates may apply to any time, past, present, or future measurements. Statistical estimation finds a statistical measure of a population from the corresponding statistics of the sample. It is an estimate because it's not certain that the sample is an exact reflection of the entire population. An estimate draws a conclusion from the study of representative cases.

This quick overview of research sources and definitions will help you gather the information you need to decide what business you want to be in, what is a good location, how much money will it cost to start, and more. The following resources will help you understand business concepts more and find statistical sources.

REFERENCES

(Starred titles discussed in the chapter)

■ Print Resources

Berinstein, Paula. *Business Statistics on the Web*. CyberAge Books, 2003. 244p. ISBN 0-910965-65-X. $29.95.

Berinstein illustrates how to search the Internet to find statistics about companies, markets, and industries in this handy reference guide. Chapters are organized under broad topic areas such as Statistics Basics, U.S. Industry Sources, Non-U.S. Industry Sources, Market Research Sources, and Company Information. Dispersed between the chapters are sometimes lengthy case studies that illustrate the breadth and depth of information you can find on the web. The last chapter, which covers estimating your company's numbers that you don't yet have, will be especially useful for small businesses.

Boettcher, Jennifer C. and Gaines, Leonard M. *Industry Research Using the Economic Census: How to Find It, How to Use It*. Greenwood Publishing Group, Inc., 2004. 305p. ISBN 1-57356-351-X. $85.00.

This guide will help beginners use the Economic Census to recognize trends in different industries, provide help for marketing and targeting sales, as well as understand the key economic indicators of the U.S. economy. This handbook explains the Census's concepts, methods, and vocabulary in everyday language and will help users locate needed Census data. The authors also explain how business executives and researchers use the industry data. Use this resource as a place to begin researching your industry.

**Dun & Bradstreet. *Industry Norms and Key Business Ratios*. Annual. $409.00.

This annual resource is very expensive but some libraries still purchase it for their business collections. D&B analyzes nearly 800 business lines and can help small businesses make financial projections. If you haven't been able to find financial norms for your industry, try this resource.

Fallek, Max and Solie-Johnson, Kris. *How to Set Up Your Own Small Business*. American Institute of Small Business, 2003. 850p. ISBN 0-939069-71-7. $159.95.

This large two-volume set covers the basic principles of getting into, operating, and succeeding in a small business. Besides discussing the usual topics like buying a business or franchise, topics include site selection, advertising, personnel management, how to do market research and sales forecasting, and how to calculate your actual cost per product are also presented in good detail. The chapter on the Business Plan is particularly thorough and well organized. Appendices provide contact information on SBA Regional Offices, SCORE State Offices, and SBDC State Offices plus a sample partnership agreement and sample Limited Liability Company agreement.

**Hague, Paul. *Market Research: A Guide to Planning, Methodology, and Evaluation.* 3rd ed. Kogan Page, 2002. 278p. ISBN 0-7494-3730-8. $37.50 (with CD-ROM).

Hague presents clear, concise advice with real-life case studies on the topic of market research. Slightly distracting is the very British slant. Tools and techniques used by market researchers are described and explained so that you can use them. Learn how to use a sample to see trends in your business and your local area. Find ways to check to see that your marketing efforts are yielding results. Marketing is an essential ingredient in the successful business. Learn how to use market research to help your business grow.

Hillstrom, Kevin and Hillstrom, Laurie Collier. *Encyclopedia of Small Business.* 2nd ed. Thomson Gale, 2002. 2v. 1,061p. ISBN 0-7876-4906-6. $475.00.

Arranged alphabetically, over 500 essays cover topics such as Advertising Media on the Web, Business Start-up, Employee Compensation, Franchising, Health Insurance Options, E-commerce, Product Development, and Tax Planning. How these topics affect small business is, of course, emphasized. Bibliographic citations at the end of each topic point to additional sources of information. The Master Index at the end of volume II provides additional subject, organization, government agency, and legislation access. Written in a relevant and accessible format and manner, all types and ages of entrepreneurs will find this a useful reference.

Moss, Rita. *Strauss's Handbook of Business Information.* 2nd ed. Libraries Unlimited, 2004. 453p. ISBN 1-56308-520-8. $85.00.

Business information has experienced a revolution in the past few years, i.e., user-friendly and sometimes free access to online databases filled with company, industry, association, and government information. The basic organization of the first edition has been followed here, dividing the Handbook into two main sections: Formats and Fields of Business Information. Additionally, with the globalization of business and economies, international resources are featured in each chapter. The Format section includes guides, directories, periodicals, loose-leaf services, and electronics. Fields covered include marketing, accounting and taxation, banking, stocks and bonds, futures, insurance, and real estate. Appendices cover acronyms, federal government agencies, state agencies, and selected websites. A title and a subject index complete the volume.

Plunkett Research, Ltd. *Plunkett's Industry Almanacs and CD-ROM's.* $249.95 each.

Plunkett Research produces a growing list of industry almanacs that give researchers and business owners a variety of statistics and information. For example, the *Advertising and Branding Industry Almanac* broadly covers data and areas of interest ranging from branding strategy and trends to emerging technology and an in-depth analysis of The Advertising 350. This volume includes data on radio and television, direct mail, and online advertising as well as public relations. Trends in areas such as advertising agencies, marketing consultants, and global markets are reviewed. Contacts for business and industry leaders, industry associations, Internet resources, and magazines are provided. Examples of statistics included are worldwide advertising growth 1990–2004, advertising spending of U.S. top 10, cable and pay television revenues and expenses, and the largest entertainment industry mergers from 1985 to 2004. The company profiles are the major section, and companies are arranged alphabetically. Details for each company contain rankings within industry grouping, business description, major brands, divisions and affiliations, officers, addresses, phone and fax numbers, URLs, number of employees, locations, and growth plan statements. If your industry is covered by Plunkett Research, their almanacs are authoritative reports.

**RMA Annual Statement Studies*. Robert Morris Associates. Annual. $155.00.

These studies collect and compile current and historical financial data for almost 350 industries by company asset and sales size. An annual volume is expensive so check your library or their website for information on buying an individual industry report (www.rmahq.org). This website is also described below in online resources. Banks use this information for analyzing business loan applications. Libraries have traditionally purchased this data for their business collections but subscription costs keep rising.

Small Business Sourcebook. 2 volumes. Thomson Gale. Annual. $405.00.

This directory provides a wealth of information for the small business owner/manager. The Small Business Profiles cover 340 different small businesses. Businesses profiled include catering, cooking schools, fish farms, antique shops, bookstores, and car washes, for example. Entries contain as many as 17 subheadings, such as start-up information, edu cational programs, reference works, sources of supply, statistical sources, trade periodicals, trade shows and conventions, consultants, and franchises and business opportunities. The Small Business Topics section covers general ideas including budgets/budgeting, retailing, service industry, franchising, insurance, seasonal business, and more. Similar to the small business profiles, these entries have the same 17 subheadings and lead users to many resources relating to the topics. The State Listings and Federal Government Assistance sections list programs and offices that provide information and support to small businesses. Check your library for this practical, well-organized source.

Strawser, Cornelia J. *Business Statistics of the United States*. 8th ed. Bernan Associates, 2003. ISBN 0-89059-618-2. $147.00.

This comprehensive, classic business resource contains all kinds of data relevant to the economic performance of the U.S. economy. Historical data, including statistics on production, manufacturers' stocks, exports, prices, etc. is provided for a variety of U.S. industries. More than 3,000 economic time series, mainly from federal government sources, are included. This huge compilation of data enables users to observe past trends and provides the basis for projecting trends in the future. Part B presents a general description of NAICS and its differences from SIC before presenting detailed industry data on the NAICS basis as far back as possible, usually the early 1990s. Part D includes State and Regional Data on personal income and employment back to 1972.

**Troy, Leo. *Almanac of Business and Industrial Financial Ratios*. Aspen Publishers, Inc., 2004. 801p. ISBN 0-7355-4319-4. $139.00.

This updated business reference standard covers 50 operating and financial factors in 192 industries and derives its data from IRS figures on U.S. and international companies.

Data for each industry is subdivided into 13 categories based on company size. Troy presents all variety of factors relating to operations, operating costs, financial performance, and an array of financial factors in percentages including debt ratio, return on assets, return on equity, and profit margins. Tables are divided into 13 asset sizes to help with making comparisons.

Ultimate Small Business Guide: A Resource for Startups and Growing Businesses. Basic Books, 2004. 352p. ISBN 0-7382-0913-9. $19.95.

This small but authoritative and handy source presents a wealth of insightful tools and information for the new entrepreneur. Success stories and interviews with entrepreneurs will motivate and inspire. Briefly covered are all aspects of business creation, planning, and managing a growing new business. Find here sections on Refining and Protecting Your Idea, Finding Premises, Communicating with Customers, and more. The Figuring It Out section thoroughly covers financial statements and ratios to help the new small business person understand what an accountant is saying. The Directory is divided into subject categories such as Franchising, Market Research and Competitor Intelligence, Pricing, and Selling and Salesmanship with books and websites listed under each heading. This handy little reference work will guide entrepreneurs through the start-up process.

**U.S. Department of Commerce. Bureau of the Census. *Statistical Abstract of the United States*. Government Printing Office. Annual. Web version at: www.census.gov/statab/www/ (also available on CD-ROM).

This collection of statistics on U.S. social, political, and economic conditions provides information on various topics, such as the number of cell phones in the United States, average cost of a home in different areas of the United States, educational level in various parts of the country, fastest growing jobs, where population growth is happening, and more in over 1,400 tables and charts. First published in 1878, the data is collected from over 220 difference government and private agencies. Each chapter begins with a description of the data being presented and definitions of terms and concepts. You can use the subject index to quickly locate the statistical tables you need. Most tables present information for the past 5 to 10 years. Footnotes under the tables provide source information.

Walsh, Ciaran. *Key Management Ratios: Master the Management Metrics That Drive and Control Your Business*. 3rd ed. 400p. Financial Times/Prentice Hall, 2003. ISBN 0-273-66345-3. $24.95.

Business ratios are the standards and targets that help owners and managers work toward achieving their goals in running a successful business. Walsh proceeds to teach readers everything they need to know about key business ratios, linking them to day-to-day operations. He also covers financial statements, balance sheets, cash flow, liquidity, and cost, volume, and price relationships. Thorough and well organized, all readers will take some knowledge away from studying this book.

■ Online Resources

About.com: www.about.com/business (Accessed Fall 2005).

This site provides a treasure trove of information, links, books, and other assorted help in learning new research and management skills and improving those an entrepreneur has already developed. Finding industry research as well as articles on industries is easy. Sections cover Management 101, Management Tips, How to Manage, and more. Learn best business practices and leadership skills from experts. A related area of the site is Human Resources which helps users learn about human resources (HR) issues and managing employees.

American FactFinder: factfinder.census.gov/home/saff/main.html?_lang=en (Accessed Fall 2005).

This federal government source for information on population, housing, economic, and geographic data is easy to use and well designed. You can get a Fact Sheet for your community by just entering town, county, or zip code. A quick link gets you to the Decennial Census of Housing and Population, American Community Survey, the Economic Census, or the Population Estimates program. A couple clicks will get you to County Business Patterns, information on the NAICS code, statistics about small business from the Census Bureau, the characteristics of business owners' database, and more. A glossary, FAQs, and search function will also help you use this great, free resource.

BEOnline: Business and Economics Online: www.loc.gov/rr/business/beonline/ (Accessed Fall 2005).

Compiled by the Library of Congress Business Reference Services for researchers, under Subject Guides, you will find a lengthy list of business topics such as associations, business plans (forms), companies by industry, data sets, e-commerce, franchises, economic indicators, legal resources, and more. If you click on Associations, you are in an Associations Database that includes contacts, descriptions, addresses, and events data for the organizations listed. Over 10,000 business organizations in the United States are listed. Find here a link to the Herb Growing and Marketing Network or the Association of Bridal Consultants. Under the Title Listing, you can find Airlines on the Web, America's Business Funding Directory, American Chambers of Commerce Abroad, American City Business Journals, and more.

**BizStats.com: www.bizstats.com/ (Accessed Fall 2005).

Find Profitability and Operating Ratios for S corporations, partnerships, and sole proprietorships for industries including furniture stores, electronics, gas stations, and sporting goods. You can find Retail Industry Benchmarks such as sales per foot (SPF), average sales per foot in malls, and SPF for a three-year trend. Look at the table of Safest and Riskiest Small Businesses to see if your research agrees with this site. You can find lists of the Most Popular Small Businesses, Current Ratios and Balance Sheet Ratios by Industry, and Industry Profitability for Sole Proprietorships, for example. This site has Financial and Operating Ratios for 30,000 Industry Segments. Even if your industry is not found here, this site will show you how to do a financial and industry analysis using the figures you have gathered. CPA Patrick O'Rourke has produced the data on this well-organized, comprehensive site for small business statistics.

**Bureau of Labor Statistics (BLS): www.bls.gov/home.htm (Accessed Fall 2005).

Find here under Publications and Research Papers publications such as the *Dictionary of Occupational Titles* and the *Occupational Outlook Handbook* online. The Handbook provides training and education needed, earnings, and expected job prospects for a wide range of jobs. Help is available to write job ads, job descriptions, and more. Also find out about current government regulations and legislation in regard to employees.

**Business.gov: www.business.gov (Accessed Fall 2005).

Another government site developed to help businesses find the information they need and want. The Market Research section of this site is especially noteworthy. Links to information on major industries, population and demographic resources, plus Rural America Facts provide users with a multitude of useful resources. International trade connections are useful for global or Internet businesses too. Major categories include Laws & Regulations, Buying & Selling, Financial Assistance, Taxes, etc. Also find workplace issue information on interviewing, working environments, training, hiring procedures, and employing minors. The Site Map works like a Table of Contents and gets you where you want to go quickly and easily.

Department of the Treasury Internal Revenue Service: www.irs.gov (Accessed Fall 2005).

The IRS's Market Segment Specialization Program focuses on particular market segments, which may be an industry such as auto body and repair, a profession including ministers, or an issue like aviation tax. These Guides discuss common and unique industry issues, business practices, and industry terminology. These Guides are produced and updated on an as-needed basis so some are quite old. However, you may find that like the overview of the Bars and Restaurants industry from April 2003, the information is still useful for your business.

**FedStats: www.fedstats.gov/ (Accessed Fall 2005).

The official website of the Federal Interagency Council on Statistical Policy is a gateway to statistics from over 100 U.S. federal agencies and is well organized and easy to use. Users can find under Links to Statistics, Topic Links A–Z, MapStats, and Statistics By Geography from U.S. Agencies. MapStats provides statistical profiles of states, counties, cities, congressional districts, and federal judicial districts. The Statistical Reference Shelf, a bit further down on the home page, is a large collection of online reference sources including the *Statistical Abstract of the United States*. You will find a variety of other sources such as the *State and Metropolitan Area Data Book* and *Digest of Education Statistics*, which will provide statistics on many topics of interest to entrepreneurs. On the other half of the page, Links to Statistical Agencies, under Agencies by Subject, click Economic on the drop-down arrow to lead you to a list of Periodic Economic Censuses. Below this area, you'll find Data Access Tools, which link users to agency online databases.

**FirstGov.gov: The U.S. Government's Official Web Portal: www.firstgov.gov (Accessed Fall 2005).

Information by Topic will interest and amaze first-timers. Topics include Environment, Energy and Agriculture, Money and Taxes, Reference and General Government, and Science and Technology. Tabs at the top of the page include one for Businesses and Nonprofits. On FirstGov.gov, under the Reference Center, clicking on Data and Statistics brings up an alphabetical list of links to resources chock full of statistics. Economic Indicators is the website of the Economics and Statistics Administration, part of the U.S. Department of Commerce (www.economicindicators.gov), and it provides timely access to the daily releases of key economic indicators from the Bureau of Economic Analysis (BEA) and the Census Bureau. Also, under Data and Statistics, you can find Health Statistics,

Labor Statistics, searchable government databases, and searchable bibliographies. Spanish translation of the site is also available. You can email questions about the site and the statistics or telephone for help too. Your taxes pay for the collection, compiling, and publishing of these statistics and they are available for your use.

**Market Research, Industry Research, Business Research: www.virtualpet.com/industry (Accessed Fall 2005).

This major portal for researching companies and industries presents a step-by-step process to begin researching an industry. Here you can find sources to help you learn about legal issues, regulatory issues, competition, markets, and even the history of the industry for your new business. Additional links to Industry Portals are also available. Three other linked sites offer help on How to Learn about a Company by Examining Its Products, How to Review, Evaluate, Critique a Web Site, and How to Conduct a Patent Search.

**RMA Universe: www.rmahq.com (Accessed Fall 2005).

After 85 years in the business, Robert Morris and Associates *Annual Statement Studies* are one of the standards in business ratios. This resource will help you show investors that you understand your business and are prepared to compete. Financial ratio benchmarks are included for over 700 industries, now using the NAICS codes. Trend data is available for five years. Using this data, you can make more informed decisions for your new business.

SBDCNET: sbdcnet.utsa.edu (Accessed Fall 2005).

The Small Business Development Center National Information Clearinghouse provides timely, web-based information to entrepreneurs. Small Business Development Centers (SBDC) are located in all 50 states. SBDCs offer free, confidential business counseling. This website provides information on business start-up, e-commerce, industry research, marketing, trends, and more. Templates for business plans and marketing tools are also available. A free newsletter will help you keep up on trends in small business. Entrepreneurs will find plenty of links and information here to help them plan and run their new business.

**State and Local Government on the Net: www.statelocalgov.net/ (Accessed Fall 2005).

This site provides convenient access to all state and local government sites by listing the states alphabetically. Frequently updated, this directory of official state, county, and city government websites also provides a list of topics to choose from plus listings of government grants, with applications. Links are provided to even the smallest counties or state agencies in the nation if they have a web presence. The directory lists 10,792 websites that can be searched by state, topic, or local government name.

The Thomas Register: www.thomasregister.com (Accessed Fall 2005).

This well-known multivolume set is now available online as well. It lists data on more than 150,000 manufacturing companies in the United States and Canada by type of product, company name, and location. Find your competitors and suppliers in this comprehensive listing of North American manufacturers; search by product, service, company, or brand.

**U.S. Census Bureau: www.census.gov/ (Accessed Fall 2005).

This web page is the best place to start searching for the multitude of data produced by Census programs, publications, and statistics. The home page groups the data under

Census 2000, People, Business, Geography, Newsroom, At the Bureau, and Special Topics. Under Business, you can click on the Economic Census, NAICS, Survey of Business Owners, E-Stats, and Foreign Trade. Under People, business owners will be interested in income statistics, housing data, and more. Analyzing the Demographic Trends in the United States allows businesses to forecast future demands for their products or services. The New to Using Census Bureau Data page is very helpful in helping users locate what they need quickly. The Catalog, a Search feature, and links to related sites are also accessible on the left side of the home page. Use this site frequently to help start and grow your business.

U.S. Industry & Trade Outlook 2000: www.ita.doc.gov/td/industry/otea/outlook/ (Accessed Fall 2005).

The 2000 Outlook is the last edition available in print. However, the Outlook is moving to the web. This single-source, industry-by-industry overview of the U.S. economy includes macro forecasts for U.S. industries, highlighting trends, and top performers. Industries are covered in chapters that include historical data, trends and international competition, trade patterns, and reference lists for further research.

Valuation Resources.com: www.valuationresources.com (Accessed Fall 2005).

This commercial site provides links to many industry information resources for over 250 industries. It pulls together industry resources from trade associations, industry publications, and research firms. Topics also included are industry outlook, financial ratios, salary surveys, economic data, and public market data. Check here to see what information is available on your industry.

START-UP 3

CHAPTER HIGHLIGHTS:

- Select Your Business
- A Cautionary Note
- Research Your Business and Industry
- Find Trade Associations
- Find Newspaper and Magazine Articles, Trade Publications, and Newsletters
- Determine Your Business Structure
- Establish Your Business Identity
- Financial Statements
- Breakeven Analysis
- Business Licenses and Permits
- Business Location
- Insurance

So far, you've decided you have entrepreneurial talents and you now know where to find many different types of business and industry information, statistics, economic indicators, etc. In this chapter, we'll examine some of the sources you'll want to consult as you begin your business planning—sources that will help you in everything from selecting a type of business and determining structure to how to get licenses and permits. In general, e-commerce or e-business is not the focus of this work, but keep in mind that if you are starting a dot-com business or e-commerce, basically everything that is needed for a successful bricks-and-mortar business is needed for an e-business to be successful as well. Let the decision making begin.

SELECT YOUR BUSINESS

What type of business should you start? Many people already have an idea and just need to determine if it's viable. Experts advise choosing something related to what you love, enjoy, and won't mind spending thousands of hours and dollars working on. The first question to ask yourself is, "If you could do anything in the world, what would you truly like to do with your time, daily, twelve or more hours each day?" There are probably a number of things that will occur to you. Make a list of them, and prioritize the list.

Other leading questions that may help you in the decision-making process are, "What don't you want to do, and what did you hate about previous jobs?" These questions may help you rule out some of the ideas swimming in your head.

Another important, even vital, question is does the market need your product or service? Most businesses provide a service to individuals or companies or they manufacture a product for individuals or businesses. Can you provide something better or more affordable than what is already being offered by other businesses?

Finding the perfect fit for you with a business may be difficult, but if you lack the drive and passion to overcome challenges and obstacles, success will be elusive. Time spent determining what business you want to start is time well spent.

A CAUTIONARY NOTE

There are four common mistakes that entrepreneurs often make when choosing their business. Review the list, and remember them.

1. One is overestimating demand for your product or service; be realistic as well as optimistic.

2. The second error is inadequate planning. One of the main reasons businesses fail is that the entrepreneur has not researched and planned every step of the way.

3. The third major error is not asking for help and advice. It is vital that you recognize who can best help you with each step of developing your business plan. Get free help when possible, but don't be afraid to pay a consultant, lawyer, or accountant.

4. Lastly, inadequate funding is a major error. Seek and obtain an adequate amount of financing as inadequate funding is a difficult problem to overcome. Opening on a shoestring may sound romantic, but it's not sound business practice.

If you have several business ideas and want to check a resource that will give you an overview of them, try the *Small Business Sourcebook*. This directory provides a wealth of information on nearly 350 different choices for the small business owner/manager. Each profile provides start-up information sources, associations, educational programs, reference works, sources of supply, statistical sources, trade periodicals, trade shows and conventions, consultants, franchises, and libraries and research centers relating to businesses such as coffee shops, dry cleaners, car washes, home furnishings store, and many more. This excellent first source of current, relevant information should be consulted by every new business owner.

Small Business Sourcebook. Thomson-Gale. Annual.

This directory provides a wealth of information for the small business owner/manager. In the over 300 Small Business Profiles, users will find a long and complete list of resources including associations, licensing, trade publications, trade shows, franchises, sources of supply, etc. about the type of business from Bagel Shop to Restaurants. Each resource in a profile has a complete citation as well as a short description. Often URLs are provided or email addresses. The two-volume set helps entrepreneurs start up, develop, and grow their businesses.

A website that allows you to explore different businesses is **Entrepreneur.com (www.entrepreneurmag.com)** from *Entrepreneur Magazine.* Under Businesses to Start, you will find many ideas of current "hot" businesses, new ideas for businesses, and information on starting or growing established business lines such as restaurants or interior decorating. If you need ideas or help developing an idea, here's a great place to start.

RESEARCH YOUR BUSINESS AND INDUSTRY

Now that you've determined what you want to do and that the market needs this product or service, you need to start asking questions and doing some research to form a start-up plan. As mentioned previously, failure to plan is one of the most frequently cited reasons for small business failures. You will need to extrapolate the information on your industry, market, and competition from government reports, newspaper and magazine articles, trade associations, university studies, and other research. Some of this material is available online, and some will only be found by visiting a business research library.

Interviewing potential customers and suppliers and people already in the same or a similar business is an additional method of collecting current data. Before conducting interviews, you will probably want to identify a list of questions to ask. For example,

1. Would the interviewee be interested in this product/service that you're thinking of offering?

2. How much might they pay for it?

3. Could the product/service they currently use be improved and how?

4. What do they see as trends in this industry/business?

If you know of people already in this type of business, you might approach them to give you a few hours of their time to help you learn the ropes or offer to pay them as a consultant. Besides conducting personal interviews, a survey can also be used to ask questions of potential customers or your target market. If you can identify a similar product or service to your idea, find out everything you can about the companies involved. One way to learn from possible competitors is to become a customer and identify what they do well and what needs improvement.

To learn more about the industry your business is in, explore the Small Business Development Center National Information Clearinghouse website at sbdcnet.utsa.edu/SBIC/industry.htm. Here you will find information on many smaller and developing industries and businesses including Art, Home Services, Pets, and Toys/Games. You can easily identify your North American Industry Code or NAICS to use when you research your industry in many sources. Start your industry research at this user-friendly site.

FIND TRADE ASSOCIATIONS

Trade associations are an important resource for any new business. Everyone needs contacts or a network, and you'll be no exception when you are running your own business. Joining a trade association, such as the National Retail Federation for small retailers, relevant to your industry, and nearly every industry has one, is a great way to get access to any research they have conducted on your industry as well as a way to network with seasoned professionals. Trade association members usually receive a copy of a monthly or quarterly newsletter; this will help you find out what's happening in the industry as well as within the association. These associations exist to provide networking, pooling of resources, sponsoring of conferences, and of course, publishing special reports and statistics on their industry. They also devote time and resources to keeping tabs on and influencing what's going on at all levels of government. Trade associations can even help you find professionals, like lawyers and accountants who specialize in your industry. Below are two outstanding print sources for locating trade associations with contact information, and many libraries will have copies of one or both of these sources:

Encyclopedia of Associations. Thomson Gale. Annual. $1310.00.

This comprehensive list of national organizations provides a brief entry including names, addresses, telephone numbers, URLs, cost of membership, and a short description of their publications and members. Organizations are grouped in general subject areas. Indexes provide access to the organizations, by name, key word, and geographic area. An international directory is also available. This work is a standard in the field and one any small business owner should know about.

Small Business Sourcebook. Thomson Gale. Annual. $405.00

This directory provides a wealth of information for the small business owner/manager but here we'll concentrate on information about trade associations. In the Small Business Profiles, the second part of the entry is entitled Associations and other Organizations, and listed here are trade and professional associations that gather and disseminate information and statistics of interest to its members. For each group, you'll find the association's name, address, phone, toll-free and fax numbers, company email, URL, contact name, purpose and objective, description of the membership, and a listing of its publications with frequency.

Trade associations can also be located online. Using any search engine, such as Google or Yahoo!, you will find a wide variety of associations. A sample search might include: "trade associations" and "Connecticut" (your state) or "business associations" and "Connecticut" (your state). If too many irrelevant associations surface this way, add your industry, such as "retail grocer" or "construction" to narrow the search.[1] Another approach is to use a subject directory, such as Yahoo!'s, which can be found at the following lengthy address (dir.yahoo.com/Business_and_Economy/Organizations/Trade_Associations/). This directory lists national and international associations alphabetically, and it can be searched by keyword. The Library of Congress also sponsors Business and Economics Online+ (BEOnline+) at http://lcweb.loc.gov/rr/business/beonline/. BEOnline began in 1996 as an experimental project to provide access for Internet resources related to the practice or study of entrepreneurship and small business. BEOnline+ expands the project to include additional subject areas in the humanities and social sciences. You will find a Subject Guide on Associations, which takes you to the Associations Database. There you'll see contacts, descriptions, addresses, and events data for over 10,000 business organizations in the United States. Find here the Association of Retail Marketing Services and the National Association of Beverage Retailers to name two that come up when searching retail.

A few specific URLs for small business general associations as examples are listed below alphabetically with a short description:

Entrepreneurship Institute (TEI): www.tei.net (Accessed Fall 2005)

Established in 1976, this institute provides encouragement and assistance to entrepreneurs and unites financial, legal, and community resources to help foster success of their companies. A monthly newsletter and periodic President's Forums are available to members.

National Association for the Self-Employed: www.nase.org (Accessed Fall 2005)

The self-employed and micro-businesses (up to 10 employees) join this group for support and advocacy. Their website links to the "Entrepreneurial Connection" (http://www.entrepreneurialconnection.com) where users can find Success Skills, Trends, and other helpful information.

---

[1] When you put quotation marks around a phrase in a search engine, often the search will look for the phrase instead of each individual word. Therefore, "trade associations" would be searched by Google instead of trade and associations. Hopefully, you will get fewer hits and fewer false hits on such a search.

National Federation of Independent Businesses: nfib.com (Accessed Fall 2005)

This long-established and well-known national advocacy organization represents small, independent businesses in Washington, D.C. The NFIB aims to impact public policy at the state and federal level and be a key resource for small businesses. On their site, you can see what impact their 600,000 members have and read other articles of interest to small businesses. Members have access to discounts on business products and services. Also, anyone can access their Tools and Tips section with helpful, practical articles for the entrepreneur.

Below are listed a couple of sites for special sectors of small business owners:

The National Association for Women Business Owners: www.nawbo.org (Accessed Fall 2005)

This group has chapters located through the United States and sponsors national and regional conferences, provides networking opportunities, and sponsors awards. The Center for Women's Business Research, part of the National Foundation for Women Business Owners, produces original groundbreaking research to show the economic and social contributions of women-owned firms.

The Minority Business Development Agency (MBDA): www.mbda.gov (Accessed Fall 2005)

Through its minority business development centers, regional and district, the MBDA helps new ventures and established businesses seek working capital, startup business financing, and access to markets. It helps entrepreneurs prepare loan packages, write business plans, and create financial statements. Other key sections include Management and Technical Assistance and Education and Training. It publishes *Capital Trends*, *Demographic Trends*, *Industry Trends*, and *Export Trends*. The Resource Locator will help users locate local minority business resources. Other MBDA development programs include Native American Business Development Center, Minority Business Opportunity Centers, and Business Resource Centers.

FIND NEWSPAPER AND MAGAZINE ARTICLES, TRADE PUBLICATIONS, AND NEWSLETTERS

Start your research by doing an industry overview and then move to specific companies in that industry. Periodicals are one of the best resources for current industry statistics as well as trends in the industry and the economy that are affecting companies. For some lists of trade publications grouped by business type, visit the Idea Café at http://www.businessownersideacafe.com, and some of the publications will give you a free one-year trial subscription to see if you can use the information they provide. On the left side of the screen about half-way down, you'll see Take Out Info and below that Free Trade Publications. The number of publications listed under each subject varies, but you'll probably find something of interest related to your new business.

Another way to find trade journals online by industry is to use Direct Contact Publishing's Media Jumpstation at www.imediafax.com/jumpstation/. Just

Figure 3.1 Screenshot of Small Business Help: Business Owners Idea Café (www.businessownersideacafe.com)

select an industry under Magazine Subject, and it brings up a list. Sometimes the entire journal is available and sometimes just some of the articles. Thousands of publications can be located here. For example, *Prepared Foods Magazine* at their website, http://www.preparedfoods.com/ includes New Product Trends, Daily Food News, Industry Associations, and supplier directories. Another example is *Beverage World* at http://www.beverageworld.com/, which features annual rankings of soft drinks, bottled water, and beer.

Large periodical indexes are generally available through local libraries and are usually online. Check with your local librarian to see if the library subscribes to Proquest, EBSCOHost, or Thomson Gale's *Business Resource Center*. If you are familiar with searching the Internet, you will have no problem searching these databases. Articles on new developments and trends in industries or companies can be found by searching company names or the industry. Major business publications such as the *Wall Street Journal* will provide you with information on economic and business trends that may impact your new venture. Large city newspapers like the *LA Times*, *Washington Post*, or *New York Times* are also indexed in large periodical indexes and can be searched in the same way. Local business journals and newspapers can provide you with data on your area; usually either local indexes or the large indexes will help you find information on subjects.

Another good resource to help you investigate business ideas is John Mullins's book, *The New Business Road Test*. Use his practical advice and real-world examples to give your new business idea a better chance at success. Learn what makes a viable business model and why good business ideas fail.

Mullins, John. *The New Business Road Test: What Entrepreneurs and Executives Should Do Before Writing a Business Plan.* Financial Times/Prentice Hall, 2004. 288p. ISBN 0-273-66356-9. $24.95.

Before writing a business plan or investing any money, use Mullins's seven domains model for assessing new business ideas. Learn how to run a customer-driven feasibility study to assess that new business opportunity. Case studies use real businesses such as Honda, Enterprise Car Rental, and Starbucks to illustrate industry trends and opportunities. What are critical success factors and niche markets? Avoid the "me too" trap and more. Use his practical advice and guidance to help your new business succeed.

Determine who is your market, before you invest time and money in a business with no or a shrinking market.

See Chapter 2 for more sources of statistics and industry data. Also, if during this planning phase of starting a new business, you decide that maybe you'd like to purchase an established business, one resource you might try is BizBuySell at www.bizbuysell.com. Here you will find a great deal of information about buying and valuing an established business. Also, check Chapter 5 on Franchising.

DETERMINE YOUR BUSINESS STRUCTURE

After deciding what type of business you're going to start and researching the industry, competition, and economy, you must decide the legal or business structure. This determination is one of the most important decisions that the new business owner can make. Depending on your choice of business structure, you may be personally liable if your business is sued for tax liabilities, torturous injuries (slip and fall), or other problems. This decision can also determine your ability to sell your interest in the business, influence the ease of later capital infusions, and affect the relationship between co-owners.

The primary forms of ownership in the United States include sole proprietorship, general partnership, limited partnership, C corporation, S corporation, and limited liability company (LLC). These forms will be briefly discussed here. But if you have any doubts about which one best fits your needs, the number of owners in your business, and financial exposure you can accept, research the forms more thoroughly (check the References for print and online resources), and consult an attorney.

Sole Proprietorship

This simplest, most common form of legal structure means you are the business and the business is you. The main advantages of the Sole Proprietorship are:

1. Owner has complete authority and control, and it's the easiest and cheapest form to set up and terminate;

2. It can easily be changed to a partnership or corporation; and

3. The government tends not to regulate.

The disadvantages of a Sole Proprietorship include:

1. As owner, your personal assets are at risk and all business obligations remain on you; and

2. The business ends with death or departure of the owner.

Partnership(s)

A Partnership is a business relationship involving two or more owners who share management responsibilities, profits, and all liability. A Partnership Agreement has been compared to a pre-nuptial agreement, but is usually even more complicated. This complex agreement should be created by a lawyer and typically covers:

1. Financial contribution of each partner;

2. Management and control of each;

3. Profit/loss sharing;

4. Responsibilities and duties;

5. Term of partnership;

6. Guidelines for admitting new partners;

7. Right of first refusal or other partners have the right to purchase withdrawing partner's interest before that partner can offer it to someone else; and

8. Stated policy on how a deceased partner's interest will be handled.

A Partnership is not considered as a separate taxpayer so profits or losses are passed through individual income tax returns proportionate to the ownership percentage. (See Chapter 10, Legal/Taxes, for more information.) Two types of partnerships exist, the General Partnership and the Limited Partnership. A Limited Partnership is based on a General Partnership and consists of one or more general partners and one or more limited partners who have restricted or limited responsibilities and liabilities. Silent partner or partners is often used to describe these agreements as limited partners who have no voice in the day-to-day business operations and management. Limited partnerships are a method of obtaining investments in a business with limited financial exposure as well as limited exposure to lawsuits for the investor. Advantages of Partnerships include:

1. Shared power and responsibility along with complementary skills;

2. Partner investments bring additional funds;

3. Tax rate is lower than corporate rate;

4. Partnerships can easily be incorporated; and

5. Relatively inexpensive and easy to start and operate.

Disadvantages of Partnerships are:

1. All partners are responsible for all the other partners' liabilities and debts for the partnership;
2. The partnership terminates on death of a member unless prior arrangements are made in the initial agreement; and
3. Disagreements between partners can affect success and operation of the business.

Corporations

A C corporation is a legal entity whose organizational structure has been established in accordance with state laws and given certain rights and responsibilities. In its simplest form, a corporation can have one shareholder or stockholder who owns 100% of the stock, is chair of the board, and president of the company. The sole voting stockholder can nominate and elect individuals to serve on the board of directors. For specifics on state requirements for C corporations, check with the Secretary of State in your state. Corporations must conform to numerous regulations and file certain forms in a timely manner, so verify your state and federal procedures with a local lawyer.

Under S corporation structure, income losses, deductions, and credits of the corporation are passed through its shareholders to be included on personal income tax returns. Organizational requirements for corporate structure must still be met and maintained. The S status exists only for reporting taxes and can easily be changed to a regular corporate tax structure. Please note that not all states recognize the S corporation, which means that you would pay federal individual taxes but state taxes would be paid at the corporate rate. Check with an accountant and lawyer for recommendations on your specific situation. The advantages of Corporations are:

1. Your business has a legal life of its own.

2. It's easy to raise capital by selling stock or shares in the company or transferring stock to key employees as an incentive or benefit.

3. A corporate structure allows each owner to separate personal assets from company assets.

4. Corporations are granted tax deductions not available to other forms of businesses.

Disadvantages of corporations include:

1. Corporations have more complex start-up procedures and maintenance with higher costs to meet legal requirements.

2. If shareholders are involved, decision making can be more complex.

3. Taxes may be higher as corporate tax rates are higher than individual ones and dividends are taxed as profits and then as income to the shareholder.

Limited Liability Company

Limited Liability Company (LLC) is the newest business structure in this country. An LLC contains the tax advantages of a partnership with the limited personal liability of a corporation. An LLC must issue stock but can issue two classes of stock—for voting and nonvoting members. Advantages of LLCs include:

1. It allows an unlimited number of stockholders who need not be U.S. citizens;

2. An LLC requires less paperwork than corporations and limits the liability of the owners; and

3. An LLC avoids being taxed twice like C corporations are.

Disadvantages of are LLCs:

1. The organizing costs are as high as those of corporations; and

2. The states are interpreting the legalities of an LLC differently, which sometimes involves high fees and additional taxes.

Below are two resources to check first when you're deciding on your business structure.

Beech, Wendy. *Black Enterprise Guide to Starting Your Own Business*. John Wiley & Sons, Inc., 1999. 465p. ISBN 0-471-32454-X. $19.95.

Beech covers business structure in a very thorough chapter, including sample tax forms. A multitude of checklists, sample forms, and lists of resources enhances the book's continuing usefulness. One highlight is the testimonials of black entrepreneurs who have persevered again the odds. Readers will be motivated and inspired.

Cooke, Robert E. and Cooke, Robert A. *Small Business Formation Handbook*. John Wiley & Sons, Inc., 1999. 245 p. ISBN 0-471-31475-7. $22.95.

This comprehensive resource describes in detail the different types of business structures including sole proprietorships, partnerships, C and S corporations, and limited liability companies. The advantages and disadvantages of each type are discussed. The first part of the book helps users eliminate the types of formations a business cannot and should not use. The second section includes samples of all the necessary business and legal forms including articles of incorporation, stockholder agreements, IRS forms, and more. To make a completely informed decision on business structure, use this resource fully and consult a lawyer for recent changes in laws.

ESTABLISH YOUR BUSINESS IDENTITY

Naming or identifying your business holds it together and should be a fun, personal, and professional activity that uses your creative powers to the max. Try to find something that represents the feel of your business and is infused with your personality. Be sure to consider these aspects or issues as you brainstorm:

1. Alphabetical placement as in the Yellow Pages and other directories should be considered as a name at the beginning of the alphabet has major benefits since people often start at the top of a list and work their way down.

2. Personalization, or should you include your name or not. Whether you choose to use you name or someone else's probably depends on personal preference and the type of industry.

3. Depictive or representational names that connect to the kind of business you are in are sometimes helpful. People associate the name with the product or service.

4. A "play on words" such as puns can help or hurt your cause, but try to stay away from "too cute." A clever name that sets you apart from competitors is a real plus, but often a straightforward, informative name works best.

5. Expandability is important so don't get too specific. Adding Etc. or "and More" often gives one room for diversification.

6. Trademarkability is a complex process but in the future, you might want to consider it. See more information about trademarks on the next page and in Chapter 10, Legal/Taxes under Legalities of Business Names.

7. Internet domain availability is important even if you have no immediate plans to use the Internet. Check to see if "the name you want.com" has been registered and if not, register it immediately. One good website to use in this search is www.internic.com. If you are new to the world of domain names, this site can provide some basic information on domains and has been designed to provide the public with information regarding Internet domain name registration. See Chapter 10, Legal/Taxes again for information on registering a domain name and checking to see what ones are available. If your domain name has already been registered, you might want to consider changing it slightly or find a variation that you can register as a dot-com.

In any case, you must pay attention to the laws of business names and trademarks in selecting your name. To begin learning the basics about trademarks (and patents), start by reading the information on the U.S. Patent and Trademark Office website at www.uspto.gov. Here you will find FAQs and guidelines to help you understand the basic ideas and types of trademarks available. You can search trademarks to see if your idea has already been trademarked. You can email or call the Trademark Assistance Center with your questions too. It's possible to apply for a trademark online, but a lawyer is useful in guiding you through this tricky procedure. The site also provides a list of trademark lawyers. Depending on your chosen legal structure, you will have to follow some specific rules for registering your business's name and protecting its identity. And, in today's world of the Internet, growing national chains, and mail order, checking local sources in your state is not enough.

In Peri Pakroo's *The Small Business Start-Up Kit*, you will find an excellent chapter on Picking Winning Business Names That Won't Land You in Court. Nolo Press is the publisher of this book and on their website at http://www.nolo.com, you will find an article under Starting a Business, entitled Registering Your Business Name, by attorney Bethany K. Laurence. This article is short but thorough and will help you cover your bases. Keep in mind that if you choose a business name that has no part of your name, then you will need to file a fictitious business name statement, sometimes called an assumed business name or doing business as (DBA) name with your county or city clerk and with your state's secretary of state. Resources in Chapter 10 cover the legalities of name more thoroughly. In most "starting a business" books, there is some information on business names, but be as thorough as you can to save yourself grief later when your business is established.

FINANCIAL STATEMENTS

As you begin the process of estimating your sales and expenses for your new business, keep in mind that at this time these numbers are guesses. You must conduct your research and based on that, make your best estimates. The basics are provided here, and it is recommended that you consult several of the sources at the end of the chapter and/or an accountant to help you develop your financial plan. You will need to develop three critical financial statements as part of the planning process, and most experts suggest projecting for three years.

Start with the Cash Flow Statement. This statement monitors the changes in your cash during a set period of time. Estimate here your gross receipts on sales for the first year and then break it down into monthly income. If you know of any seasonal highs or lows for your business, include those in your estimates. Also list any invested capital. Below this, you estimate your monthly expenses. Just like a home budget, you include utilities, insurance, supplies, raw materials, taxes, any loan payments, travel, etc. Then subtract your expenses from your income each month. This tool is very important because if you run out of cash, you could be out of business. Monitor your cash flow at least monthly, if not weekly when you first begin your business.

The Income Statement is similar to the cash flow statement and presents the proverbial bottom line. It is sometimes referred to as a Statement of Profit and Loss and is really quite simple. Write down the total revenue you expect to receive from selling your products or services, and then subtract the total cost of operating your company. This number is your net profit. This statement will show your company's financial performance over a period of time.

Finally, the Balance Sheet details a company's assets (cash, inventory, equipment), liabilities (accounts payable, loans), and capital (equity in the business). It tells you just how much money you'd have left if you sold absolutely everything and then paid every last one of your debts. Everything your company owns are its assets, the amounts you owe are your liabilities, and the difference between the two is the equity in your business. Financial information will help you develop a realistic budget and develop a vision for growth. With these three financial statements, you can also compare your company with other companies and with industry averages through financial ratios.

The best resource for help in preparing these three important financial statements is by Peri Pakroo with the citation listed below.

Pakroo, Peri. *The Small Business Start-Up Kit*. 2nd ed. Nolo Press, 2003. 250p. ISBN 0-87337-924-1. $29.99.

Her chapter on Financial Statements is especially useful. Using real-life case studies, Pakroo illustrates important issues. Learn what the numbers mean and how to calculate them. Chapters on federal, state, and local start-up requirements, on insurance and risk management, and on taxes are also treasure troves of practical, useful information for every new business owner. Additionally, a CD-ROM, which includes a multitude of useful forms, is included with the book.

For a great website to help you develop and use financial statements, try Edward Lowe's Peerspectives at peerspectives.org. The article titled How to Analyze Your Business Using Financial Ratios will help you understand "financial ratio analysis," comparing it to "batting averages for business." Learn how to calculate Operating Ratios, Liquidity Ratios, and Solvency Ratios, for example. Another article titled Taking the Financial Pulse of Your Business, explains things like Debt to Equity, Current Ratio, and Asset Composition Ratio.

BREAKEVEN ANALYSIS

In addition to financial ratios, every small business owner needs to know how to conduct a breakeven analysis. When planning a new business or making decisions about offering new products or services, entrepreneurs need to find out at what point they will begin making money. The breakeven point is where the income from sales exactly equals all the fixed and variable costs incurred in doing business. More sales will result in profit, and fewer sales will result in loss. Once you know all your costs and have estimated the selling price, you can calculate how many products or hours of your time you will need to sell to break even, or cover all your costs. When you know what you need to sell, you can look at market demand and competitors' market shares to determine if it is realistic to expect to sell that much. Breakeven analysis helps you think through the impact of price and volume relationships. A higher price for your product or service will achieve breakeven with fewer sales, but a lower price may attract more customers.

The further above breakeven that a business can operate, the greater its margin of safety is. Once you have determined your price and defined the breakeven volume that you need to sell, you can set an annual target, broken down by monthly targets, to determine how to generate a reasonable profit.

To monitor the progress of your business, you might want to plot targets for sales and actual sales on a graph. If your business is not achieving its targets, you can take remedial action immediately. A business owner should review sales volumes and income regularly to ensure that you are making a profit. Adjusting your sales price or increasing marketing efforts are two actions that can affect your business's profitability. Once again refer to Peri Pakroo's book, *The Small Business Start-Up Kit*, mentioned a few pages back for more help on estimates to figure your breakeven point. A good website for all things "accounting" is Business Town.com at http://businesstown.com/accounting/projections.asp.

The article Break-Even Analysis thoroughly explains why an analysis is important and then walks you through an example using fixed and semi-variable expenses. Also find ways to lower your breakeven volume.

BUSINESS LICENSES AND PERMITS

The list of businesses and professions that must be licensed varies by state, as does the list of businesses needing a permit in order to operate. Virtually every business owner will have to acquire a county, city, state, and/or federal license. You may need a seller's permit and federal I.D. number depending on your industry and local requirements. Seller's permits are required in states that impose sales tax. Each state uses a different agency to issue such permits. You may also need a permit to handle flammable materials, a food-service license, or others. Don't think that if you have an e-commerce or Internet business that you are exempt from business licenses and permits; check with these agencies to see what's required.

Start by calling your city or county clerk's office or checking with your local Chamber of Commerce and these may lead you to a state office. Securing the appropriate licenses for your business can be a challenging task. Most entrepreneurs will need a local or "municipal" license and some type of filing with their state. Call or visit the appropriate licensing departments in your area for information on fees and necessary forms. Planning and Zoning departments often review license applications to determine whether the area's zoning ordinances permit your type of business in that jurisdiction. Besides providing government agencies with a tax-collecting strategy, licensing and permits show your customers that you have complied with local regulations. Generally speaking, it can take from two to eight weeks to obtain the necessary permits and licenses.

BUSINESS LOCATION

Business location can be a major issue for retail operations and restaurants, so if you're planning one of these types of businesses, you must determine if your customers will be coming to you and how visible you need to be. For some businesses, success is based on choosing a strong, visible, accessible, and high-traffic location. On the other hand, some businesses are not impacted by location, and you can work from your home or any rented location. If your business has special needs (e.g., catering or mail-order food business), or if you've outgrown your basement or garage, you might look into a small business incubator. Incubators offer commercial space to start-up businesses at a below-market rate in order to foster entrepreneurism. They have different sponsors, usually universities, economic development groups, or state and local governments. New incubators open every month, and some are now located in rural areas as well as cities. The basic services offered sometimes include (these will vary so check with your own locale):

1. *Low-cost flexible space and leases.* Key words here are low cost, usually below-market rate, and flexibility, giving a new business space to grow if needed quickly.

2. *Shared business equipment and services.* Expensive equipment such as fax machines, copiers, computers, and services such as bookkeeping, reception, and word processing are often among the choices offered. Sometimes access is included in the rent and sometimes it is pay as you use.

3. *Business and technical assistance.* A team of experts or network of community support may help entrepreneurs in areas such as business planning, engineering, patent protection, and marketing.

4. *Financial assistance.* Expert help in preparing to secure a loan or gain access to federal and state research and development funds may be provided.

5. *Networking.* Associating with other small business owners in the incubator allows you to bond with people facing the same set of problems and issues your company may face. The mentoring and access to business contacts provided may be the most important value of an incubator. Partnerships with other businesses in the facility may be advantageous to your business.

To see if an incubator might be a fit to help your business off to a good start, analyze the costs and services, as well as policies and procedures. Business incubators screen new businesses and accept companies that are likely to succeed, have sufficient financing, are committed to success, will benefit from the incubator's help, and are able to build a growing business. Check out the website of the National Business Incubation Association (NBIA) at www.nbia.org for more information on incubators, locations in your area, and help in determining if one is right for your business.

If you're a dot-com entrepreneur, please keep in mind that operating an e-business from home or an office does not mean you can skip licensing. Like a bricks-and-mortar business, a license will legitimate and establish your business in the view of local, state, and federal governments. If you have an income, you must pay taxes, and if you have a loss, you will want to use it to save you on taxes. Local licenses are easy to obtain and inexpensive. For more information on starting an e-business, check out *Entrepreneur Magazine's* website at www.entrepreneur.com. Tim W. Knox's article on No Exemptions for E-Businesses is excellent, and one of their how-to guides is entitled How to Start an E-Business.

INSURANCE

All businesses need business insurance to protect against losses. Uninsured losses will threaten your financial situation, so don't cut corners here. The type of insurance you buy depends on the specific coverage you need. Ask other business owners in your area which insurance agents or brokers they would recommend. Get quotes from several agents to compare quotes and gain a perspective on which types of insurance your business needs. Some types of insurance include business owner's policy (BOP), property, malpractice, liability, product liability, health, and business interruption. Property insurance usually covers vehicle damage, comprehensive damage, fire, crime, and inland marine. Liability covers general liability, but there's also product liability, automobile, and "umbrella" insurance to consider. To learn more about the types of insurance that would apply to your business, check out the Insurance Information Institute's website at www.iii.org or check with an insurance agent. The Institute's site answers questions like how to save money on business insurance, whether you need professional liability insurance, what does a business owner's policy cover, and more.

Everyone has different ways of thinking and working. Below is a list of resources that can help you work through the procedures of kick starting your first business venture. Try several to see which one(s) works best for you. For researching your industry, go back and look at references listed in Chapter 2 for additional assistance. Remember planning is the key to a successful business. Good luck!

REFERENCES

(Starred titles discussed in the chapter)

■ Print Resources

**Beech, Wendy. *Black Enterprise Guide to Starting Your Own Business*. John Wiley & Sons, Inc., 1999. 465p. ISBN 0-471-32454-X. $19.95.

Beech covers business structure in a very thorough chapter, including sample tax forms. A multitude of checklists, sample forms, and lists of resources enhances the book's continuing usefulness. The chapter on Choosing a Business Form is easy to understand and thorough. If you're considering buying a business, Chapter 14 will help you find and investigate the possibilities open to you. The chapter on a web presence is also still very useful. One highlight is the testimonials of black entrepreneurs who have persevered again the odds. Readers will be motivated and inspired.

Browning, Robert. *Setting Up and Running a Limited Company: A Comprehensive Guide to Forming and Operating a Company as a Director and Shareholder*. 4th ed. How To Books, 2004. 192p. ISBN 1-85703-866-5. $22.75.

Because LLCs are relatively new business structures, many business owners have more questions about them, and this book sets out the pros and cons of an LLC. Find out how to proceed and operate a limited liability company if that's the structure you choose. Browning explains the responsibilities of shareholders and directors, how to prepare financial records, find venture capital, and dissolve an LLC gracefully. Though aimed at the U.S. market, the book does have a slight British approach. Well written and clearly organized, see if Browning can help you with your LLC.

**Cooke, Robert E. and Cooke, Robert A. *Small Business Formation Handbook.* John Wiley & Sons, Inc., 1999. ISBN 0-471-31475-7. $22.95.

This comprehensive resource describes in detail the different types of business structures including sole proprietorships, partnerships, C and S corporations, and limited liability companies. The advantages and disadvantages of each type are discussed. The first part of the book helps users eliminate the types of formations a business cannot and should not use. The second section includes samples of all the necessary business and legal forms including articles of incorporation, stockholder agreements, IRS forms, and more. Steps users should take to protect themselves from incurring penalties from local, state, and federal agencies are also enumerated. To make a completely informed decision on business structure, use this resource fully and consult a lawyer for recent changes in laws.

daCosta, Eduardo. *Global E-Commerce Strategies for Small Business.* MIT Press, 2001. 230p. ISBN 0262041901. $24.95.

daCosta lays out the steps for beginning a global small business. Using examples from seven companies located in six different countries, he details the purchasing process and customer service, explains how to research new business opportunities and markets, recommends ways to utilize the web and other forms of new technology, and provides ideas for overcoming obstacles to international trade for small companies. Written in a casual, readable style, readers on all levels will gain something from this optimistic view of the global marketplace.

Duoba, John L. and Gada, Paul (eds.). *Launching Your First Small Business; Make the Right Decisions During Your First 90 Days.* 2nd ed. CCH Inc., 2003. 201p. ISBN 0-8080-0859-5. $14.95.

The purpose of this book is to lead entrepreneurs through the process of starting their first business. The first part, Clearing the Preliminary Hurdles, helps readers answer questions like what do you want from self-employment, is there a market for your business idea, and can you afford to go into business? Chapters cover the topics of matching your skills with current opportunities in the marketplace, selecting professionals, marketing your business concept, and equipping and staffing the right facility and location. Especially useful is Chapter 10, Figuring the Cost of Opening Your Doors. A companion website, CCH Business Owner's Toolkit Online at www.toolkit.cch.com provides a wealth of interactive forms and spreadsheets to customize for your business.

**Encyclopedia of Associations Thomson-Gale. Annual $1310.00

This comprehensive list of national organizations provides a brief entry including names, addresses, telephone numbers, URLs, cost of membership, and a short description of their publications and members. Organizations are grouped in general subject areas. Indexes provide access to the organizations, by name, key word, and geographic area. An international directory is also available. This work has become a standard in its field.

Esser, Teresa. *The Venture Café.* Warner Books, 2001. 292p. Index. ISBN 0-446-52783-1. $24.95.

Esser is a young member of the MIT entrepreneurial community and has gathered case studies of small business successes and failures in order to explore the nature of the entrepreneurial spirit. Along the way and using real-life stories, she teaches readers how to find funding, attract good employees, use the press, and set up a vesting schedule.

Friedman, Caitlin and Yorio, Kimberly. *The Girl's Guide to Starting Your Own Business*. HarperResource, 2004. 272p. ISBN B0002RQ1Q8. $21.95.

Full of practical, frank, and useful advice and presented in a straightforward, breezy style, this guide covers all the basics using charts, quizzes, checklists, worksheets, and interviews. In addition, they cover proposals, presentations, payroll taxes, selecting a lawyer and an accountant, and venture capital, with an emphasis on networking and public relations. Their knowledge and zeal is contagious.

Gilderson, Linda D. and Paauwe, Theresia. *Self-Employment: From Dream to Reality*. 2nd ed. JIST Works, 2003. 144p. ISBN 1-56370-922-8. $16.95.

The worksheets and exercises provided here encourage a practical, hands-on approach to learning. Gilderson and Paauwe present key business concepts in a simple-to-understand manner with clear examples. The chapter on Understanding Financial Statements is particularly well done. All areas of start-up are covered and presented in an organized manner. If you want to be your own boss, this book will help you on your way to success.

Goodridge, Walt. *Turn Your Passion into Profit*. 2nd ed. Passion Profit Co., 2004. 338p. ISBN 0-9745313-2-4. $29.95.

This inspiring work advises readers to follow their passion. Goodridge, a writer for *Entrepreneur Magazine, Black Enterprise*, and others, motivates readers and provides the steps needed to achieve success as an entrepreneur. All the basic areas of starting and growing a small business are presented. Practical, down-to-earth advice to make the move from employee to self-employed business person is provided in a logical, well-organized format.

Hashemi, Sahar and Hashemi, Bobby. *Anyone Can Do It: Building Coffee Republic from our Kitchen Table—57 Real Life Laws on Entrepreneurship*. Capstone, Ltd., 2003. 224p. ISBN 1-841122041. $24.95.

This sister, a lawyer, and brother, an investment banker, team built Coffee Republic, the original High Street coffee chain in the United Kingdom. They left the security of well-paying jobs to follow the entrepreneurial dream. Here they chronicle the development of the business plan, raising money, opening the first store, taking the company public, and finally today's inspirational success where Coffee Republic has over 100 outlets and thousands of employees. Small business ownership is time consuming but if you're successful, the rewards are tremendous as illustrated by this team.

Holden, Greg. *Starting an Online Business for Dummies*. 3rd ed. For Dummies, 2002. 384p. ISBN 0-7645-1655-8. $24.99.

As in other books of this series, readers find the basics of starting a business on the Internet. E-commerce survival stories, best practices, and other resources to help you develop your new business are provided. Good tips on selecting an online host, understanding website design, establishing a graphic identity, providing customer service, and providing various payment options. Some coverage of legal matters, trademarks, copy-righting, and taxes are included. If you like the For Dummies format and are thinking of joining the e-commerce world, this book will work for you.

Hupalo, Peter I. *How to Start and Run Your Own Corporation: S-Corporations for Small Business Owners*. HCM Pub., 2003. 208p. ISBN 0-9671-624-4-0. $22.95.

This thorough, instructional explanation of S corporations shows why this business structure may be right for your business. He also employs dozens of examples to illustrate the key issues involved in choosing a business structure and how to manage it later. Learn the role of bylaws and how to minimize taxes and issue shares. Hupalo explains how to fill out the 1120S Corporate Income Tax form as well as Social Security and Unemployment Insurance for officer salaries. A chapter on Attracting Angel Investors for your Corporation is also included.

Judson, Bruce. *Go It Alone*. HarperBusiness, 2004. 207p. ISBN 0-06-073113-3. $23.95.

Not as practical as some of the other titles listed, this book convinces readers that using the array of current technology such as email, the WWW, and outsourcing many aspects of a small business, it has never been easier to start your own business. Judson lists the principles of success, dispels the myths about start-up, discusses when to quit your day job, and encourages learning from mistakes. Using many real-life examples, Judson encourages you to recognize your core competency and use it in your daily work.

Kawasaki, Guy. *The Art of the Start*. Portfolio, 2004. 226p. ISBN 1-59184-056-2. $26.95.

For those thinking about starting a business, Kawasaki's GIST's (Great Ideas for Starting Things), which open each chapter, will help turn any idea into action. In a casual, entertaining style, Kawasaki discusses such basics as selecting a company name, writing business plans, establishing partnerships, building brand identity, and more. Kawasaki, a well-known figure in Silicon Valley, is very familiar with the needs of technology start-ups so be sure to consult this title if that's where you're headed. Easy to read and understand, let Kawasaki get you off to a great start.

Levonsky, Rieva. *Start Your Own Business*. 3rd ed. McGraw-Hill, 2004. 800p. ISBN 1-932156-65-8. $24.95.

Full of worksheets, tip boxes, charts, graphs, and illustrations, Levonsky's book provides practical, hands-on techniques to get you started in your own business. Learn how to conduct market research, develop a system for keeping your books and doing your taxes, create a winning business plan, and learn about choosing a name and leasing versus buying equipment. Chapters are short and to the point. If you're a new entrepreneur with little or no business education or experience, this book will help you with the basics.

Lientz, Bennet P. and Rea, Kathryn P. *Start Right in E-business: A Step by Step Guide to Successful E-business Implementation*. Academic Press, 2001. 326p. ISBN 0-12-449977-5. $44.95.

Based on over 50 e-business implementation projects, each chapter provides detailed guidelines for helping transform a business into an e-enterprise. Highlights include nine principles for e-business implementation, 13 specific actions to include, plus a chapter on technology, management, vendors, and organizational issues. Practical information is written in a user-friendly format.

McKnight, Thomas K. *Will It Fly? How to Know if Your New Business Idea Has Wings...Before You Take the Leap*. Prentice Hall, 2003. 332p. ISBN 0-13-046221-7. $24.95.

This unique title helps entrepreneurs evaluate their ideas. Using 44 crucial success indicators, readers can refine and prepare their ideas to maximize their chances of success. For each element, readers learn what to evaluate, how important it is, how to uncover the information needed, and how to improve the score. McKnight covers pricing strategy, competition, outsourcing, management, products or services, operations, and personnel. Use this practical book before you start your business plan.

Montgomery, Vickie L. *The Smart Woman's Guide to Starting a Business*. Career Press, 1998. 287p. ISBN 1-56414-368-6. $15.99.

With practical advice, insight, and encouragement, this revised edition covers a variety of basic concepts and start-up issues and challenges such as startup options, business plans, marketing, accounting, technology, and employees. Well organized and written in easy-to-understand language, this title presents chapters that will help readers understand concepts and use the advice presented quickly and easily.

**Mullins, John. *The New Business Road Test: What Entrepreneurs and Executives Should Do Before Writing a Business Plan*. Financial Times/Prentice Hall, 2004. 288p. ISBN 0-273-66356-9. $24.95.

Before writing a business plan or investing any money, use Mullins's seven domains model for assessing new business ideas. Learn how to run a customer-driven feasibility study to assess that new business opportunity. Case studies use real businesses like Honda, Enterprise Car Rental, and Starbucks to illustrate industry trends and opportunities. What are critical success factors and niche markets? Avoid the "me too" trap and more. Use his practical advice and guidance to help your new business succeed.

Norman, Jan. *What No One Ever Tells You about Starting Your Own Business*. Upstart Publishing Company, 1999. 221p. ISBN 1-57410-112-9. $17.95.

Norman's collection of short tales of adventures and misadventures in starting a business will teach you lessons about business start-up painlessly. Enjoyable to read, the stories are grouped in major topic areas such as The Money Chase, Management Issues, and Marketing. At the end of each section, a collection of Tips summarizes ideas presented through the stories.

**Pakroo, Peri. *The Small Business Start-Up Kit*. 2nd ed. Nolo Press, 2003. 250p. ISBN 0-87337-924-1. $29.99.

Besides covering the basics, Chapter 3, Picking Winning Business Names That Won't Land You in Court, is an outstanding collection of information and advice on trademarks, names, and domain names. Her chapter on financial statements is also very useful and thorough as is the chapter on Choosing a Legal Structure. Chapters on federal, state, and local start-up requirements, on insurance and risk management, and on taxes are also treasure troves of practical, useful information for every new business owner. Appendix A provides contact information for an assortment of business and tax-related agencies for each of the 50 states. Appendix C is a collection of Tear-Out Forms for the new business owner. Additionally, a CD-ROM is included with the book and contains useful tax forms and a partnership agreement. Pakroo's outstanding book is mentioned many times throughout this book as it really provides essential advice to new entrepreneurs in many areas of starting a new business and is a worthwhile purchase.

Rogak, Lisa. *The Compete Small Business Start-up Guide*. John Wiley & Sons, Inc., 2004. 256p. ISBN 0-471-67957-7. $14.95.

Here Rogak concentrates on finding the ideal business idea for each entrepreneur by matching personality and skills. There is an excellent chapter on selecting the best business structure to meet your goals and match your individual circumstances. Choosing a bank and selling your business are also thoroughly covered. Rogak presents a realistic, detailed picture of the life of an entrepreneur.

**Small Business Sourcebook*. Thomson-Gale. Annual. $405.00.

You'll find a wealth of information for the small business owner/manager in this guide, but here we'll concentrate on trade associations. In the Small Business Profiles, the second part of the entry is entitled Associations and Other Organizations, and listed here are trade and professional associations that gather and disseminate information and statistics of interest to its members. This resource lists the association's name, address, phone, toll-free and fax numbers, company email, URL, contact name, purpose and objective, description of the membership, and its publications along with frequency. Also in the Small Business Profiles, users will find a long and complete list of resources grouped under categories like licensing, trade publications, trade shows, franchises, sources of supply, etc. about any type of business from Bagel Shop to Restaurant. Each resource in a profile has a complete citation as well as a short description. URLs or email addresses are provided. The two-volume set helps entrepreneurs start up, develop, and grow their businesses.

Stephenson, James. *Ultimate Homebased Business Handbook: How to Start, Run and Grow Your Own Profitable Business*. Entrepreneur Press, 2004. 404p. ISBN 1-932-5310-2-5. $23.95.

This handy guide will help you start your own venture in your kitchen or spare room. Every stage of business creation is covered but the chapter on setting up your business legally is especially noteworthy. Stephenson provides how-to tips, ideas, and tools to organize and develop a winning business strategy. Operations, collections, taxes, licenses, and increasing sales are presented thoroughly and in layperson's language. And, if you haven't determined what kind of business to start, good ideas are also available here. This useful book will help many new entrepreneurs.

Strauss, Steven D. *Business Start-Up Kit*. netLibrary, 2003. ISBN 0-585-44549-4. $19.95.

Strauss's business model teaches an entrepreneur what steps to take to start and run a successful business. Included here are proven strategies, tips, worksheets, and forms to fill out. The first three chapters concentrate on how to choose and do what you love and Chapters 4 through 20 explain success strategies. Learn about how to write an outstanding business plan and financial planning for your start-up. Thorough coverage of this complex challenge is presented clearly.

Turner, Marcia Layton. *The Unofficial Guide to Starting a Small Business*. John Wiley & Sons, Inc., 2004. 432p. ISBN 0-7645-7285-7. $16.99.

This well-written manual for the entrepreneur explains selling services, hiring and firing, networking, taxes, business insurance, and more. Learn where to find office space, how to keep overhead and expenses down, find cheaper supplies and temporary help, and how to do market research. The business plan chapter is complete and easy to understand with "tried-and-true templates." The section discussing the growth of a small business will help many make the transition through the "I am the business" stage. The checklists and illustrative examples are particularly noteworthy. Tools and References at the end of each chapter will help you find more assistance for areas where you need it.

Tyson, Eric and Schell, Jim. *Small Business for Dummies.* 2nd ed. John Wiley & Sons, Inc., 2002. 432p. ISBN 0-7645-5481-6. $21.99.

This enterprising guide explains how to write a business plan, manage your costs and your time, create the right legal framework for your business, find financing, and understand financial statements. Financial ratios and how to determine them are also well covered in plain, simple language. The "For Dummies" format includes tear-out cheat sheets, top ten lists, and dashes of fun and humor.

The Ultimate Small Business Guide: A Resource for Startups and Growing Businesses. Basic Books, 2004. 501p. ISBN 0-7382-0913-9. $19.95.

This large collection of how-to's, step-by-step objective lists, and enlightening FAQs covers all aspects of planning, launching, managing, and growing your small business. Sections cover Refining and Protecting Your Idea, Communicating with Your Customers, Selling Online, and Managing Yourself and Others. Financing, pricing, cash flow, ratios, and assets are thoroughly and carefully covered in a section called Figuring It Out. The Directory at the end of the book leads users to more resources.

Online Resources

American Express Small Business Exchange: http://www133.americanexpress.com/osbn/ Landing/informyourdecisions.asp?us_nu=subtab (Accessed Fall 2005).

Small business owners will find help here on management, finding money, and marketing. This outstanding site has information on managing debt, business plans, and SBA loans. The article under Financial Management, entitled Business Valuation Methods, explains the various common methods used to come up with a value for a small business. The Starting a Business section tells users about structuring their business as well as some information on types of insurance.

**BEOnline: Business and Economics Online: www.loc.gov/rr/business/beonline/ (Accessed Fall 2005).

Compiled by the Library of Congress Business Reference Services for researchers, under Subject Guides, you will find a lengthy list of business topics like associations, business plans (forms), companies by industry, data sets, e-commerce, franchises, economic indicators, legal resources, and more. If you click on Associations, you are in an Associations Database, which includes contacts, descriptions, addresses, and events data for the organizations listed. Over 10,000 business organizations in the United States are listed. Find here a link to the Herb Growing and Marketing Network or the Association of Bridal Consultants. Under the Title Listing, you will find Airlines of the Web, America's Business Funding Directory, American Chambers of Commerce Abroad, American City Business Journals, and more.

**BizBuySell: www.bizbuysell.com (Accessed Fall 2005).

This very useful, practical website not only lets you find businesses for sale on the Internet, but provides a wealth of articles on valuing and buying a business. Search for a business to buy here if you've decided through the planning process that you'd like to start with an established business. The Common Questions and Answers covers things like seller financing, how can I help my business sell, and what do business brokers really do? Business brokers can be located from the site.

BizStats.com: http://www.bizstats.com/ (Accessed Fall 2005).

Here you can find Profitability and Operating Ratios for S Corporations, Partnerships, and Sole Proprietorships for industries like furniture stores, electronics, gas stations, and sporting goods. You can find Retail Industry Benchmarks like sales per foot (SPF), average sales per foot in malls, and SPF for a three-year trend. Look at the table of Safest and Riskiest Small Businesses to see if your research agrees with this site. Find and study lists of the Most Popular Small Businesses, Current Ratios and Balance Sheet Ratios by Industry, and Industry Profitability for Sole Proprietorships, for example. This site has Financial and Operating Ratios for 30,000 Industry Segments. Even if your industry is not found here, this site will show you how to do a financial and industry analysis using the figures you have gathered. CPA Patrick O'Rourke has produced the data on this terrific site for small business statistics.

BFI Business Filings Inc.: www.bizfilings.com (Accessed Fall 2005).

This large site provides detailed information on incorporating, listing advantages and disadvantages, forms needed, advice on where to incorporate, and publication requirements. LLCs are also discussed in detail. The Small Business Information section covers many subjects related to start-up, taxes, and legal issues. Business Tools provides sample forms and agreements from CCH Incorporated. Ask Alice! is a series of columns where small business owners ask questions about issues they've encountered from computer encryption to finding a business incubator. Learn how to select an accountant and an attorney.

**Business Owners Idea Café: www.businessownersideacafe.com (Accessed Fall 2005).

Developed by successful entrepreneurs and authors of published guides on starting a business, the large site presents short articles on all aspects of small business or entrepreneurial life. The main divisions include CyberSchmooz, Starting your Biz, Running Your Biz, Take Out Info, Classifieds, The "You" in Your Biz, De-Stress and Have Fun, About Idea Café, and Join Idea Café. Here you can find experts to answer your questions or discuss your current business crisis. You'll find sample business plans, financing help, business forms, and business news.

**BusinessTown.com: www.businesstown.com (Accessed Fall 2005).

This large business information site has sections on Managing a Business, Home Businesses, Internet Businesses, Accounting, Selling a Business, and more. The articles are not lengthy but quite thoroughly cover their subject. Under Accounting, you will learn basic concepts, how to budget, how to plan and project, and more. Also it has links to a variety of Financial Calculators at www.dinkytown.net. Useful site and not too commercial, use it to help you in any area where you need more information.

**Direct Contact Publishing's "Media Jumpstation:" www.imediafax.com/jumpstation/ (Accessed Fall 2005).

This large site is terrific for locating trade journals. Just select an industry under Magazine Subject and it brings up a list. Sometimes the entire journal is available and sometimes just some of the articles. Thousands of publications can be located here.

Edward Lowe PEERSPECTIVES: peerspectives.org (Accessed Fall 2005).

This nonprofit organization promotes entrepreneurship by providing information, research, and education. Use this site to find practical articles on marketing, finances, human resources (HR) management, and legal issues and taxes. Networking possibilities include conferences and educational seminars listed here. Although aimed at second-stage business, the Foundation provides good basic help too. The newsletter, *PeerSpectives*, is well worth subscribing to for inspiration.

eHow.com – Running a Business: www.ehow.com (Accessed Fall 2005).

This huge site contains articles on every phase of starting and running a business from incorporating a business, creating a market survey, filing for a copyright, finding cheap advertising, deciding when to quit your day job, and leasing office space to opening particular types of businesses such as garden centers, car washes, kennels, and online businesses. Articles are short and to the point to get you started in the right direction. Links to related or relevant topics expand on the basic article.

Entrepreneur's Reference Guide: www.loc.gov/rr/business/guide/guide2/ (Accessed Fall 2005).

The Library of Congress's Business Reference Services staff originally compiled this guide and it has been updated by Robert Jackson. This large collection of how-to books, reference books, and directories covers a number of topics including start-up, raising capital, managing your business, HR, and more. Find resources here to help you get started and manage your small business.

**Entrepreneur.com: www.entrepreneurmag.com (Accessed Fall 2005).

Maintained by *Entrepreneur Magazine*, this site supports new businesses and growing companies. Under First Steps, learn how to evaluate your idea and determine if there's a market for your business. Start Up Topics include location, naming your biz, and business structure. Especially strong in franchising and home-based businesses, you can get expert help on a variety of topics including toolkits for specific kinds of businesses like herb farms, B&Bs, and consulting firms. Find ready-made business forms here too in the FormNet section.

**Entrepreneurship Institute (TEI): www.tei.net (Accessed Fall 2005).

Established in 1976, this institute provides encouragement and assistance to entrepreneurs and unites financial, legal, and community resources to help foster success of their companies. A monthly newsletter and periodic President's Forums are available to members.

Entreworld: www.entreworld.org (Accessed Fall 2005).

Sponsored by the Kaufman Center for Entrepreneurial Leadership at the Ewing Marion Kauffman Foundation, Entreworld's editorial team assigns each article to one of three channels: Starting Your Business, Growing Your Business, and Supporting Entrepreneurship. Easy-to-navigate and updated daily, users can email SCORE volunteers, a counseling organization of retired executives who work through the SBA, for help with starting their business or developing a business plan. Access The Resource Database or Entrepreneur's Search Engine to find current information on the web that has been selected, reviewed, and organized. This site contains no advertising; the only agenda here is to promote the growth and understanding of entrepreneurship in America.

Health Insurance Association of America (HIAA): www.hiaa.org (Accessed Fall 2005).

This site offers an online guidebook entitled *Insurance Guide for Business Owners*, located under Consumer Information. Here you will find information on group health insurance, tips on choosing quality coverage, and a checklist to help evaluate the different types of coverage available. Other guides discuss long-term care insurance and disability income insurance. Get accurate insurance information here.

Home Business Magazine: www.homebusinessmag.com (Accessed Fall 2005).

The Business Start-Up category accessible through the frame on the left side of the screen provides a wealth of articles on starting various types of small businesses in your spare room or kitchen. Advice and ideas on Business Start-up, Management, and Marketing and Sales are also included. Technology issues are presented clearly, and telecommuting is a huge trend that is also explored thoroughly. Retirement planning contains good articles and advice.

**Insurance Information Institute: www.iii.org (Accessed Fall 2005).

This site has plain English answers to questions like how do I insure my home business, what's the difference between cancellation and non-renewal, and how do I find the right agent? Click on Business at the site and the list of questions on business insurance will appear. Find information on annuities, health, disability, life, home, and auto as well. The I.I.I.WIRE provides basic information that is not slanted toward a particular company.

**InterNIC.com: www.internic.com (Accessed Fall 2005).

This website was established to provide public information in regard to Internet domain name registration services and is updated frequently. A directory lists the ICANN-accredited (Internet Corporation for Assigned Names and Numbers) registrars; for more information on ICANN, go to their website at www.icann.org. InterNIC's FAQs will answer many of your questions about registering a domain name and the competitive registration environment.

Michigan Electronic Library (MEL): mel.org (Accessed Fall 2005).

This huge small business portal has links to dozens of sites. Under the Business, Economics & Labor section, you will find groups of links under topics like Entrepreneurs/Venture Capital, Home Business, and Small Business. Related topics include Advertising and Marketing, Information Technology, Management, Patents and Trademarks, and Taxation.

**The Minority Business Development Agency: www.mbda.gov (Accessed Fall 2005).

Through its minority business development centers, regional and district, the MBDA helps new ventures and established businesses seek working capital, start-up business financing, and access to markets. It helps entrepreneurs prepare loan packages, write business plans, and create financial statements. It publishes *Capital Trends, Demographic Trends, Industry Trends*, and *Export Trends*. Other MBDA development programs include Native

American Business Development Center, Minority Business Opportunity Centers, and Business Resource Centers.

MoreBusiness.com: www.morebusiness.com (Accessed Fall 2005).

Basic sections on this site include Startup, Running SmallBiz, Templates, and Tools. The Templates section provides sample business contracts and agreements, business and marketing plans, press releases, and business checklists. Users will find sample marketing plans for specific businesses like car washes, rental clothing stores, catering, and health and fitness programs; some plans are free and some are offered for a fee.

**National Association for the Self-Employed (NASE): www.nase.org (Accessed Fall 2005).

The self-employed and micro-businesses (up to 10 employees) join this group for support and advocacy. Their website links to the Entrepreneurial Connection (http://www.entrepreneurialconnection.com) where users can find Success Skills, Trends, and other helpful information. Begun in 1981 and with over 200,000 members, NASE offers group rates on insurance, political representation, and resources for the self-employed.

**The National Association for Women Business Owners (NAWBO): www.nawbo.org (Accessed Fall 2005).

This group has chapters located throughout the United States and sponsors national and regional conferences, provides networking opportunities, and sponsors awards. The Center for Women's Business Research, part of the National Foundation for Women Business Owners, produces original groundbreaking research to show the economic and social contributions of women-owned firms.

**National Business Incubation Association (NBIA): www.nbia.org (Accessed Fall 2005).

This organization aims to advance business incubation and entrepreneurship by providing education, information, advocacy, and networking resources for professionals helping early-stage companies. Entrepreneurs will visit this site to find a business incubator in their state or city where they can rent space to start their new business venture. Users click on Links to Member Incubators to search your locale for an incubator. Tips for Entrepreneurs is also useful.

**National Federation of Independent Businesses (NFIB): nfib.com (Accessed Fall 2005).

Since 1943, this long-established and well-known advocacy organization has represented small, independent businesses in Washington. The NFIB aims to impact public policy at the state and federal level and be a key resource for small businesses. On their site, you can see what impact their 600,000 members have and read other articles of interest to small businesses. Members have access to discounts on business products and services. Also, anyone can access their Tools and Tips section with helpful, practical articles for the entrepreneur.

**Nolo Press: www.nolo.com (Accessed Fall 2005).

This commercial site provides a good collection of free articles written by lawyers generally. Nolo's legal self-help books, now often accompanied by CD-ROMs, are outstanding, and you will find useful information and advice on the site as well as invitations to buy their products. For answers on questions about patents, trademarks, and copyrights, browse the Small Business Law Center.

**SBDCNET: sbdcnet.utsa.edu (Accessed Fall 2005).

The Small Business Development Center National Information Clearinghouse provides timely, web-based information to entrepreneurs. Small Business Development Centers (SBDC) are located in all 50 states. SBDCs offer free, confidential business counseling. This website provides information on business start-up, e-commerce, industry research, marketing, trends, and more. Entrepreneurs will find plenty of links and information here to help them plan and run their new business.

Service Corp of Retired Executives (SCORE): www.score.org (Accessed Fall 2005).

SCORE (Counselors to America's Small Business) is an organization of volunteer members that provides business advice to small businesses throughout the nation. Visiting their website, you can receive free counseling via email. Click on Ask SCORE, search the specialties of the counselors, and select a counselor with the specific expertise you need. The Business Toolbox provides important links and a template gallery with many templates to help the new business owner. Business counseling and workshops are offered at 389 SCORE chapter offices across the United States. To find a SCORE office near you visit the website or call (800) 634-0245.

Small Business Administration: www.sba.gov (Accessed Fall 2005).

This official government site offers a wealth of resources and programs for starting and growing a small business. Under Startup Basics, users will find an Entrepreneurial Test of 25 questions that will help them in doing a personal evaluation of their possible success in their own business. Other major sections cover business planning, financing, managing, marketing, employees, taxes, legal aspects, and business opportunities. Find here online forms, business plans, loan information, and many publications. Some contents are available in Spanish.

Small Business Advisor: www.isquare.com (Accessed Fall 2005).

This large site has lots of articles and advice for entrepreneurs just getting started in business. The Small Biz FAQs answer many of the basic questions like should I incorporate in Delaware and why do so many businesses do, do I need a Federal ID number, and do I need a business license? Tax Advice is another major section as well as Checklists for Success. Find articles on pricing your product or service, steps to improve sales, and how to build customer loyalty. Books, Business Services, and a Glossary add value. The U.S. Government and State Information are also very helpful. Use this site to help you get started right.

Small Business Notes: www.smallbusinessnotes.com (Accessed Fall 2005).

Here you will find articles on starting or buying your first business as well as planning, management, and legal issues. Explore articles on business incubators as well as marketing and choosing a business name. Basic articles contain links to fuller explanatory articles on a wide variety of topics like business models, recordkeeping, etc. A useful site for many topics related to small business and entrepreneurship come here for answers to basic and more complex questions.

Smartbiz.com Small Business Resource: www.smartbiz.com (Accessed Fall 2005).

This large site is organized into six major sections, including Smart Moves, Heads Up, Network, Tech Center, Form Fetcher, and Smart Links. Users will find business forms like Daily Cash Flow, Employee Disciplinary Action, Employee Time Sheets, Sample Business and Marketing Plans, and Collection Letters. Sample policies like Drug Test, Smoking, Safety, Time Off, and Workplace AIDS are also provided. The Network section will prove useful to many new entrepreneurs.

**U.S. Patent & Trademark Office: www.uspto.gov (Accessed Fall 2005).

This large, easy-to-use site will help entrepreneurs gain a basic knowledge of the trademark and patent processes. Find tips on conducting a search for registered patents and trademarks plus those pending or rejected. Use this site to begin your search for a unique business name.

Wall Street Journal **Center for Entrepreneurs:** www.startupjournal.com/ (Accessed Fall 2005).

WSJ's Startup Journal is an authoritative site that has a section entitled How-To, and entrepreneurs will find there a great deal of help deciding if they are entrepreneurs and how to get started in business. Collected here are many articles about different aspects of starting a business such as legal structure, finding a name, business plan tools, and more. The sample business plans are very thorough and will really help new business owners fill in the gaps in their own plans. Articles on important issues such as Should You Hire an Accountant will also get entrepreneurs off on the right foot. Continually updated and well written, this site is useful to all entrepreneurs.

**Yahoo! Business and Economy: dir.yahoo.com/Business_and_Economy/ (Accessed Fall 2005).

Especially important categories are organizations, e-commerce, software, and use tax issues. This large site includes a wealth of information with good international coverage on a wide variety of topics. Under Organizations, users will find listings for trade associations in nearly every industry. Under its small business site (smallbusiness.yahoo.com) the e-commerce section covers online shopping centers, privacy seal programs, and digital money. For industries it covers manufacturing as well as the retail industry. Check this site for current, accurate business information.

YOUR BUSINESS PLAN   4

CHAPTER HIGHLIGHTS:

- What Is a Business Plan?
- Sample Plans: Where to Find and How to Use
- Essential Elements of a Business Plan
- Format Your Plan
- Review, Update, Change Your Business Plan
- The Executive Summary

Writing a business plan is not an event; it's an ongoing, essential process. Remember the adage: "Failing to plan is planning to fail." It can be a daunting, time-consuming task, but creating a business plan is crucial to the success of your business. Find the method of creating and maintaining a business plan that works for you. Planning is a strategy for survival. The real value of creating a business plan is the process of researching and thoroughly thinking through your plan for a new business in a systematic manner. Remember a business plan is a living document and should continually be revised and updated.

WHAT IS A BUSINESS PLAN?

What is in this essential document, and why must it be written down? The well-prepared plan raises numerous critical questions and then discovers answers to those questions. A business plan allows you to gain control over your business and enables you to promote a competitive advantage over industry rivals. Because it describes the basics of your business's operations and forecasts, the format should be easy to read, understand, and change.

Your business plan requires market research on an ongoing basis. The world of business, your industry, and your business will constantly change, and you must be alert and aware of trends and economic changes that affect your business. Your business plan communicates your vision and ideas to others, and it will continually change and grow with you and your business. Obviously, it cannot be kept in your head, but must be committed to paper. Don't worry about writing complete sentences or using perfect grammar, just start writing down your thoughts and ideas and use the plan as an organizing tool.

Occasionally, potential dot-com entrepreneurs ask if they must do a business plan. The answer is an emphatic "yes." In the overall scheme of things, nothing is different in starting a dot-com business from a bricks-and-mortar business, so they usually will not be mentioned separately. Remember, whether you're dot-com or bricks and mortar, there is no substitute for business planning to ensure your success.

How to begin? Take an objective and unemotional look at your business idea. State the mission of your business. Why does or should your business exist? What is the purpose of your business? Conversely, state what your mission is not. Profit is not a goal or a mission but an outcome of the successful achievement of your mission. Emphasize the thing or things that set your business apart from others.

SAMPLE PLANS: WHERE TO FIND AND HOW TO USE

Now is a good time to look at some resources specifically designed to help you make and write your business plan. One of the best places to start on the Internet is Bplans.com at (http://www.bplans.com). Here you'll find over 50 free sample business plans as well as helpful tools and know-how for creating a business plan. Sample plans, even if for the same business you plan to open, should not be simply copied. A sample plan suggests categories of things for you to consider. A business plan defines and reveals the relationship between the business and the entrepreneur, you. A sample plan tells you what must be included in a well-written document. Take a careful look at the financial section in the sample plan as it can help you in developing your financial plans.

Another good site for business plan guidance is sponsored by Inc. Magazine (http://www.inc.com/guides). This site provides two plans for business planning: one is an in-depth look at each section of a plan and the other is a quick guide to building and improving your plan. Also, you may find the Small Business Administration sample business plan at http://www.sbaonline.sba.gov useful. Its business plan section was written by Linda Pinson, who is a well-known author on business planning. You'll also find her business plan book listed in the References at the end of this chapter. An exceptionally good, current book on business plans is *Business Plans That Work* by Jeffry A. Timmons, Andrew Zacharakis, and Stephen Spinelli. Using this work will enable you to create a plan that crystallizes and legitimizes your ideas for customers, investors, and yourself. In the For Dummies series, Steven Peterson and Peter Jaret have written an outstanding resource entitled *Business Plans Kit for Dummies* (with a CD-ROM). In an easy-to-use, easy-to-follow humorous manner, the authors lead you through the steps of writing a business plan for all types of businesses including nonprofits as well as plans for businesses in later stages of development or who need restructuring. The CD-ROM contains lots of forms, government documents, sample bylaws, and more. For new entrepreneurs, this package will help them along the path to success.

Figure 4.1 Screenshot of Business Plan Software & Free Sample Business Plans (www.bplans.com)

ESSENTIAL ELEMENTS OF A BUSINESS PLAN

The essential parts of a business plan include:

1. *Cover Page* contains name of business, brief description or mission statement, Business Plan as title, date written, your name (and contact information if you want to list different ones from your business), and the address

and phone number for the business. If you have a business logo, it should be included here.

2. *Table of Contents* is the name of each section and the page number where the section begins and subheadings if needed for clarity. The purpose of this page is to get your readers to the section that they are most interested in reading.

3. *Executive Summary* identifies the key ideas you want to emphasize (write this after your plan is finished). Summarize all sections briefly as this should be just a page or two in length. As many readers will only read this section, it is very important that it be done well. This section is expanded upon later on in this chapter.

4. *Business Overview* describes the services and/or products you'll be selling, legal structure, and some short-term and long-term goals. Focus here on customer benefits.

5. *Business Environment* identifies all the major aspects that affect your company's situation that are beyond your control such as how your industry operates including industry regulation, intensity of your competition and who they are, and the movement and trends of the marketplace.

6. *Marketing Plan* describes how to get the products or services to your targeted consumer or market. Also describe your pricing philosophy and competitive advantage, if any. Describe how you will promote your business and its wares (advertising).

7. *Financial Plan* tells your story in numbers. You will include a projected balance sheet and a profit and loss statement which shows when you anticipate profits to start and how long you can afford to absorb losses. Here is where you show your start-up and operating cash needs.

8. *Outside Advice* lists those individuals you plan to hire such as insurance agents, lawyers, accountants, and/or bankers.

9. *Supporting Documents* includes any contracts, agreements, or leases that you feel are important to the operation of your business.

After reading through the list of sections in a business plan, start a list of things you need to research in connection with your business and preparing your business plan. Set a deadline for completion. Ask someone to read it and comment on your work, so you'll have a reason to write and complete your plan in a timely fashion. Often professional business planners will suggest that a short section on Exit Strategies be included for a complete business plan. Check Chapter 13, Growing Your Business and Moving On, for suggestions on possible contingencies to plan for when leaving your business. Life does not follow our plan but occasionally throws a curve such as a death, divorce, upturn or downturn in the economy, etc., and you should be prepared to consider your business options.

If you would like to compare your plan to other business plans, try Anne McKinney's book, *Real Business Plans and Marketing Tools: Including Samples to Use in Starting, Growing, Marketing, and Selling Your Business*. She presents useful plans for a brew pub, home-based wholesale company, and janitorial supply company, 17 different business plans in all, to help you compare and develop your own plan.

McKinney, Anne. *Real Business Plans and Marketing Tools: Including Samples to Use in Starting, Growing, Marketing, and Selling Your Business*. PREP Publishing, 2003. 224p. ISBN 1-885288-36-0. $24.95.

Designed to help entrepreneurs prepare paperwork relating to starting, marketing, and growing a business, McKinney presents real business plans for 17 different types of businesses including a hair salon, auto body shop, home-based wholesale company, and janitorial supply company, for example. Readers will also find samples of financial statements and other documents used to obtain bank loans and equity financing. This title will help new business owners in their strategic planning.

FORMAT YOUR PLAN

Keep your audience in mind as you prepare your formal business plan. In order to make your plan more readable and improve the readers' comprehension of your vision, use headings and subheadings when you begin a new topic area and for key or important points. This practice improves the eye appeal and readability of your plan. Numbered lists are also effective in breaking up long blocks of text and increasing impact. Bulleted lists bring information across clearly and concisely. If you can produce or obtain good graphics, use pie charts, graphics, or other pictorial devices to illustrate the numerical parts of your plan. Be succinct and to the point but completely describe your business vision and include all the necessary parts of a good business plan.

REVIEW, UPDATE, CHANGE YOUR BUSINESS PLAN

Be committed to continually reviewing and updating your plan. Note in your calendar to "Review business plan" in six months or less if you know things will change sooner. Business events that should trigger an update of your business plan include:

1. Something in your business changes such as you hire an employee, you add a new product or service, or you take on a partner.

2. Your target market or customer base changes and you make a change in your product line or price or inventory that reflects this change and meets a new need or request.

3. Technology continues to change and some of its changes will affect the way you do business such as new software packages, Internet resources, desktop environments, or new hardware.

Experts who critique business plans frequently state that entrepreneurs are not realistic. Try not to be overly enthusiastic and inflate your potential or expectations. Be precise, concise, and clear but demonstrate a thorough knowledge of the market and the competition and your industry as a whole. Emphasize what is different or unique about your venture and find a niche. For help with keeping your plan current, find Mike McKeever's book:

McKeever, Mike. *How to Write a Business Plan*. 7th ed. Nolo Press, 2005. 256p. ISBN 1-4133-0092-8. $34.99.

This logically organized, thoughtfully presented book uses examples and worksheets to help entrepreneurs prepare a successful business plan. Included are business plans for a small service and a manufacturing business. A business plan is a dynamic document that needs constant revision to keep you and your business current. His explanations of the breakeven analysis and sales forecasting are very thorough and easy to understand. The chapter on Selling Your Business Plan will especially help those interested in obtaining financing for their new venture. This new edition has good new online and offline resources to help the new entrepreneur plan her or his business.

THE EXECUTIVE SUMMARY

This snapshot of your company's history, objectives, financial status, industry overview, and marketing plan is sometimes the only section people will read carefully. It must be a complete, yet brief, overview of your entire plan; and it must be very well written. It must be specific, exciting, and succinct. Grab your readers' attention. Cover the type of business you have/want, what you hope to achieve, how you hope to achieve it, and your capabilities.

First, outline your business's philosophy, goals, and commitments. Identify the type of business you have such as a new or existing business or a franchise. Define your legal structure with name, location, hours of operation, and years in operation, if any. Name the principal owner(s). State the objective of the business plan. What do you need to help you accomplish your business goals? What business opportunity have you identified? If you need start-up capital or a bank loan, state the amount and explain generally how the money will be used. Don't forget to include the potential return on investment, along with the proposed payback period. Also, mention the industry overview, target market, and competitive advantage.

Although this document appears at the beginning of your business plan, you should prepare it last, because it summarizes the deep learning that has taken place through the planning process. You have identified your niche in the market, researched and analyzed your industry, and are ready to launch and grow a business. If you're having trouble writing the Executive Summary, take a look at Linda Pinson's book, *Anatomy of a Business Plan*, for help in writing this snapshot of your business so that it will capture the attention and interest of your readers.

Pinson, Linda. *Anatomy of a Business Plan*. 6th ed. Dearborn Trade, 2004. 288p. ISBN 0-7931-9192-0. $22.95.

This user-friendly guide includes three sample business plans, plus blank forms to help you write a thoughtful, thorough, and professional business plan. Pinson believes that the Executive Summary should grab attention, and she presents ways for you to do just that. This new edition includes a resource section to help businesses research financial and marketing information so essential for an outstanding plan. Also find guidelines for updating and packaging your plan.

Below are resources to help you learn how to write a business plan and where to get help in preparing your plan. Sample several different resources and find one that helps you work through the process.

REFERENCES

(Starred titles discussed in the chapter)

Print Resources

Bangs, David H. *The Business Planning Guide*. 9th ed. Dearborn Trade, 2002. 256p. ISBN 0-7931-5409-X. $24.95.

Bangs, a well-known entrepreneur and business writer, continues to update this classic work. He includes two complete sample business plans. Find here step-by-step strategies for compiling the data relevant to your business plan from sources inside and outside your company. Learn to analyze current market conditions and deal with risks and opportunities. Bangs helps you analyze your industry and forecast revenues and expenses.

Covello, Joseph and Hazelgren, Brian. *Your First Business Plan*. 4th ed. Sourcebooks, Inc., 2002. 160p. ISBN 1-4022-0002-1. $14.95.

Covello and Hazelgren present step-by-step instructions for writing your business plans as well as tips on avoiding common mistakes. They teach readers how to read and understand financial statements along with illustrating how they are developed. Using a simple question-and-answer style, they help you create a plan that will meet lender or investor standards. Learn why "business owners who fail to plan, plan to fail."

Dethomas, Art and Grensing-Pophal, Lin. *Writing a Convincing Business Plan*. 2nd ed. Barron's Educational Series, 2001. 272p. ISBN 0-764-11399-2. $16.95.

Short and concise, the authors walk entrepreneurs through the process of writing a business plan, step-by-step. How to complete the industry analysis, the marketing and sales plan, the organization plan and the financial plan are detailed. Learn to analyze your business idea and state your plans simply in writing.

Gilderson, Linda D. and Paauwe, Theresia. *Self-Employment: From Dream to Reality*. 2nd ed. JIST Works, 2003. 144p. ISBN 1-56370-922-8. $16.95.

The worksheets and exercises provided here encourage a practical, hands-on approach to learning. Gilderson and Paauwe present key business concepts in a simple-to-understand manner with clear examples. The chapter on Understanding Financial Statements is particularly well done. In the Appendix, the business plan for Cathy's Cleaning Service, Inc. is clearly written and complete. The business plan could be used as a model for a less complicated new business too.

Gorman, Robert T. *Online Business Planning: How to Create a Better Business Plan Using the Internet, Including a Complete, Up-to-Date Resource Guide.* Career Press, 1999. 224p. ISBN 1-564-14369-4. $17.99.

The focus of this title is to make the web accessible to entrepreneurs who want to use it to create a better business plan. Learn how to search the web more efficiently and effectively for the information you need. Gorman also covers what to include in an effective business plan and provides many samples of what good business plans look like and include. He includes a number of online resources on contract workers, obtaining loans, location selection, marketing strategies, and more. Use this book and the web to write your business plan.

**McKeever, Mike. *How to Write a Business Plan.* 7th ed. Nolo Press, 2005. 256p. ISBN 1-4133-0092-8. $34.99.

This logically organized, thoughtfully presented book uses examples and worksheets to help entrepreneurs prepare a successful business plan. Included are business plans for a small service and a manufacturing business. The chapter on writing your marketing and personnel plans is particularly helpful for the marketing section of a business plan. Before proceeding with the marketing plan, McKeever suggests you return to your written business description to see if it still is an accurate statement of how you view your business or if the thinking and writing experiences between chapters have changed your current ideas. A business plan is a dynamic document that needs constant revision to keep you and your business current. His explanations of the breakeven analysis and sales forecasting are very thorough and easy to understand. The chapter on Selling Your Business Plan will especially help those interested in obtaining financing for their new venture. This new edition has good new online and offline resources to help new entrepreneurs plan their business.

**McKinney, Anne. *Real Business Plans and Marketing Tools: Including Samples to Use in Starting, Growing, Marketing, and Selling Your Business.* PREP Publishing, 2003. 224p. ISBN 1-885288-36-0. $24.95.

Designed to help entrepreneurs prepare paperwork relating to starting, marketing, and growing a business, McKinney presents real business plans for 17 different types of businesses including a hair salon, brew pub, auto body shop, home-based wholesale company, and janitorial supply company, for example. Readers will also find samples of financial statements and other documents used to obtain bank loans and equity financing. This title will help new business owners in their strategic planning.

Napier, Albert H. *Business Planning for the Entrepreneur.* South-Western, 2005. 278p. ISBN 0-324-22097-9. $27.95.

This new textbook really emphasizes business plan writing and can be very helpful to someone new to this process. Besides teaching readers how to create a business plan, Napier presents many real-life examples or case studies. A series of exercises walks readers through all the parts needed in the process of writing a plan. Thorough and deliberate, new entrepreneurs can learn from this title.

**Peterson, Steven. *Business Plans Kit for Dummies*. John Wiley & Sons, Inc., 2001. 360p. ISBN 0-7645-5365-8. $34.99.

This kit helps you put your business plan to work. Every chapter has checklists and forms. The examples in the case studies illustrate how real-life businesses succeed. The analysis of business plans for businesses that didn't make it is an unusual and useful feature. An excellent sample business plan is included in Chapter 16. Chapter 17 lists 10 final questions to ask about your business plan before you show it to anyone or decide it is complete. Every entrepreneur will want to test his or her plan. Plus the CD-ROM with its wealth of forms and useful documents will help entrepreneurs in many areas of their business.

**Pinson, Linda. *Anatomy of a Business Plan*. 6th ed. Dearborn Trade, 2004. 288p. ISBN 0-7931-9192-0. $22.95.

This user-friendly guide includes three sample business plans, plus blank forms to help you write a thoughtful, thorough, and professional business plan. Pinson believes that the Executive Summary should grab attention and she presents ways for you to do just that. This new edition includes a resource section to help businesses research financial and marketing information so essential for an outstanding plan. Also find guidelines for updating and packaging the plan.

Rogak, Lisa. *The Complete Small Business Start-up Guide*. John Wiley & Sons, Inc., 2004. 256p. ISBN 0-471-67957-7. $14.95.

Here Rogak concentrates on finding the ideal business idea for each entrepreneur by matching your personality and skills. A succinct sample business plan is one of the highlights of this well-written book. There is an excellent chapter on selecting the best business structure, including subchapter S corporations and LLCs, to meet your goals and match your individual circumstances. Choosing a bank and selling your business are also thoroughly covered. Rogak presents a realistic picture of the life of an entrepreneur.

Rule, Roger. *Rule's Book of Business Plans for Startups*. 2nd ed. Entrepreneur Press, 2004. 460p. ISBN 1-932531-05-X. $18.95.

This well-written, thorough guide covers writing a business plan section by section. Learn how to convert facts and figures into a readable, compelling description of your business in business language. Each step of the plan is covered thoroughly, and Rule turns complicated tasks into logical step-by-step processes using clear, concrete examples. Sample plans included cover wholesale, service, manufacturing, nonprofit, home-based, and retail businesses. Discover recent trends in business start-up financing. Particularly outstanding are the chapters on Industry Analysis and Financial Pro Formas. Learn why a business plan is an essential tool for any business to be successful and how to create an exceptional plan.

Stutely, Richard. *The Definitive Business Plan*. Financial Times/Prentice Hall, 2002. 312p. ISBN 0-273-65921-9. $27.00.

This excellent work has a more international focus and viewpoint and is written by a UK businessman. Some of the terminology is slightly different but the basics are the same. Stutely presents many short case studies to illustrate the use or importance of sections or strategies in business planning, which often target misconceptions. Stutely also includes many quotes and proverbs, which will help the important ideas and concepts of business planning stick in your mind. This outstanding work will help you write a great business plan.

**Timmons, Jeffrey A., Zacharakis, Andrew and Spinelli, Stephen. *Business Plans That Work*. McGraw-Hill, 2004. 128p. ISBN 0-07-141287-5. $16.95.

Based on work with hundreds of entrepreneurs and entrepreneurial ventures, this book illustrates a proven, innovative, and strategic approach to writing a business plan. Business planning allows practitioners to anticipate the resources required and the pitfalls that may arise in their new business. Learn how to write, adapt, focus, and revise your business plan. An entire chapter is devoted to each section of a business plan and each includes exceptional samples for those sections. Chapters on the industry and the competition and the start-up team are particularly practical. The Financial Plan chapter will guide new entrepreneurs through the process of generating realistic financials. Flow charts and tables illustrate every step in the development of an outstanding and complete business plan.

■ Online Resources

About.com: about.com/business (Accessed Fall 2005).

This large site has many different parts but the Small Business Information and Business Plan Writing sections are especially well done. Find articles about the importance of writing a plan and how to complete a useful plan. There's a business plan FAQ and more. Location selection advice is provided as well as many downloadable business forms. Some industry information can be accessed here as well. Continually updated and well organized, this site will help you write your business plan and continue to plan your business activities.

Bplans.com: www.bplans.com (Accessed Fall 2005).

This well-established, frequently updated site, sponsored by Palo Alto Software, Inc., is the best for help in writing your business plan. The section entitled Write a Business Plan contains articles; calculators on cash flow, starting costs, breakeven, and more; a business plan template; and executive summary and mission statement help plus access to Expert Advice. Currently 60 free plans are viewable online. Fully searchable, users can quickly find topics that they need, such as getting your plan funded and business plan legalities. Another nice feature is that they offer a Business Planning Audio for auditory learners. Other sections include Finance and Capital, Marketing and Advertising, Buying a Business, Market Research, and a monthly Newsletter. Bplans.com is a useful, practical site that also offers fee-based experts and assistance.

Business Know-How: www.businessknowhow.com/bkhstartup.htm (Accessed Fall 2005).

This large business website has a great page on Starting a Business. One article is on How to Use Graphs and Charts in Your Business Plan, and helps entrepreneurs decide when and where in their plan to use graphs and charts. A handy checklist helps you remember what to do and when to do it. Also included is information on business loans, employment forms, templates and productivity tools, and web design and content. Check out this site when working on your business plan.

Business Owners Idea Café: www.businessownersideacafe.com (Accessed Fall 2005).

Developed by successful entrepreneurs and authors of published guides on starting a business, the large site presents short articles on all aspects of small business or entrepreneurial life. The main divisions include CyberSchmooz, Starting Your Biz, Running Your

Biz, Take Out Info, Classifieds, The "You" in Your Biz, De-Stress and Have Fun, About Idea Café, and Join Idea Café. Here you can find experts to answer your questions or discuss your current business crisis. You'll find sample business plans, financing help, business forms, and business news.

Business Plan Center: www.businessplans.org (Accessed Fall 2005).

The main sections of this website include Business Plan Software, Sample Business Plans, Planning Guidelines, Web Resources, and a List of Consultants. The library of business plans was compiled from the finalists or winners in the University of Texas's student business plan competition. The sample plans are grouped by type: Internet Services, Services, and Products. The Guidelines for Business Planning links users to articles written by experts, who analyze business and marketing strategies and the parts of business plans such as the mission statement, pricing, financial statements, and marketing strategy.

Entrepreneurs' Help Page: www.tannedfeet.com/bizplan.htm (Accessed Fall 2005).

Find here help with business plans, financial statements, legal structure and legal forms, marketing and public relations (PR), human resources (HR), and strategy. Designed, created, and published by a group of young professionals in Chicago, Entrepreneurs' Help page does not claim to substitute for professional advice and judgment but provides information to entrepreneurs to get them started in the right direction. Experts detail the 11 things that really matter when preparing your business plan and provide 10 "painless" steps to writing a business plan. Articles are usually not lengthy but ask questions to help the new business person start thinking about what is needed and what questions will be asked of him or her. Down-to-earth advice from peers is often the most valuable.

Entrepreneur.com: www.entrepreneur.com/howto/bizplan (Accessed Fall 2005).

Under Startup Topics, Business Plans, *Entrepreneur Magazine* provides a wealth of information and assistance to the new entrepreneur. A thorough understanding of the need and finding the right type of business plan to fit your business and your style of planning and working is very important; this site guides you through the process. Learn how to determine your goals and objectives and how a plan will help you achieve them. Assess your company's potential and plan for growth. Besides a sample plan, Entrepreneur leads you to consultants, associations, government agencies, and software to help you develop the best business plan possible. Additionally, the site also helps users find free places for start-up help and mentors for advice during the start-up phase. Use this outstanding site often during the planning and opening of your new business.

How to Supercharge Your Business Plan: www.expert-zine.com/business_plan.html (Accessed Fall 2005).

You're convinced that you need to write a business plan, have written a plan, but now how good is it? This 19-point checklist is presented in a logical, well-organized manner. Find out if you included the essential ingredients of an outstanding plan and/or how you can improve your plan. Expand areas that are important to investors. Make your executive summary outstanding.

**Inc.com: www.inc.com (Accessed Fall 2005).

The publishers of *Inc* magazine present a large directory of articles by topic targeting many problems, concerns, and decisions confronting new business owner/managers. Their section on business plans is precise and practical. Particularly strong is the article on writing your Business Description; write out the problem your business solves for its customers and then describe how your business solves your customers' problem. As stated earlier, the Executive Summary is a critical section in the business plan. Get advice here on what not to include in it. Simple but effective advice is the hallmark of this outstanding, easy-to-use site.

PowerHomeBiz.com: *www.powerhomebiz.com/financing* (Accessed Spring 2005).

This large, small business site has many outstanding sections including Starting a Biz, Business Ideas, and Growing a Biz. One especially good article is entitled How Much Do You Need to Start Your Small Business? The Section on Angel Investors and Venture Capital includes informative articles such as the one entitled Find Yourself an "Angel," and Why Investors Say "No." The articles on e-commerce are worth checking out if you're interested in a virtual business. Must-Have Books are listed with some articles and Recommended Tools and Software as well. This established, well-organized site will help new entrepreneurs with financing and other parts of starting a new business.

**Small Business Administration: www.sba.gov (Accessed Fall 2005).

This official government site offers a wealth of resources and programs for starting and growing a small business. Under Startup Basics, check out the areas you need help with while doing your business planning. Other major sections cover business planning, financing, managing, marketing, employees, taxes, legal aspects, and business opportunities. Find here online forms, sample business plans, loan information, and many publications. Some contents are available in Spanish. Also parts of the SBA program are the Small Business Development Centers (SBDC) at www.sba.gov/sbdc. SBDCs are located in every state and deliver counseling and training for small businesses in the areas of management, marketing, financing, and feasibility studies.

Service Corp of Retired Executives: www.score.org (Accessed Fall 2005).

SCORE (Counselors to America's Small Business) is an organization of volunteer members that provides business advice to small businesses throughout the nation. Visiting their website, you can receive free counseling via email; ask to have a counselor look at the first draft of your plan. The Business Toolbox provides important links and a template gallery with many templates to help the new business owner with several parts of a good business plan. Like the SBA site, solid business planning help is available here.

SBDCNET: sbdcnet.utsa.edu (Accessed Fall 2005).

The Small Business Development Center National Information Clearinghouse provides timely, web-based information to entrepreneurs. Small Business Development Centers (SBDCs) are located in all 50 states. SBDCs offer free, confidential business counseling. This website provides information on business start-up, e-commerce, industry research, marketing, trends, and more. Entrepreneurs will find plenty of links and information here to help them plan and run their new business.

WebSite 101 (Expanding Your Business to the Web): website101.com (Accessed Fall 2005).

This huge, helpful site has a large collection of articles entitled Business Planning Articles for Entrepreneurs. Two very useful articles are on common business plan mistakes. WebSite 101 takes surveys of its users and other groups, tallies results, and presents them on the website; they also collect surveys with results from other researchers and present them. This site is very dynamic and contains a wide variety of practical, realistic data. Free, online tutorials are also available here. Besides their own tutorials, they link to other huge tutorial sites. Learn to write a business plan, step-by-step, to use software like Frontpage or MSOffice, to buy health insurance, and how to buy and sell on Ebay. Some of the sites offer one or two free tutorials and then want you to purchase books, more classes, or advanced instruction; as always, buyer beware.

Yahoo! Small Business Resources: smallbusiness.yahoo.com (Accessed Fall 2005).

Under Getting Started on the far right-hand side of this large site, the section on Business Plans is full of good links to articles on the basics, the risks, the need for updating, the financials, and the importance of a good Executive Summary. Special guidance is presented for home-based businesses and e-businesses, which are very popular today. The site is fully searchable and the listing of new articles covers a wide range of relevant information including, for example, hiring an email marketing firm and choosing a web host. And, in fact, Yahoo! presents a whole section on e-commerce and the many decisions involved in setting up a store online. This useful large site is a good place to start learning about planning your new business.

UPS AND DOWNS OF FRANCHISING

5

CHAPTER HIGHLIGHTS:

- Types of Franchises
- Uniform Franchise Offering Circular
- Researching Franchise Opportunities
- Advantages and Disadvantages
- Franchising and You!
- Visit a Franchise Trade Show
- A Final Cautionary Note

A franchise is not a separate type of small business entity. A franchise is a contractual licensing and distribution arrangement between two businesses, in which the franchiser (the owner of a business concept) gives the franchisee (another business person) the right to own and operate a business based on that concept. Franchisees borrow from another entrepreneur's success and pay for their experience. So, if you don't have the experience and expertise to start a business from scratch, another option is buying a franchise, utilizing another business owner's established business idea and plan. Franchisees rarely go bankrupt, and franchises can be found in nearly every industry in the United States and globally, in various sizes and requiring varying amounts of financial investment. Franchising is very popular and continues to expand. The two major reasons franchisees fail are undercapitalization and absentee ownership.

TYPES OF FRANCHISES

Two main types of franchise operations exist for the independent entrepreneur. The first one is the Entire Business Format (EBF), or turnkey package, where the franchiser grants the franchisee a license to use the logos, trademarks, business know-how, copyrights, trade secrets, standard operating procedures, purchasing power, etc. of the franchiser. The franchisee is required to pay a franchise fee plus start-up costs, ongoing royalty fees, and operating expenses (inventory, rent, etc.). The franchiser provides site selection assistance, job training, an operating manual, volume purchasing, and advice on marketing, management, personnel, and finance issues. Some franchisers offer workshops, newsletters, a toll-free telephone number for technical assistance, and other services. In an EBF, the business identities of the franchiser and franchisee are merged so the public perceives each outlet as a part of a large chain of identical outlets all offering the same goods and services. The franchiser exercises a great deal of control over the business operations of the franchisees.

The second type of franchise is the Product and Trade-Name Franchise, which involves the distribution of a product through a dealer, usually limited to an exclusive geographic distribution area. This franchise is limited to selling only the products included, such as ice cream, soft drinks, candy, etc., but does utilize the recognition and notoriety accompanying the franchise name and history. Some tire stores are also a good example of this type of franchise. Some other support services may be offered to the franchisee but generally assistance is limited and only minor control over the franchisee's business operation is exerted. Each franchisee is free to use its own business style and distribution techniques. In the end, franchising is a relationship business with franchiser, customers, other franchisees, suppliers, attorneys, bankers, and family.

UNIFORM FRANCHISE OFFERING CIRCULAR

The exact services provided to franchisees are described in the Uniform Franchise Offering Circular (UFOC). Under the Federal Trade Commission (FTC) Franchising and Business Opportunity Ventures Trade Regulation Rules (FTC rules) franchisers must provide franchisees with full disclosure of all the information they need to make an informed and rational decision about purchasing the franchise in a document called the UFOC. Under the FTC rules, franchisers must supply the complete franchise agreement at least five days before the franchisee signs any forms or issues any money. The terms in this document are uniform and nonnegotiable. Read and understand it thoroughly. The UFOC contains 23 items of information about the franchise. Key points to identify include:

1. When the company was founded and date of incorporation,

2. Franchise fees,

3. Litigation history,

4. Renewal dates,

5. Start-up costs,

6. Earnings claims,

7. Territory rights, and

8. Grounds for termination to name a few.

Much of this same information will be in the Franchise Agreement, but you may want to know these things before you even consider this franchise. Jane Applegate, in *The Entrepreneur's Desk Reference*, lists eight key questions that the franchisee need to know, such as what are the fees, is the territory you're buying exclusive, can the franchiser bypass the franchisee's outlet, what happens if the franchiser merges with another business, what are the online issues, exactly what training and support are provided, does the franchise sponsor an association of franchisees, and what happens if you die, become disabled, or want out of the franchise agreement? Be clear on what you want from a franchise before you make any commitments. The citation for Applegate's book is listed below.

Applegate, Jane. *Entrepreneur's Desk Reference*. Bloomberg Press, 2003. 399p. ISBN 1-5766-0086-6. $24.95.

This easy-to-use guide is an alphabetical compilation of answers, solutions, advice, and ideas for small business owner/managers, covering over 300 topics from the basics such as accounting, taxes, marketing, and networking to more advanced concepts including buyout contracts, joint ventures, and employee benefits and problems. Applegate, one of the United States top small business experts, provides a comprehensive guide that entrepreneurs will refer to often.

RESEARCHING FRANCHISE OPPORTUNITIES

One outstanding resource for entrepreneurs and new franchisees is Franchising: Franchise411 at (www.franchise411.com). Franchise411 is the Internet home of Franchise Profiles and Franchise Profiles International. This online library and resources center will help you understand what franchising is and how to take advantage of everything it has to offer. Find here a thorough explanation of UFOCs, the FTC's rules, state registration information, and international franchising. Links to dozens of sites presenting franchise opportunities in the United States and internationally are included though some need updating. Articles on franchise ratings, franchise politics, global franchising ins and outs, and more are included.

However, the FTC does not require that franchisers register with the Commission in order to conduct business. Some states impose registration rules; check with your Secretary of State office for requirements in your state. States usually grant or deny a franchiser the right to franchise its operations in their state. This state approval only means the state could not find any reason to refuse the franchiser's application. Because buying a franchise involves considerable risk on your part, you will want to research a franchise opportunity thoroughly.

ADVANTAGES AND DISADVANTAGES

Looking at the big picture, what are the advantages and disadvantages of purchasing a franchise? Advantages of purchasing a franchise include:

1. Business ownership

2. The economic power of immediate name recognition;

3. Assistance in finding financial support or even providing financial assistance;

4. Reduced risk of failure;

5. Advertising assistance and publicity both locally and nationally;

6. Reduced costs for equipment and inventory through bulk buying power;

7. Help with site selection and possibly development of your facility;

8. Basic business training plus sometimes advanced training in marketing, management, and training for employees;

9. And finally, the operations manual.

Disadvantages of buying and running a franchise include:

1. The high cost of purchasing plus the ongoing costs;

2. Loss of control and inflexibility over such things as facility look and layout, method of operation including hours of operation, vendors, pricing, advertising campaigns, and facility location;

3. Continuing to follow the restrictive franchise agreement; and

4. Sharing in parent company's image when things go wrong.

Again, you have to ask yourself what is most important to you. Do you follow the rules? Realize and accept that franchisees are not rebels or independent thinkers but team players.

FRANCHISING AND YOU!

If you have decided you want to investigate franchising further, how do you begin? Well, if you know already exactly what kind you want to acquire, contact a franchisee in your community or state to see if they might be interested in selling their outlet, or contact the franchiser directly. Also check them out on some of the websites listed in the resources in this chapter to see what different organizations and other franchisees are saying about them. Another important resource is the business and trade press. Has an article on them appeared in the *Wall Street Journal* or other business publication? Search the Internet. Visit your local library.

Attend seminars sponsored by the International Franchise Association; find locations on their website for upcoming franchise seminars and shows with dates for events all over the country at http://www.franchise.org. Besides seminars, users will find sections like Franchise Basics, Franchise Resources, and the FTC

Figure 5.1 Screenshot of International Franchise Association (www.franchise. org)

Guide to Buying a Franchise. This large site links to specific companies that sell franchises as well as to information about franchising in general. Use this site to start your search for information on a franchise.

Call the Better Business Bureau to see if there are complaints about the franchiser or contact the Attorney General in your state, neighboring states, or the state where the franchiser is based. Be sure to thoroughly research any franchise you are seriously interested in because research now will save time and money in the future.

VISIT A FRANCHISE TRADE SHOW

In order to talk to many different franchisers and industry experts in one location, attend a franchise trade show or exposition. These shows often offer workshops and seminars to teach you about the industry and explore its advantages and disadvantages. Some exhibitors may use hard-sell tactics so it's probably worth your time to do some preliminary investigation before attending one of these shows. Develop a budget or investment range and some business goals. At the show, comparison shop for opportunities that meet the criteria you've developed. Remember you are just investigating possibilities and will need to do a great deal more research before coming to a decision and selecting a franchise to purchase. Your local chamber of commerce may be aware of trade shows coming to your area or state.

Another place to check is FranchiseHandbook.com (www.franchise1.com). This site lists shows by date and covers the world. Shows are sponsored by different vendors so if you have several franchises you want to research, see if they'll be exhibiting at the show you're thinking of attending. Research beforehand can always save you time and money.

A FINAL CAUTIONARY NOTE

Some common misconceptions franchise buyers should avoid include the following:

1. A large industry does not assure success; careful planning, research, training, site selection, and marketing are essential for any business to be successful.

2. If you are the first franchisee for a company, be extra careful. If after a good deal of research, sign on only if you are very confident that the business can replicate its success.

3. Always hire a lawyer to read the agreement with you before you sign; lawyers are necessities—not luxuries.

4. All franchise systems are not the same so find one that fits your philosophy of doing business, investment limits, and management style.

5. Every business venture involves risk so plan to work long hours to implement the franchiser's business plan and succeed.

If you want to use books or the web to find a franchise that matches your talents, tastes, and investment capital, below are many places to check. The business of franchising has really proliferated on the web, and with the explosion of American exports of franchises to many other countries, international opportunities are also often listed. Find and use several of the resources listed below.

REFERENCES

(Starred titles discussed in the chapter)

 Print Resources

**Applegate, Jane. *Entrepreneur's Desk Reference*. Bloomberg Press, 2003. 399p. ISBN 1-5766-0086-6. $24.95.

This easy-to-use guide is an alphabetical compilation of answers, solutions, advice, and ideas for small business owner/managers, covering over 300 topics from the basics such as accounting, taxes, marketing, and networking to more advanced concepts including buyout contracts, joint ventures, and employee benefits and problems. Applegate, one of the United States top small business experts, provides a comprehensive guide that entrepreneurs will refer to often.

Bond, Robert E. and Woo, Stephanie. *Bond's Franchise Guide 2004*. 15th ed. Source Book Publications, 2004. 496p. ISBN 188713736X. $29.95.

Covering 45 distinct business categories, profiles of franchises supply a description of the business with number of operating units and geographic distribution; capital requirements including initial investment and total investment; detailed space needs and staffing levels; initial training and start-up assistance detailed as well as ongoing support; evaluation statements from current franchisees; and specific areas of geographic expansion. This directory is one of the first places a prospective franchise buyer should search.

Dugan, Ann, ed. *Franchising 101*. Dearborn Trade, 1998. 280p. ISBN 1-57410-097-1. $22.95.

Though becoming a bit dated, this thoughtful, thorough guide explains how to find, buy, operate and grow a successful franchise. Full of checklists, forms, worksheets, and sample strategies to help readers evaluate an opportunity, develop forecasts and budgets, estimate start-up costs, and identify financing sources. The Association of Small Business Development Centers (ASBDC) helped develop this resource and uses it in its training and development seminars throughout the United States. Part I, Choosing Your Franchise, helps you find a good opportunity that fits your personality, skills, and aptitudes and is likely to succeed in the market you are considering. Part II, Acquiring Your Franchise, helps readers through the process of purchasing a franchise and especially alerts readers to parts of franchise agreements that are overlooked, misunderstood, or ignored. Additionally, the chapter on Negotiating a Lease will help individuals new to such legal contracts. Ann Dugan, the editor, also walks franchisees through a business plan for a franchise. Part III, Managing Your Franchise, gets the new franchisee off to a good start by providing additional guidance in business management and building on the training provided by the franchiser. The chapters on taxes and insurance and communication with your franchiser will also prove beneficial to most new franchisees.

Keup, Erwin J. *Franchise Bible: How to Buy a Franchise or Franchise Your Business*. 5th ed. McGraw-Hill, 2004. 288p. ISBN 1-932156-62-3. $22.95.

Franchise lawyer Keup explains how to assess your suitability for running a franchise, investigate franchisers, interview existing franchisees, and understand the legal terms and documents associated with franchising. The checklists and worksheets Keup has prepared will be useful to readers as well. The Appendices contain sample franchise documents for UFOCs, franchise agreements, background data for circulars and agreements, state franchise information guidelines for many states, and UFOC guidelines. The second half of Keup's book tells readers how to franchise their business, but this section is also of interest to new franchisees.

Klueger, Robert F. *Buying and Selling a Business*. 2nd ed. John Wiley & Sons, Inc., 2004. 249p. ISBN 0-471-65702-6. $16.95.

Learn how to evaluate a business by analyzing financial statements. Find out what the key considerations should be when buying a franchise and how franchises differ from other small businesses. This step-by-step guide will help readers understand what buyers are looking for and what sellers need to tell prospective buyers and how to present it. Discover tips on negotiating for price, timing, stock and asset agreements, and noncompetitive agreements. New tax law changes are also covered.

Levonsky, Rieva and Conley, Maria Anton. *Ultimate Book of Franchises*. Entrepreneur Press, 2004. 540p. ISBN 1-9321-5686-0. $23.95.

Over a thousand companies are listed for the prospective franchisee to survey. The authors provide in-depth facts and figures such as company size, financial ratings, training and support provided, qualifications needed to obtain a franchise, and contact information. Practical, how-to advice on buying your first franchise is presented in an easy-to-understand, organized manner.

McKinney, Anne. *Real Business Plans and Marketing Tools: Including Samples to Use in Starting, Growing, Marketing, and Selling Your Business*. PREP Publishing, 2003. 224p. ISBN 1-885288-36-0. $24.95.

Designed to help entrepreneurs prepare paperwork relating to starting, marketing, and growing a business, McKinney presents real business plans for 17 different types of businesses including a hair salon, brew pub, auto body shop, home-based wholesale company, and janitorial supply company. Also included is the franchise application for a convenience store. Readers will also find samples of financial statements and other documents used to obtain bank loans and equity financing. This title will help new business owners in their strategic planning.

Rule, Roger C. *No Money Down: Financing for Franchising*. PSI Research, Oasis Press, 1998. 240p. ISBN 1-55571-462-5. $19.95.

Though becoming a bit dated, this book clearly explains the ins and outs of starting and paying for a franchise. Beginning entrepreneurs will find help in developing a business plan and help finding different sources of financing. Part One outlines the preliminaries of financing, discussing your credit potential, developing financial statements that lenders can read and understand, and describing the necessary investment requirements for a franchise. Part Two walks readers through developing a franchise business plan. Part Three covers equity or debt financing and how to professionally package your proposal and present it. Concise and well written, this comprehensive resource will help beginners.

Seid, Michael and Thomas, Dave. *Franchising for Dummies*. For Dummies, 2000. 378p. ISBN 0-76455-160-4. $19.99.

Yes, that's Wendy's International's late owner, Dave Thomas, who was the co-author for this useful guide that outlines in typical fashion the basics, development procedures, running the business, and moving forward. One highlight of this practical guide is the approach to franchiser/franchisee disagreements. Seid and Thomas suggest sitting down with the franchiser, discussing your concerns, and negotiating a way to settle the problem. Thomas recommends that training is an ongoing activity for employees and franchiser because you can always improve. This book will help new franchisees make the most of the time and money invested in a franchise.

Small Business Sourcebook (SBS). Thomson-Gale. Annual. $405.00.

This directory provides a wealth of information for the small business owner/manager. The Small Business Profiles cover 340 different small businesses. Businesses profiled include catering, cooking schools, fish farms, antique shops, bookstores, and car washes, for example. Entries contain as many as 17 subheadings, such as start-up information, educational programs, reference works, sources of supply, statistical sources, trade periodicals, trade shows and conventions, consultants, and franchises and business opportunities. The Small Business Topics section covers general ideas like retailing, service industry, franchising, and more. Under restaurants, SBS lists nearly 200 franchises. The State Listings and Federal Government Assistance sections list programs and offices that provide information and support to small businesses. Check your library for this practical, well-organized source.

Thaler, John. *The Elements of Small Business: A Lay Person's Guide to the Financial Terms, Marketing Concepts, and Legal Forms That Every Entrepreneur Needs.* Silver Lake Publishing, 2005. 354p. ISBN 1-56343-784-4. $24.95.

Specializing in small business law, this lawyer and small business owner presents tools, tips, and advice to help you get your business off to a smooth and legal start. Chapters are thorough and cover topics such as Franchises, Business Equipment, Business Plans, Insurance, Computers and E-Commerce, and Marriage and Divorce. Each chapter concludes with a list of resources. Over 20 appendices provide forms and sample reports such as registration for a fictitious business name, operating agreement for an LLC, financial statements, etc. This well-written book will help more entrepreneurs.

Tomzack, Mary E. *Tips and Traps When Buying a Franchise.* 2nd ed. Source Book Publications, 1999. 236p. ISBN 1-88713-712-2. $19.95.

Tomzack helps readers determine the best franchise for their personal finances and lifestyle. She helps new franchisees avoid last-minute deal breakers and navigate the legal maze to understand the fine points of franchise agreements. This insightful work contains tips and explanations of all aspects of buying a franchise.

Online Resources

American Express Small Business Exchange: http://www133.americanexpress.com/osbn/Landing/informyourdecisions.asp?us_nu=subtab (Accessed Fall 2005).

Small business owners will find help here on management, finding money, and marketing. This outstanding site has information on managing debt, business plans, fraud protection, and SBA loans. The article under Financial Management entitled Business Valuation Methods explains the various common methods used to come up with a value for a small business. The Starting a Business section tells users about structuring their business as well as some information on types of insurance.

American Franchisee Association: www.franchisee.org (Accessed Fall 2005).

Founded in 1993 and now with over 16,000 members, this association promotes the economic interests of small business franchisees, assists in the formation of franchisee associations, and provides support and assistance to its members. It provides information on legislation such as the Small Business Franchise Act and other legislative activities affecting franchisees. Resources for legal and business issues are provided. The article on Buying a Franchise is outstanding, and Find a Franchise Attorney is useful also. A monthly newsletter is provided to members. This trade association is useful for all new franchisees.

Be The Boss: www.betheboss.com (Accessed Fall 2005).

This international site, Americas, Europe, and Asia and Australia included, provides a large directory of franchise opportunities. Franchises can be searched by category and/or investment level. Links are also provided to industry publications and business plans for franchises plus a pre-investment checklist and using your 401(k) for buying a franchise. Easy to use and well organized, franchisees searching for an opportunity will find them here.

Bison1.com: www.bison1.com (Accessed Fall 2005).

This well-researched and organized site helps would-be franchisees learn about purchasing a franchise, profiles many franchises in a variety of industries, and even provides a franchise self-test. Franchises are grouped alphabetically, by categories, or premium opportunities. Under Franchise Resources, articles on Franchise Trends are brief but informative, industry experts give advice and discussion groups are available under Franchise Forum, and news, industry links, and a bookstore can also be accessed. This worthwhile, useful site is sponsored by a variety of advertisers.

Entrepreneur.com: www.entrepreneurmag.com (Accessed Fall 2005).

Maintained by *Entrepreneur Magazine*, this site supports new businesses, franchisees, and growing companies. Under First Steps, learn how to evaluate your idea and determine if there's a market for your business. Start Up Topics include location, naming your biz, and business structure. Especially strong in franchising and home-based businesses, you can get expert help on a variety of topics including toolkits for specific kinds of businesses like herb farms, bed and breakfasts, and consulting firms. A unique feature is looking at franchises by the training they offer. Also, search franchises by categories like low cost, top global, and fastest growing. A Franchise Zone magazine and a Franchise Coach are available.

FindAFranchise.com: www.bizquest.com/findafranchise/ (Accessed Fall 2005).

This user-friendly site calls itself The Internet Franchise Search Engine, and is sponsored by BizQuest. Here users can browse 1,200 franchises, find the hottest or trendiest franchises, find franchises for sale, or search through a wide variety of categories such as Children's Franchises, Educational Franchises, or Home Services Franchises. An alphabetical list is also available. Franchise financing information as well as other franchise resources are also provided. A list of low-cost franchises is also available. Lots of well-organized balanced information is presented.

Franchise America: www.franchiseamerica.com (Accessed Fall 2005).

This huge site opens the door to hundreds of franchise opportunities. Find franchises by categories including Automotive Opportunities, B2B Franchises, China Opportunities, eBusiness, Hot Dog Franchises, Outdoor Travel, Senior Care, Under $20,000, Vending, and more. Lists of International Franchise and Franchisee Associations with contact information are provided. Sign up for a free account to explore thousands of franchises, home-based or conventional.

Franchise.com: www.franchise.com (Accessed Fall 2005).

This large site provides information for franchise buyers, franchise owners, franchisers, and suppliers. You can search or view by category, license, or franchise name. Find lists such as Star Opportunities, New Arrivals, and Premier Listings. Also provided are a Resale Franchise Directory, Lender Directory, and Attorney Directory. Several calculators and Franchise Events are also useful to new franchisees. This site is international so you can find opportunities globally. The Research Center has articles on Finding Financing Fast, New Franchise Success Rate, and How Do I Choose the Right Franchise? Use this site to investigate franchising.

FranchiseGator.com: www.franchisegator.com (Accessed Fall 2005).

Search here for conventional franchises and multi-unit franchise opportunities. Besides franchise offerings and Franchise FAQs, users can access a Franchise Consultant and Franchise Financing. The Featured Articles section offers brief articles on a range of related topics. Frequently updated and easily searchable, users will return to this site to learn more about franchises.

**FranchiseHandbook.com: www.franchise1.com (Accessed Fall 2005).

This online directory lists shows by date and covers the world. Shows are sponsored by different vendors so if you have several franchises you want to research, see if they'll be exhibiting at the show you're thinking of attending. Franchise opportunities and companies are described with contact information. Franchise industry news and a list of franchises for sale are also available.

Franchise Info Mall: www.franchiseinfomall.com (Accessed Fall 2005).

Another large franchise directory, Franchise Info Mall is available on the web. This one has over 100 franchise categories that can be searched. It lists the top 100 franchises, the top 500, and the top 200 international franchises. Franchise Expos are listed as well as Franchise attorneys and consultants. A few franchise-related articles are also presented.

FranchiseSolutions: www.franchisesolutions.com (Accessed Fall 2005).

This unique site lists Franchise Resales, plus allows franchisees to sort franchise opportunities by cash requirements and industry category. Users can also check out Unique Franchises and Home-based Franchises. The Franchise Advice and Resources section includes franchise success stories and advice on starting and managing a successful franchise. Original articles and news on franchising and franchises are also accessible. This site also selects Franchises for Women. A wealth of information is available and nicely organized.

Franchising.org: www.franchising.org (Accessed Fall 2005).

This useful site provides links to many other informative and helpful sites on getting started in franchising. Articles, advice, and information on shows and franchising news are also presented. Links to general business information and resources are also included.

**Franchising: Franchise411: www.franchise411.com (Accessed Fall 2005).

This online library and resources center will help you understand what franchising is and how to take advantage of everything it has to offer. Find here a thorough explanation of UFOCs, the FTC's rules, state registration information, and international franchising.

Upcoming franchise seminars and shows and events with dates all over the country are listed. Links to dozens of sites presenting franchise opportunities in the United States and internationally and information about franchising in general and specific franchises. Articles on franchise ratings, franchise politics, global franchising ins and outs, and more are included. Check out the 20 Red Flags of Franchising to help you consider the advantages and disadvantages of a franchise.

Inc.com: www.inc.com (Accessed Fall 2005).

The publishers of *Inc* magazine present a large directory of articles by topic targeting many problems, concerns, and decisions confronting new business owners/managers. Their section on business plans is precise and practical and applies to a franchise business plan, too. Their section on Buying a Business or Franchise includes 10 Common Mistakes of Prospective Franchisees, which should be read by every prospective franchisee. Simple but effective advice is the hallmark of this outstanding, easy-to-use site.

Info Franchise News: www.infonews.com (Accessed Fall 2005).

The International New Franchise Opportunities teaches its users about franchising, franchisers, and being a franchisee. Also available here is The Franchise Annual Directory: Online. One main section is How to Investigate Franchises; it links to many important sources of information such as government agencies, the American Bar Association, and the North American Securities Administrators Association. Franchisor associations worldwide are listed with contact information. Over 20 pages of information to help users find out about a franchise before signing an agreement is included. The list of items under Dangerous Contract Terms from a Franchisee's Perspective is very enlightening and may help a franchisee avoid many problems.

**International Franchise Association: www.franchise.org (Accessed Fall 2005).

If you are thinking of or have purchased a franchise, this site contains a comprehensive database with links to over 800 companies. Many details about buying and running an individual franchise are provided. Its publication, *Franchise Opportunities Guide*, is outstanding. IFA's Franchise Discussion Forum allows users to discuss best practices, answer questions and ideas for new and existing franchisees, locate and contact international franchise groups, and exchange ideas and news on technology. Under Guidance, find a free Franchise Basics course and a list of Key Questions to Ask. Here you can also search franchises by investment dollar amount needed. You will find educational opportunities here as well as news affecting the franchise industry. This easy-to-use, large site spotlights all information related to franchising.

Nolo Press: www.nolo.com (Accessed Fall 2005).

This commercial site provides a good collection of free articles written generally by lawyers. Find here information on the legal aspects of buying a franchise. Nolo's legal self-help books, now often accompanied by CD-ROMs, are outstanding, and you will find useful information and advice on the site as well as invitations to buy their products. For answers on questions about patents, trademarks, and franchising, browse the Small Business Law Center.

USA Franchise Directory: www.franchisedirectory.com (Accessed Fall 2005).

This large directory allows users to request brochures directly from franchises that interest you, to send emails to sales representatives, and of course, to access the franchise's websites. Franchising statistics provided are current and interesting. A Canadian Franchise Directory is also provided.

***Wall Street Journal* Center for Entrepreneurs:** www.startupjournal.com/ (Accessed Fall 2005).

WSJ's Startup Journal is an authoritative site that has a tab on its homepage for Franchising. Collected here are articles about international franchises, the most successful franchisees, franchise rankings, various types of businesses that have been franchised, and more. Practical advice and real-world case studies are highlights of the well-written and timely articles. Continually updated and well organized, this site is useful to all entrepreneurs and franchisees.

Yahoo! Small Business Resources: smallbusiness.yahoo.com (Accessed Fall 2005).

Under Getting Started on the far right-hand side of this large site, the section on Franchises contains a great many useful links to articles on purchasing a franchise, questions to ask other franchisees in the chain, franchise funding sources, and researching a franchise opportunity. Also, under Business Tools, there's a Franchise Search option that allows the user to search by category and/or investment dollar amount ranges. If you are considering the franchise option, this site will help you get started learning about the world of the franchise.

In this particular area, I have found another type of website. I am not recommending these sites but they might be helpful to some users.

FranChoice: www.franchoice.com (Accessed Fall 2005).

The FranChoice program is a consultation program that is similar to working with a realtor when you buy a house. An industry expert works with the prospective franchisee to find a good match in terms of the type of franchise to buy and run. Fees are paid by franchisers. Franchise consultants help you select and evaluate a franchise opportunity, including reviewing and explaining the UFOC.

FranNet: www.frannet.com (Accessed Fall 2005).

A similar service to FranChoice is FranNet. This site is a bit larger with testimonials, events, helpful tips, news, and links to other sites. If you want to use one of these services, it's probably good to shop around on the Internet and find the best deal you can for the service you need.

RAISING CAPITAL

6

CHAPTER HIGHLIGHTS:

- What Will It Cost?
- Sources of Seed Capital
- Traditional Sources of Loans
- Angel Investors
- Venture Capital

As a new business owner, a key factor in starting or growing your business is your ability to obtain financing. You need start-up capital or "seed money" to finance every aspect of this venture from securing a location to business cards. Start by carefully analyzing these costs to determine how much money you'll need. Remember that undercapitalization is one of the most common reasons small businesses fail.

WHAT WILL IT COST?

Using the business plan that you're developing and your own instincts as to what is the least you can do and the most you can afford, make a list to start deciding what you already have and what you have to rent or purchase. The list will include:

- Office equipment,
- A space in which to conduct business,
- Computer,
- Furniture,
- Telephone service,
- Utilities,
- Product inventory,
- Business licenses and permits,
- Insurance,

- Advertising,
- Professional fees, and
- Miscellaneous expenses.

As in figuring any budget, you'll have priorities to establish and choices to make, but figuring a budget first and deciding where to cut corners will help you in the day-to-day management of your business. Collect the information to make these figures as accurate as possible. If you completed your three financial statements for your business plan already, you should have most of this data at your fingertips. If you're still having trouble estimating start-up costs, try consulting the Entrepreneur's Guidebook Series at (www.patsula.com/businessplan-guides/). Under Financial Plan in guidebook #78 titled Start-up Costs, you'll find a lengthy and thorough guide to estimating start-up costs.

If your opening estimate is greater than your available resources, you will have to consider different sources for the necessary capital. Be very careful about using retirement savings to fund your new business. There's always a risk to any new venture, so consider every possibility, and then weigh your alternatives carefully. You know your financial needs; prepare to present your financial request in the most professional manner you can devise, regardless of how you decide to pursue the necessary capital.

SOURCES OF SEED CAPITAL

Family and Friends

A variety of methods can be used to raise seed capital. Probably the least expensive route is to tap family and friends. If your business is too small or too new to get other financing, this may be the best route. Inform them as to how much interest you can pay and when they will be paid back. Put the loan terms in writing and treat this loan as any other. Also tell them how much of your own funds are invested in the business.

A Note of Caution

Be sure motives and expectations are clear with family and friends—the price of losing a valuable relationship is very high. Treat them as professionally as you would a banker or a potential partner. Clearly outline the repayment schedule and keep updating them as your business situation changes.

Partner(s)

Acquiring a partner is often used as a means to bring into the business someone who has the funds needed for start-up. Go back to the chapter on business structure to see if this type of financing would work for your business.

Life Insurance

Life insurance policies that have a cash surrender value are a source of money that you can borrow, and sometimes the interest rates are lower than market rates. However, before you borrow against your policy, be sure you understand all the conditions outlined in the policy.

Home Equity Loan

If you own your own house, a home equity loan can be a source of capital for your new business. Call several lenders for the lowest rates and find out if there are any "hidden costs" you'll have to pay at closing. If you use a home equity loan, consider it a business loan that uses your house as collateral that will enable you to write off the interest as a business expense. Check with your accountant to see if you can and how to do this correctly.

TRADITIONAL SOURCES OF LOANS

Debt Financing

Financing is generally grouped into two separate types. First decide if you are looking for "debt financing," which is money you borrow, or "equity financing," which is money acquired from investors and/or savings. If you decide to convince a bank or credit union to lend you the money for your business, present your financial needs and expectations precisely, showing exactly where the money will be used and how and when it will be repaid. If you have collateral to offer to guarantee the loan, include that information. Also include financial information about you, any partners, or any key employees you have.

Most financiers check five criteria, known in the banking industry as the five "C's" of credit, when reviewing your request for a loan:

1. *Cash flow* or the money coming in and going out of your business is a major consideration. Provide projected cash flow statements as well as historic financial reports if possible.

2. *Capital* or how much of your own money is invested in your business. The standard amount that banks usually require is 30% of the total projected startup costs.

3. *Collateral* or what property can be used to secure this loan that could be seized by the lender if the borrower defaults or fails to repay the debt. Among the personal assets you could use as collateral are inventory, life insurance policies, real estate, and stocks and bonds.

4. *Credit* or what is your current credit history, both business and personal. As in personal credit history, lenders like to see four or five years of credit experience before considering your business for a commercial loan.

5. *Character* or what are your personal financial investments or past and present lender relationships. Sometimes banks will ask for references from other professionals such as lawyers or accountants with whom you have worked in the past.

Obtaining a bank loan is a challenging task for a new business owner but with a solid well-documented business plan, persistence, and patience, your chances of success improve greatly.

Even though you make a presentation for a business loan, banks are more likely to give you a personal loan to use for business purposes. One strategy that may work is to ask for a very small business loan that you agree to pay back in 180 days or a year. This type of short-term business loan, which needs to be repaid with interest within a set period of time, is sometimes called a demand loan, as the lender can call it in at any time. Once you have established a record of prompt payments, just as in your personal credit history, your business credit history is being established in this manner. *Entrepreneur Magazine*'s website at www.entrepreneur.com/bestbanks presents a list of "best small-business-friendly banks" that are more likely to lend you the funds you need. Further down the page, you'll find the Top 100 Venture Capital Firms list also. More information about Venture Capital is provided later in this chapter. Another section of Entrepreneur.com presents a guide to raising money for more assistance in obtaining the capital you need.

After you have established a business credit history, a bank may provide a line of credit that you can draw against. Through this type of agreement, your business has a set amount of credit, called revolving credit, which you can draw upon. A line of credit provides you with the flexibility to meet cash flow crises and day-to-day expenses but it, of course, has to be paid back and you pay interest on the outstanding balance. Revolving credit is replenished every time you make a payment. There is no charge for having a line of credit, just for using it.

Today some financial institutions are offering small businesses credit cards to finance start-up expenses as well as operating expenses. However, due to their interest rates, credit cards are often the most expensive small business financing there is. Financing your business on credit cards may save time and allow you to keep business expenses separate from personal ones. But be forewarned, without very careful management, credit card debt can quickly put you out of business.

The Small Business Administration (SBA) also has numerous guaranteed loan programs available for start-ups and small businesses, but they are generally associated with banks so you still have to apply for the loans through banks. Visit the SBA's home page at www.sba.gov and select the Financing button at the top of the page to learn about programs like the 7(a) Loan Guaranty, Microloan Program, Minority Prequalification Loan Program, and others. In recent years, the SBA loan package process has been simplified for loans less than $100,000 so you may want to check them out. The Microloan Program provides short-term loans of up to $35,000 and is only available in selected locations in most states. Small Business Investment Companies (SBICs) are government-operated investment firms that provide venture capital to small businesses. SBICs are licensed by the SBA, and you will find information about them on the SBA's website.

A Cautionary Note

SBA loan guarantees differ in a few important ways from loans made by other lending institutions:

1. These loans take longer and require more paperwork.

2. The loan funds won't be released in one check. Canceled checks, invoices, or purchase orders may be required before funds are released.

3. Personal assets or jointly owned assets may have to be used as personal guarantees to get the loan.

4. An SBA-guaranteed loan may carry a higher interest rate than a conventional bank loan; the benefit of an SBA guarantee is that the lender extends the term of the loan beyond the usual time period, for example, seven years instead of five.

5. The SBA charges lenders an annual servicing fee and a guaranty fee and those percentages may be passed on to the borrower by the lending institution.

6. The SBA makes a special effort to make minority-owned, women-owned, or veteran-owned businesses aware of SBA programs, but there is no special pot of money or special considerations for those enterprises.

When you consider what type of loan to apply for, it's good to keep these items in mind.

Equity Financing

Since debt financing is often difficult for small start-up businesses to obtain, let's now look at equity financing.

"Equity financing" is an exchange of money for a share of business ownership. Equity capital gives its contributor an ownership interest in the assets of the business and a share of its future income. You do not incur debt with this form of financing, and you do not have to repay a set amount of money at a particular time. The contributor often wants a voice in how the business is run so you do give up some control over your business. Two main sources for equity financing are "angel investors" and venture capital firms.

ANGEL INVESTORS

An "angel investor" is a wealthy private individual or groups of businesspeople or professionals who provide early-stage capital to new companies, especially companies who can improve the community, and who usually invest in regional or local companies within a specific industry or area of business interest or expertise. Generally speaking, these investors are more patient than venture capitalists, who often want to make 10 times their investment back in less than five years. Prepare a pitch to an angel in the same manner as you approach a bank. Once again, an outstanding business plan can help you succeed.

How does one locate an angel investor? This step can be difficult as angel investors don't advertise. Start by networking with local entrepreneurs, lawyers, and accountants. Show your business plan to many local individuals and follow every lead you're given to connect with leaders of the community. Angel investors are beginning to create a network and the place to start looking is at the website www.angelsummit.org. This site lists these groups by state and also lists their websites. Another resource for learning about angel investors and investing is *Angel Investing: Matching Startup Funds with Startup Companies*, by Mark Van Osnabrugge and Robert J. Robinson. Here you'll find out how to match your new business to angel investors as well as additional sources of information.

Van Osnabrugge, Mark and Robinson, Robert J. *Angel Investing: Matching Startup Funds with Startup Companies*. Jossey-Bass, 2000. 422p. ISBN 0-7879-5202-8. $32.00.

Using personal interviews, anecdotal evidence, and over 300 research studies, the authors describe who angel investors are, how they operate, and where they can be found. The differences between angel investors and venture capitalists are thoroughly detailed. Learn how to match your new venture to financing sources. Find tips on writing your business plan to obtain financing. Appendix One is a detailed list of matching services in the United States. The lengthy bibliography is a great source of additional information resources. This work can help you obtain financing for your new business.

See other sites at the end of the chapter where you may be able to locate an angel investor.

VENTURE CAPITAL

Venture capital is the money invested in young, rapidly growing businesses. Venture capital firms pool money from private investors and expect a high annual return (20 to 40%) on their investment and usually invest in companies for a period of three to seven years. Venture capital firms often focus on a certain industry and invest at a particular stage of the company's development. "Seed capital" is needed at the start-up stage. "Early stage financing" is designed to fund the early growth stage after the company is delivering a product or service. The final stage is "expansion stage financing," when the company needs funds to expand into new markets or product lines. As your business grows, you may need venture capital to help you finance changes that you need to make to expand your operation. The cost of this type of financing is high and may require you to sell off large portions of your business with a resulting loss of control. Sometimes when a venture capitalist decides to exit a business, an initial public offering (IPO) of your company's stock is used to continue financing the business. Investigate the pros and cons of venture capital very carefully before seeking this type of financing. When you want to find a venture capitalist or venture capital firm, check with your attorney, banker, or other local business owners to get a personal recommendation if possible.

You may also want to check the National Venture Capital Association at www.nvca.org. This trade association provides advocacy, education, and networking opportunities for the U.S. venture capital industry. The directory provides access to venture capital organizations regionally throughout the United States. Another classic reference on venture capital is David Gladstone's *Venture Capital Handbook*. Learn how to obtain venture capital as he walks you through the process and the forms including commitment letters, loan agreements, promissory notes, and stock purchase warrants.

Gladstone, David. *Venture Capital Handbook*. Rev. ed. Prentice Hall, 2002. 424p. ISBN 0-13-065493-0. $39.00.

Gladstone explains the venture capital process for entrepreneurs, using insights and actual examples he gained from his experience as a venture capitalist. Learn how to develop a business plan with obtaining venture capital in mind. Here each step in the process to obtain venture capital funding is discussed. Advice on attracting investors, accelerating the investment process, and building long-term relationships with investors is included. Many checklists are included to help you to keep track of all the homework and paperwork needed to work with venture capitalists. This revised edition also considers the impact of the Internet and new technologies on the marketplace and the venture capitalist industry. Well written and to the point, the information is easy to understand and well organized. This handbook is a classic on venture capital.

Listed in the resources at the end of the chapter you will find more sources of information on venture capital.

If you would like to read further about sources that can help you obtain many types of financing, the *Inc Magazine* site (www.inc.com/magazine) has two very good articles on the topic: 20 Tips for Finding Money Now and A Hitchhiker's Guide to Capital Resources.

REFERENCES

■ Print Resources

Amis, David and Stevenson, Howard. *Winning Angels: The 7 Fundamentals of Early Stage Investing*. Prentice Hall, 2001. 304p. ISBN 0-273-64916-7. $29.00.

This practical guide reduces the art of angel investing to the basics. Entrepreneurs will benefit from reading this work before they seek funding. Learn what investors are looking for in new businesses and provide it. Fifty venture capitalists and entrepreneurs were interviewed to provide the advice presented. Learn how to attract financing to your business venture.

Beroff, Art and Moyers, Dwayne. *Where's the Money: Sure-Fire Financing Solutions for Your Small Business.* Entrepreneur Press, 2001. 370p. ISBN 1-891984-54-3. $14.95.

These two finance experts guide readers to sources of financing and even to the best types of financing for specific businesses. Covered here are more than 25 financing sources with pros and cons of each source and risk factors associated with them so entrepreneurs can find the money their new business needs. Discover the ins and outs of borrowing against your home. Also provided are tips for writing financial statements to appeal to different audiences, filling out loan applications that get approved, and anticipating investor questions and how to answer them.

Burk, James. *Financing Your Small Business.* Sourcebooks, Inc., 2004. 256p. ISBN 1-57248-450-0. $17.95.

Burk covers the major topics for obtaining financing in a well-organized, readable style. The business start-up checklist is useful as are the sample business plan and sample formation documents for a corporation and for a limited liability company. An entire chapter is devoted to Equity Financing, which thoroughly explains what a potential investor is looking for before deciding to invest in a company. Angel investors are described in detail along with a description of how they and venture capitalists evaluate a business. This comprehensive reference guide will help new and old entrepreneurs obtain financing.

Burton, E. James and Bragg, Steven M. *Accounting and Finance for Your Small Business.* John Wiley & Sons, Inc., 2000. 288p. ISBN 0-471-32360-8. $29.95.

New business owners need to learn how to track cash flow, analyze key financial information, compile tax liabilities, and determine and control their insurance requirements. Detailed, step-by-step guidance leads readers through proven strategies and techniques for managing a small business. Checklists, ready-to-use forms, and sample spreadsheets with real-world examples in each chapter are provided to assist in the learning process. This valuable reference work will serve as a refresher for established business owners as well.

Carlini, Ronald J. and Moss, Therese Carlini. *Smooth Sailing to Venture Capital Funding.* Venture Capital Strategies, 2005. 174p. ISBN 0-9760908-5-6. $19.95.

The Carlinis focus on teaching entrepreneurs and companies how to evaluate their business model and measure it against what the financial community is currently funding. Identify your company's strengths and eliminate the weaknesses to attract investors and build a strong, profitable company. This book identifies the obstacles to obtaining financing and helps entrepreneurs and small businesses, in general, overcome them and successfully obtain the needed financing.

Evanson, David R. *Where to Go When the Bank Says No: Alternatives for Financing Your Business.* Bloomberg Press, 1998. 280p. ISBN 1-576600-173. $24.95.

Evanson explains to small business owners how to search for equity capital. He covers IPOs, angel investors, venture capital, overseas financing, and incubators in great detail. Especially noteworthy are the chapters on Presenting Financials and Preparing Business Plans. The explanations of financial ratios and statements, complete with charts and lists, will enlighten many entrepreneurs. Appendixes include a private equity capital directory, a list of universities with leading entrepreneurship programs, and the overview of securities laws influencing private and exempt transactions. This book is a great place to start your search for the capital your business needs.

Fallek, Max and Solie-Johnson, Kris. *Finding Money for Your Small Business: The One-Stop Guide to Raising All the Money You Will Need*. 2nd ed. American Institute of Small Business, 2003. 163p. ISBN 0-939-0697-2-5. $24.95.

Find more than 50 sources of funding for small business enterprises. Sources include banks, grants, commercial loan companies, the Small Business Administration, and non-traditional sources. Learn new sources of funding for entrepreneurs that are friendly to small businesses.

**Gladstone, David. *Venture Capital Handbook*. Rev. ed. Prentice Hall, 2002. 424p. ISBN 0-13-065493-0. $39.00.

Gladstone explains the venture capital process for entrepreneurs, using insights and actual examples he gained from his experience as a venture capitalist. Learn how to develop a business plan with obtaining venture capital in mind. Each step in the process to obtain venture capital funding is discussed. Advice on attracting investors, accelerating the investment process, and building long-term relationships with investors is included. Many checklists are included to help you to keep track of all the homework and paperwork needed to work with venture capitalists. This revised edition also considers the impact of the Internet and new technologies on the marketplace and the venture capitalist industry. Well written and to the point, the information is easy to understand and well organized. This handbook is a classic on venture capital.

Gompers, Paul A. and Lerner, Josh. *The Money of Invention: How Venture Capital Creates New Wealth*. Harvard Business School Press, 2001. 320p. ISBN 1-57851-326-X. $29.95.

Venture capital industry experts Gompers and Lerner provide an analysis of this unique and mysterious industry. Venture capital is incredibly important to our economy as innovation is always difficult to finance, take to market, and translate into value. The relationship between venture capital and entrepreneurs is put into a meaningful framework. Learn how this industry operates and how to take advantage of opportunities in it.

Green, Charles H. *The SBA Loan Book*. Adams Media Corporation, 2000. 218p. ISBN 1-5806-2202-X. $12.95.

Green answers questions such as how to increase your odds of getting a loan, how to present your business to lenders, and how to appeal the lender's denial. This down-to-earth, logical resource walks users through the process of loan applications. Find out how to be successful no matter what type of loan you need or want to obtain.

Green, Charles H. *Streetwise Financing the Small Business: Raise Money for Your Business at Any Stage of Growth*. Adams Media Corporation, 2003. 384p. ISBN 1-5806-2765-X. $19.95.

This new book by Green presents innovative ideas for raising money for small businesses. He covers traditional methods as well as creative ones for obtaining the funds a small business needs to start or grow. Chapters cover determining your capital needs, determining the risk versus the reward, creating impressive financial statements, and setting realistic business goals. Find out how to obtain funds through various loans and leases, private lenders, government agencies, and liquidating assets. Learn what bankers are looking for and need to know about your business and also learn about alternatives to bank financing here.

Koehler, Dan M. *The Ultimate Insider's Guide to SBA and Other Loans.* Entrepreneur Press, 2004. 278p. ISBN 1-932156-90-9. $23.95.

This helpful guide enables new entrepreneurs to navigate the red tape involved in preparing a successful loan application. Discover what to emphasize when putting together your business loan package and avoid common mistakes. Many forms and worksheets, such as a sample small business loan application, are included. Understand how the SBA can help and how to find a preferred certified lender. User-friendly and informative, this guide will help you obtain a loan.

Koplovitz, Kay. *Bold Women, Big Ideas: Learning to Play the High-Risk Entrepreneurial Game.* Public Affairs, 2001. 288p. Index. ISBN 1-58648-107-X. $26.00.

Koplovitz provides expert advice on formulating a successful business plan or a winning pitch for venture capitalists to obtain financing. Readers will be inspired to launch and finance a successful new business venture by Koplovitz's crisp businesslike analysis of doing business in today's economy. A highlight is the practical list of resources at the end of the book that will help beginners learn about and find financing sources.

Kotler, Philip, Kartajaya, Hermawan, and Young, S. David. *Attracting Investors: A Marketing Approach to Finding Funds for Your Business.* John Wiley & Sons, 2004. 246p. ISBN 0-471-64656-3. $29.95.

The three sections included cover an introduction and overview of the capital markets, describe how capital markets operate, and describe how marketing concepts and tools can help your business attract the capital you need. Learn about the different sources of funds and how investors and lenders decide whom to back from among all the applicants. Chapter 3, Early-Stage Financing: The Role of Business Angels, is especially important for entrepreneurs starting a new venture. Notes at the end of each chapter will lead readers to more sources of information. Written clearly and succinctly, this book will prove valuable when trying to secure financing.

Mohr, Angie. *Financial Management 101: Get a Grip on Your Business Numbers.* Self-Counsel Press, Inc., 2004. 176p. ISBN 1-55180-448-4. $14.95.

Mohr helps new entrepreneurs plan the financial end of their business from the first financial statements through budgeting for advertising. Learn to measure your business success and how to find new opportunities. The chapter on ratio analysis will help readers learn what basic ratios tell them, what to do when ratios indicate a problem, and how to integrate ratios into your management reporting system. Case studies are presented throughout the book to help readers understand the importance of the concepts presented.

Mohr, Angie. *Financing Your Business.* Self-Counsel Press, Inc., 2004. 184p. ISBN 1-55180-583-9. $14.95.

Designed for new business owners, Mohr presents information on how to raise capital for your small business in a brief, easy-to-understand manner. Follow Mohr as she leads you step-by-step through the process and explores all the options for finding money for your business. Don't let your business fail because it's undercapitalized. Checklists and worksheets are provided to help walk readers through the more complicated procedures. This well-organized and well-written book will help anyone understand the financial issues involved in starting and running a business.

O'Hara, Patrick D. *SBA Loans: A Step-by-Step Guide.* John Wiley & Sons, Inc., 2002. 384p. ISBN 0-471-20752-7. $27.95.

This thorough and very comprehensive guide includes every SBA loan, program, and service available to small businesses. Step-by-step, O'Hara takes you through the process of preparing a successful loan request for both a new or established business and offers help on developing an outstanding business plan for your new business. Updated loan application forms are also provided. Every type of SBA loan financing available is covered in detail. A complete explanation of the financial data needed for the Operating Plan Forecast is covered in detail. Sample forms and checklists are in every chapter. As useful as the 11 chapters are, the 11 appendixes are equally useful: Appendix C covers the Ten Rules of Advertising, Appendix F How to Write a Successful Yellow Pages Ad, and Appendix H The Business Plan. If you are considering working with the SBA on financing your business, consult this book as it will help you work through the process as smoothly as possible.

Peterson, Ron. *When Venture Capitalists Say "No": Creative Financing Strategies and Resources.* Comanche Press, 2003. 272p. ISBN 0-9728246-1-8. $29.95.

This compilation of techniques, funding sources, and helpful advice is written for entrepreneurs. Peterson uses hundreds of stories of successful business development to illustrate his points. He includes websites and thousands of sources of money from around the world with contact information. Well organized and written in layman's terms, entrepreneurs and growing small businesses will find many sources of start-up capital here.

Pratt, Stanley E. *Pratt's Guide to Private Equity Sources.* Annual. Thomson Venture Economics. $660.00.

This comprehensive, classic library reference, formerly known as *Pratt's Guide to Venture Capital Sources*, and now combined with the *Directory of Buyout Financing Sources*, includes both venture and buyout sources of financing. The 2004 edition contains more than 4,500 listings including U.S.-based and foreign-based firms. Information on the venture capital industry and guidelines for companies seeking financing are provided in the sections on the Background on Private Equity and How to Raise Private Equity. Perspectives provides insight into the characteristics private equity investors look for in their clients as well as an entrepreneur's view of the private equity process. Following the text is the directory with detailed information about private equity companies. An index of firms by location and an executive index follow the directory.

Reiss, Bob. *Low Risk, High Reward: Starting and Growing a Business with Minimal Risk.* Simon & Schuster, 2000. 336p. ISBN 0-684-84962-3. $27.50.

Reiss starts out with a carefully compiled list of 10 personal attributes entrepreneurs should possess and explains why each personal attribute contributes to the likelihood of success. Reiss' chapter on Numeracy discusses cash flow and the importance of updating cash flow statements as well as including an example of a cash flow statement in the appendix. His chapter on Getting the Money thoroughly covers the best sources of start-up capital. Full of practical suggestions and insights, this guide will help all entrepreneurs but especially those with little experience and little money.

Timmons, Jeffrey, Spinelli, Stephen and Zacharakis, Andrew. *How to Raise Capital: Techniques and Strategies for Financing and Valuing Your Small Business*. McGraw-Hill, 2005. 245p. ISBN 0-07-141288-3. $16.95.

The authors identify the financial life cycles of new ventures, provide entrepreneurs with a framework for financial strategies, and illustrate the investor's perspective when considering investing in a new venture. Entrepreneurs will learn how to find, contact, and work with funding sources from SBA lenders to venture capitalists. Besides learning the ins and outs of obtaining debt capital, entrepreneurs will learn how to manage debt. Also highlighted are key mistakes that defeat small businesses. Learn how angel investors or venture capitalists think and predict what to expect from them. The authors present many real-life examples of entrepreneurial success and failure. Learn how to finance your idea and create the financial foundations necessary for long-term success. This outstanding reference is useful for all new ventures needing financing.

The Ultimate Small Business Guide: A Resource for Startups and Growing Businesses. Basic Books, 2004. 501p. ISBN 0-7382-0913-9. $19.95.

This large collection of how-to's, step-by-step objective lists, and enlightening FAQs covers all aspects of planning, launching, managing, and growing your small business. Sections cover Refining and Protecting Your Idea, Communicating with Your Customers, and Selling Online. Financing, pricing, cash flow, ratios, and assets are thoroughly and carefully covered in a section called Figuring It Out. The chapters on creating a balance sheet, cash flow statement, and profit and loss account will help new entrepreneurs understand and produce these essential financial reports.

**Van Osnabrugge, Mark and Robinson, Robert J. *Angel Investing: Matching Startup Funds with Startup Companies*. Jossey-Bass, 2000. 422p. ISBN 0-7879-5202-8. $32.00.

Using personal interviews, anecdotal evidence, and over 300 research studies, the authors describe who angel investors are, how they operate, and where they can be found. The differences between angel investors and venture capitalists are thoroughly detailed. Learn how to match your new venture to financing sources. Find tips on writing your business plan to obtain financing. Appendix One is a detailed list of matching services in the United States. The lengthy bibliography is a great source of additional information resources. This work can help you obtain financing for your new business.

Vinturella, John B. *Raising Entrepreneurial Capital*. Elsevier, 2003. 300p. ISBN 0-12-722351-7. $54.95.

Assuming that an entrepreneur understands financial statements, has selected his or her business, and knows how to write a business plan, this work presents both sides of the debt versus equity decision, the financing options available to smaller businesses, and avenues that can lead to rapid growth such as venture capital, angels, incubators, and

IPOs. Discover how to attract private equity investment and improve your company's marketability. Taking a global view, Vinturella includes case studies from Europe, Latin America, and the Pacific Rim to illustrate the theories presented. Capital raising strategies, financial management, and budgeting are important concepts to small businesses, and this work will help you understand them better.

Walter, Robert. *Financing Your Small Business*. Barron's Educational Series, Inc., 2004. 368p. ISBN 0-7641-2489-7. $18.95.

If you are a new entrepreneur, this work will provide you with practical advice on how to create a solid financial foundation for your business. Walter describes how to attract venture capital and private equity, deal with banks and investment firms, and should your business progress, how to deal with public and private offerings of stock shares. One chapter covers Timing Issues of Different Financings. Sample term sheets, engagement letters, and letters of intent, which cover many different types of financing, are provided.

■ Online Resources

About.com: www.about.com/business (Accessed Fall 2005).

This large site has many different parts but the Small Business Financing section contains good articles on getting a loan, cash flow management, and sources of equity financing. Also find tips on insurance and tax questions or decisions. Many downloadable business forms as well as some industry information can be accessed here as well. Continually updated and well organized, this site will help you find information on financing options as well as budgeting and planning your finances.

American Express Small Business Exchange: http://www 133.americanexpress. com/osbn/Landing/informyourdecisions.asp?us_nu=subtab (Accessed Fall 2005).

Small business owners will find help here on management, finding money, and marketing. This outstanding site has information on managing debt, business plans, fraud protection, and SBA loans. The article under Financial Management entitled Business Valuation Methods explains the various common methods used to come up with a value for a small business. The Starting a Business section tells users about structuring their business as well as some information on types of insurance.

Active Capital: activecapital.org (Accessed Fall 2005).

The Angel Capital Electronic Network (ACE-Net) was created by the SDA in 1995. ACE-Net has become Active Capital to more accurately explain the proactive role it takes in helping small businesses connect with private capital. As they explain on their website, if you are a successful entrepreneur and your company's cash reserve is not keeping up with your company's growth, you may qualify to be listed on this database. Learn how to enroll and complete the application process online if you qualify.

**Angel Capital Association: www.angelsummit.org (Accessed Fall 2005).

Looking for an angel investing group in North America? Start your search here. This peer organization of angel investing organizations holds annual summits and regional meetings to develop best practices and encourage collaboration. ACA is currently a program of the

Kauffman Foundation. The Directory lists Angel Organizations regionally in the United States and also in Canada.

Asset Alternatives: www.assetnews.com (Accessed Fall 2005).

This private equity website contains news and networking opportunities involved in the venture capital industry. Read articles about investment firms and what companies they're investing in currently. The *Galante's Venture Capital and Private Equity Directory* is available for sale. Virtual seminars on international issues related to venture capital and private equity investment are also available as are newsletters and reports.

Business Finance: www.businessfinance.com (Accessed Fall 2005).

This large website includes more than 4,000 business loan and capital sources. You choose to search the In Business, StartUps, or Buyers sections with sources categorized for you. Microloans, business credit cards, equipment leasing, SBA small business loans, venture capital, construction loans, and investment banks are all included. Besides searchable Business Resource databases, you'll find Workbooks and other tools. This large, well-organized site is easy to use and provides a wealth of financing information.

Business Know-How: www.businessknowhow.com/bkhstartup.htm (Accessed Fall 2005).

This large business website has a great page on Starting a Business, as well as lots of information on Business Loans, cash flow, and planning for taxes. A handy checklist helps you remember what to do and when to do it. Also included is information on human resources (HR) training and tools, employment forms, templates and productivity tools, and web design and content. Check out this site when starting and running your business.

Entrepreneur.com: www.entrepreneurmag.com (Accessed Fall 2005).

Maintained by *Entrepreneur Magazine*, this site supports new businesses and growing companies. Find many good articles on financing your new business. Two important areas of this page are listed at the top, Management and Business Coaches. Here you'll find lists of articles covering various topics in management such as trends in management, time management, managing employees, and more. Business Coaches can help you through difficult times in your business life. Start Up Topics include organization and managing, finding a location, naming your biz, and business structure. Find ready-made business forms here, too. Use this site whenever you need help in determining what to do next.

**Entrepreneur's Guidebook Series: www.smbtn.com/businessplanguides/ (Accessed Fall 2005).

Defining real entrepreneurs as managers who adopt key behaviors developed by understanding key market concepts and theories and who are successful because of their planning and researching skills, this site discusses why people become entrepreneurs and the type of life entrepreneurs generally lead. Here you will discover what your entrepreneurial talents are and common traits of successful entrepreneurs. Explore this website for more good ideas.

Home Business Magazine: www.homebusinessmag.com (Accessed Fall 2005).

The Money category accessible through the frame on the left side of the screen provides a wealth of articles on money management for any type of small business. Articles thoroughly discuss accounting, investing, taxes, and controlling costs. The article on Managing Cash Flow for Improved Profits is an excellent example of the good ideas and advice presented. Articles on Business Start-up, Management, and Marketing and Sales are also included.

**Inc.com: www.inc.com (Accessed Fall 2005).

The publishers of *Inc* magazine present a large directory of articles by topic targeting many problems, concerns, and decisions confronting new business owner/managers. Especially outstanding are their current articles on financing your new business. Their articles on marketing and advertising are informative and practical. Simple but effective advice is the hallmark of this outstanding, easy-to-use site.

**National Venture Capital Association: www.nvca.org (Accessed Fall 2005).

This trade association provides advocacy, education, and networking opportunities for the U.S. venture capital industry. The NVCA supports entrepreneurial activity and innovation and aims to increase the visibility and awareness of the industry as well as its importance to the U.S. economy. The directory provides access to venture capital organizations regionally through the United States. Another section of the directory covers venture capital organizations outside the United States. Each entry includes a brief description and the web address. Its affiliate group, the American Entrepreneurs for Economic Growth (AEEG) is the nation's largest network of emerging growth companies with 14,000 members.

Online Women's Business Center: www.onlinewbc.gov (Accessed Fall 2005).

This site of the SBA's Office of Women's Business Ownership strives to help women business owners but provides a great deal of information free to all. Under Business Basics on the left side of the home page, you will find Financing Your Business. Numerous topics in the Finance Center on types of loans, how to qualify for a loan, links to SBA loans, and more can be located here. A wealth of information and links will help you develop a financial plan, budget, and learn more about most financial issues in running your own business.

PowerHomeBiz.com: www.powerhomebiz.com/Index/financing.htm (Accessed Fall 2005).

This large, small business site has an outstanding section on Getting Financing for Your Small and Home Based Business. The Section on Angel Investors and Venture Capital includes informative articles such as the one entitled Find Yourself an "Angel," and Why Investors Say "No." There is even a special section on Micro Loans. Must-Have Books are listed with some articles and Recommended Tools and Software as well. This established, well-organized site will help new entrepreneurs with financing and other parts of starting a new business.

**Small Business Administration: www.sba.gov (Accessed Fall 2005).

This official government site offers a wealth of resources and programs for starting and growing a small business. Under Startup Basics, users will find an Entrepreneurial Test of 25 questions that will help them in doing a personal evaluation of their possible success in their own business. Other major sections cover business planning, financing, managing, marketing, employees, taxes, legal aspects, and business opportunities. Find here online forms, business plans, loan information, and many publications. Some contents available in Spanish.

VC Fodder: www.vcfodder.com (Accessed Fall 2005).

This new website has many sections including Raise Capital, Dr. VC-Get Advice, Resources, Hot Content, Community, and more. The Angel Capital section is a listing of angel groups and early stage funds available. Links to Featured Sources of Early Stage Capital change frequently and the list of Other Angel Capital Sources continues to grow. A lengthy article explains Learn How to Work with VC Fodder. Venture Capital 101 is an introduction to the entire subject of venture capital. Check this site for ideas on raising capital and developing your financial model.

vFinance.com: www.vfinance.com (Accessed Fall 2005).

This commercial site allows visitors to search for Venture Capital or Angel Investors. Free business plan sample templates are provided for entrepreneurs in the Business Plan Center. Users can post business plans for viewing by potential investors. Also, users can research lists of lenders, investment banks, and angel investors, as well as get information on venture capital sources, accountants, lawyers, and others. The *Venture Capital Resource Directory* is continually updated and checked for accuracy.

MARKETING AND ADVERTISING

7

CHAPTER HIGHLIGHTS:

- Your Marketing Plan
- Four P's of Marketing
- Where to Find Market Research
- Write Your Marketing Plan
- Marketing Activities

Marketing is about how you communicate with customers and prospective customers, often called your audience or target market. Most marketing involves promoting a combination of products and services. The most important word in marketing is consistency. Decide up front on how you want to be perceived and remembered so you can create a consistent look and presence. Send a clear message describing how your product or service will improve the life of your customer or make it easier. In today's multi-tasking, dual-income lives, saving time often outweighs saving money. If your product or service can save both, it's a good bet for success.

The purpose of marketing is to plan and carry out a variety of strategies to inspire new customers to give you a try and encourage current customers to return. Remember that creativity is more important than money in marketing a new venture. Marketing includes research, distribution, pricing, advertising, and promotion as well as sales. If you are new to market research, find a copy of *Market Research Made Easy* by Don Doman to get you started. This book walks you through the basics of market research from finding the data through analyzing and interpreting your data to developing a marketing plan. Worksheets, case studies, and samples help you along the way.

Doman, Don and Dennison, Dell. *Market Research Made Easy*. 2nd ed. Self-Counsel Press, Inc., 2004. 160p. ISBN 1-55180-409-3, $14.95.

Market research is described by the authors as a process of asking questions or finding existing information about the market, the competition, and potential customers. Written for the first-time, do-it-yourself market researcher, the authors guide readers step-by-step through marketing your first business. Worksheets and explanations in non-technical language help you decide if you want to consult a professional, how much you want to spend, and help you gather and analyze data to create a marketing strategy. Learn how to write a questionnaire. Various real-life case studies scattered throughout bring home the importance of market research and doing it well. The authors ascertain that the most difficult part of market research is that it can burst your bubble, demolish a cherished idea, but it will save you money and point you in the right direction.

YOUR MARKETING PLAN

Your marketing plan is a key component of your business's strategy for success. The well-prepared marketing plan specifies what is unique about your product and/or service. It identifies the size of your expected or target market, by segment, and the share you can reasonably expect to capture. It lists major competitors, why customers buy from them and why not (strengths and weaknesses), their sales, growth rates, and market shares. It also describes your most likely customers, why they will or should buy from you, what sets you apart from your competitors, and which forms of promotion and advertising will most effectively reach them. Lastly, it includes a timetable, budget, and means for measuring results. Marketing without a plan wastes money and time.

Defining your competition is very important. What companies are currently selling something similar if not exactly the same as what you want to offer? It's important to identify them and research everything you can about them. Chapter 12, Competitive Analysis, delves deeply into competitive intelligence and competitive advantage. Knowledge of your competitors is important as you can learn how to get more customers, learn how they impact your business, and learn from their mistakes. Competitors influence your position in the market and how quickly or slowly your business grows.

FOUR P's OF MARKETING

Marketing research is an integral, essential part of business planning. It can be gathered by both statistical research and observation or, ideally, a combination of both. Remember to answer the questions relating to the four P's of marketing:

1. *Product or Service.* What are you offering and what do consumers want? Market research determines what consumers are buying and why; identify why consumers will buy your product over that of your competitors.

2. *Pricing.* How much must you charge for your product or service, and is it a competitive price? Market demand must be considered. Pricing is closely regulated and subject to public scrutiny. Can you balance sales volume and price to maximize income?

3. *Place.* This identifies not only the geographic area where you will market your product or service, but what sales channels you will employ to

promote and sell your product or service. This item is also often called distribution.

4. *Promotion.* How will you position your product or service in the market? It involves personal selling, sales promotion, and advertising in print, broadcast, or other media. Market research will help you define the media to which your customers are most receptive.

WHERE TO FIND MARKET RESEARCH

To know your market, start with observation and use what are called "primary market research sources." Look closely at what products and services consumers purchase; and find out when, where, why, and how they buy them. Define your information needs. What do you need to know about your potential market?

Observation

Now start collecting data and then analyze your findings. Talk to other individuals in your industry. Talk to the competition. Ask how they got started. Ask what trends they see happening in the industry. Talk to potential suppliers. Get a good feel for your industry and the market in your state, county, or city. This process is ongoing as long as you're in business; keep tabs on what is happening in the market and the industry. Market research takes time.

Secondary market research is extracted from industry studies, books, magazines or trade publications, and other published sources. Look for basic demographic information as a starting point.

Local, State, and Federal Government Agencies

As discussed in Chapter 2, use American Factfinder produced by the U.S. Census Bureau on their website at www.factfinder.census.gov. You can find statistics on age, sex, geographic region, marital status, income, and more. See how many people live in a particular county or zip code. You can also find the median age and median household income. You can see how many households earn over $10,000 a year or $75,000 a year. Find out how many families of four live in a particular zip code. Knowing income statistics and the size of the household can indicate the buying power of consumers in your area. If your product or service is family oriented, you want to know how large the possible market is now and possibilities for growth. Using industry studies, though not tailored to your specific needs, can give you insights into the customers in your industry. Find trends in your industry; how much has it grown in the past five years? From the American Factfinder page, check out the Economic Census (produced every five years) for your industry and the Survey of Current Business. Sales and employment statistics are indicators of market size and company performance.

Another great resource from the U.S. Census Bureau is County Business Patterns. Learn about the businesses in your area. Below is a detailed example of how this web resource can be used.

Start at censtats.census.gov/cbpnaic/cbpnaic.shtml and select a zip code.

This section is now called Zip Code Business Patterns and presents data on the total number of establishments, employment, and payroll for over 50,000 5-digit zip code areas throughout the nation. Let's say 87059 for Tijeras, New Mexico. What comes up are the statistics for the most recent year available, 2002, but you can go back three to four years. First you'll see a table with the total number of establishments, number of employees, first quarter payroll in $1,000s, and annual payroll in $1,000s. Now, look below that at the larger table. Let's look at the column labeled the Industry Code Description. Let's say we want to start a Bed & Breakfast so we'll look at Accommodation & Food Services, Industry Code 72 (that's the first two digits of the NAICS code). We see that there are 4 establishments in this zip code, and the next columns tell us the Number of Establishments by Employment-size class, either 1–4, 5–9, 10–19, etc. Click on the far left column, Detail. Detail breaks the NAICS code down into Full-service Restaurants, Limited-service Restaurants, and Drinking Places (alcoholic beverages). So there are no B&B's in this zip code, which may be good news. On the

---

U.S. Census Bureau

North American Industry Classification System (since 1998)

County Business Patterns   Select a state   Go

County Business Patterns provides data on the total number of establishments, mid-March employment, first quarter and annual payroll, and number of establishments by nine employment-size classes by detailed industry for all counties in the United States and the District of Columbia.

Employers without a fixed location within a state (or of unknown county location) are included under a "statewide" classification at the end of the county tables. This incomplete detail causes only slight understatement of county employment. The independent cities in Virginia, and the cities of Baltimore, MD; Carson City, NV; and St. Louis, MO, are treated as separate counties.

Zip Code Business Patterns (Enter ZIP Code) [   ]   Go

ZIP Code Business Patterns presents data on the total number of establishments, employment and payroll for more than 40,000 5-digit ZIP Code areas nationwide. In addition, the number of establishments for nine employment-size categories is provided by detailed industry for each ZIP Code.

Most ZIP Codes are derived from the physical location address reported in Census Bureau programs. The Internal Revenue Service provides supplemental address information. Those employers without a fixed location or with an unknown ZIP Code are included under an "Unclassified" category indicated by ZIP Code 99999.

Metro Business Patterns Go

Metro Business Patterns provides data on the total number of establishments, mid-March employment, first quarter and annual payroll, and number of establishments by employment-size classes by detailed industry for all Metropolitan Statistical Areas (MSAs) and New England County Metropolitan Areas (NECMAs). As defined by the United States Office of Management and Budget (OMB), an MSA is made up of at least one large city (50,000 population or more), and includes the county or counties in which it is located. Adjacent and other nearby counties meeting certain criteria are also included in the MSA. NECMAs are used in this data series as a county-based alternative to the usual city- and town-based New England MSA classifications.

County Business Patterns by 4-digit Standard Industrial Classification

Technical Support
TechSupp@census.gov
301-763-7710 Voice
301-457-1296 Fax

Census Bureau Links: Home · Search · Subjects A-Z · FAQs · Data Tools · Catalog · Census 2000 · Quality · Privacy Policy · FYI · Contact Us
USCENSUSBUREAU
Helping You Make Informed Decisions

Figure 7.1 Screenshot of CenStats Databases (censtats.census.gov/cbpnaic/cbpnaic.shtml)

Detail page, another column has popped up which is Compare. Click on Compare for Accommodation & Food Services. Compare shows us how many Accommodation & Food Services places are in nearby zip codes. There we see Cedar Crest, a town about 10 miles away has 10 establishments; Edgewood, 10 miles away in another direction has 9, etc. Use these statistics to help determine the viability of your new business idea.

Because a B&B is a tourism business, you would want to explore the Tourism Industry Statistics for New Mexico and Bernalillo County to try to track the number of overnight visits or visitors to continue your market research. Remember the State Data Center (SDC) program, as discussed in Chapter 2. The SDC is a cooperative program between the states and the Census Bureau; at the URL www.census.gov/sdc/www/, you can click on your state and see a list of Census State Data Centers, where you will find people to help you access and use your state's data. Contact the SDC in your state for training and technical assistance in accessing and using Census Bureau data for your market research.

For local information, don't forget the chamber of commerce, county or city clerk, other local business organizations, and of course, the local library. If you're marketing a service business, you might check with other service-type businesses in the area to see if they would share some of their local data or try local media sources. Creativity in finding sources of information is always helpful. Network with other business owners to see what sources they have used.

Trade and Professional Associations and Trade Journals

Refer back to Chapter 2, Research, Statistics and Information Gathering, to locate many sources to find and use trade publications. Joining a trade association will provide you with access to industry data and trends as well as provide opportunities to network with business owners with similar interests.

The Library

Besides the federal government online, visit the business section of a local library, or a larger public library or public university library in your state. Ask what industry, company, or market share resources are available for the public to use. Visit several times and ask for help. If the library purchases the *Editor and Publisher Marketing Guide* (Editor & Publisher, annual), you will find statistical data for U.S. and Canadian cities that publish one or more daily newspapers. Tables based on publisher estimates include Disposable Income per Household and more. Another well-known commercial publisher of marketing statistics and data is Standard Rate and Data Service (SRDS). While they publish a number of outstanding volumes, the *Lifestyle Market Analyst* correlates demographic characteristics with consumer behavior patterns. This volume takes interests, hobbies, and activities such as bicycling, fishing, gambling, and reading and combines them with demographic and geographic data. *The Survey of Buying Power* published each year as a special issue (September) of *Sales and Marketing Management* magazine contains regional and state summary data, retail sales, media statistics, and effective buying income (EBI) of households. The EBI, developed by *Sales and Marketing Management*, is defined as personal income less personal income tax and non-tax payments or disposable income. Many of these publications are very expensive and therefore may be difficult to find in your area.

However, most libraries will have some good resources for you to use or check out on market research or marketing small businesses. See the list of resources at the end of this chapter, and Chapter 3, Start-Up, to get started.

Local Media and Organizations

Don't forget that local newspapers, radio stations, television stations, and business-related magazines are great resources for gathering demographic information about potential target markets. They can provide you with information and statistics about economic trends, tax issues, advertising, and readership or viewership.

Look for networking opportunities by joining the local chamber of commerce and volunteering for committees. Share information and ask questions. Community groups often have information concerning local habits and markets. Find other local merchant associations or trade groups. Be active in your community.

WRITE YOUR MARKETING PLAN

Now, having gathered your research, it's time to write down your plan. Generally, a marketing plan contains the following sections:

1. *Business Environment*: Describe your company's and your competition's strengths and weaknesses and the key to success in your industry today. (Sometimes called a SWOT analysis, read more about this in Chapter 12, Competitive Analysis.)

2. *Overview of the Marketplace*: Identify how fast the market is growing, what's causing the growth, and present your forecast for the immediate future.

3. *Market Opportunities*: Identify the opportunities in the industry and market that you will use to your advantage.

4. *Business Description*: Outline current products or services and the demographics of your customer base as well as your vision of how your business will grow.

5. *Sales*: Set sales targets for the coming year including number of customers or unit sales and projected total sales dollars.

6. *Marketing Program:* Describe here your planned methods of marketing your product(s) or services. For each tool, indicate monthly activities for the coming year with estimated costs.

For some practical, detailed help in writing your marketing plan, *Marketing Plans That Work* by Malcolm McDonald and Warren J. Keegan, provides a step-by-step guide to preparing and executing your first plan. Pricing, distribution, and sales are also thoroughly covered.

McDonald, Malcolm and Keegan, Warren J. *Marketing Plans That Work.* 2nd ed. Elsevier, 2001. 264p. ISBN 0-7506-7307-9. $27.95.

New chapters in this second edition emphasize e-commerce and technology in marketing strategies. Readers will learn how to prepare a marketing plan that ensures unique value is created for the market and competitive advantage for the business. Flow charts and graphs are used to illustrate mapping and strategic assessment tools. Well organized, the step-by-step approach leads readers through the marketing process.

A good website for help with marketing is Edward Lowe's PeerSpectives at http://edwardlowe.org/indexa.htm. The section entitled Defining and Serving a Market explains how to anticipate customer needs, keep an eye on your competition, and write a practical marketing plan. Once again, the *Entrepreneur Magazine* site (www.entrepreneur.com) proves to be very useful with sales and marketing plan forms as well as articles to help the new entrepreneur. For dot-com businesses, the WebSite MarketingPlan.com website at www.websitemarketingplan.com for help in getting started is highly recommended. See the resources at the end of the chapter for more books and websites with sample plans and more help and advice. Don't forget to review and update your marketing plan on a regular basis just as you would your business plan. What would you do differently? What new goals does your business have or need?

MARKETING ACTIVITIES

As a new business, attracting customers is critical. The first and free option is "word-of-mouth" marketing. Work with your current customers and encourage them to spread the word. Good customer service will generate repeat business, and happy customers will talk to their friends and relatives. Ask your customers for referrals. Keep the concerns of your customers in mind, and let them know you care. Keeping your customers happy will make your business successful.

◼ Public Relations

Publicity in a local publication is another way to generate discussion. Send out press releases to all such publications announcing your new enterprise and what it offers. Whenever your company wins an award, introduces a new product, or hires a new employee, send a press release. Help promote a community event. Send a pitch letter to editors suggesting that you write an article on a subject related to your new business. Marcia Yudkin has written an entire book entitled *6 Steps to Free Publicity* in which she details many different ways to attract media attention. Use this book and/or brainstorm with family and friends how you can generate publicity for your new business.

Yudkin, Marcia. *6 Steps to Free Publicity*. Rev ed. Career Press, 2003. 272p. ISBN 1-56414-675-8. $19.99.

This small guide is packed with inspirational ideas and tips to bring visibility to your new venture. Chapters explain how to create and distribute a news release, write "advertorials," cope with reports and information overload, concoct creative angles, images, and exploits, and make time to publicize. Well written with more than a touch of humor, learn how to get media attention at no cost to you.

■ Advertising and Promotion

Advertising is a type of marketing where a business pays for a certain amount of space in a newspaper or magazine, or airtime on radio or television in order to present its message to an audience. If you open a retail store or restaurant, you will want to make advertising a priority. Otherwise, try to hold off on placing ads, and try other forms of promotion. Take some time to establish goals for your ads and a budget. Determine what publication or publications would be most effective in generating customers for your business. Remember to run at least six ads, or you'll be wasting money. People need to see something at least three times in print before it makes an impression. Be consistent—companies often change their ads just when customers are beginning to read, remember, and possibly act on the message. Also, try to develop a method or response mechanism to analyze the results of your advertising efforts.

Direct mail is another vehicle of advertising, but it is very expensive. If you have a targeted group of people or businesses, such as singles between the ages of 21 and 35 with an annual income of more than $30,000 (rather than just anyone over 21), direct mail is more cost effective. Focus on the three M's when using the mail to market your product or service. The three M's are:

1. The Market, which is the number of identifiable people who need your product or service enough to make a purchase;

2. The Message, which are the words, images, or special offers used to get attention and get the customers to take action; and

3. The Mailing List, which are the people who receive the mailing and how closely they match to the types of people who have a need or desire for your product or service.

If all these 3 M's are in sync, the mailing is likely to get good results. Do a series of smaller test mailings before you consider a large bulk mail effort to determine the effectiveness of your marketing piece and your mailing list. Keep testing with small samples until you have a handle on what copy, offers, and mailing list works for your business. Be sure to include a response mechanism in each mailing to help you track the results of the mailing. For example, "mention this flyer for a 20% discount." Coupons, discounts, and giveaways are the most frequently used methods. Be sure to weed out those names from future mailings that respond the least or not at all.

Like ads, a series of direct mail pieces sent to a select group generates a better response than a single flyer or postcard sent indiscriminately. Another form of direct mail is marketing via email. Though cost-effective, remember that unsolicited email is viewed as junk mail and may irritate your prospects rather than interest them. One way to avoid this is to buy advertising space on email newsletters and ezines (online magazines) that are sent out from websites that target your target audience.

Here is a brief list of inexpensive promotional ideas for a new business: leafleting house-to-house; posters; hire a sandwich board person; discounts for launch week; freebies such as rulers, bookmarks, any type of small item with the business name, address, phone, and URL on it; free samples; or a window display in a local business. Use a mixture of marketing/promotional methods to generate sales and get your business noticed.

The Internet

Related to email marketing is the use of a web page to market a business. Many consumers and business people use the Internet to research a company before deciding to patronize it. When creating a web page, be clear about providing information about your business, products, or services. Remember, it is the message that matters, not the slickness of the medium; start simple and see what happens. As in other forms of advertising, develop a method to count visitors and if possible, actual sales that result from seeing or using your web page. Be sure to use the speed and flexibility of the web to immediately adapt to changing market conditions and customer demands as a way to seize a competitive advantage. A website that's only updated annually or when the spirit moves you is very nearly worthless; on the web, timeliness is what it's about. If customers seek information on the web and find it on your competitors' site, you will lose customer loyalty. See Chapter Eight, Management, under Technology, for more information and ideas on a web page for your small business. One resource that will help you use and develop your web presence is Shel Horowitz's, *Grassroots Marketing*. He includes models for marketing budgets of $10, $100, and $1,000, and includes an entire section on the Incredible Internet.

Horowitz, Shel. *Grassroots Marketing: Getting Noticed in a Noisy World*. Rev. ed. Chelsea Green Publishing, 2004. 320p. ISBN -890132-68-3. $22.95.

Horowitz maintains that the average small business, individual, or organization needs to market very inexpensively. Learn how to identify your target market, get the message to your market, and convince the customer to do business with your company. Case histories and examples illustrate the effectiveness or ineffectiveness of many marketing vehicles for different types of businesses. Nine chapters cover using the Incredible Internet in Part IV. Chapter 21, Getting Started in Cyberspace, is particularly useful for those unfamiliar with ecommerce. An appendix of useful resources is also included. Learn how to attract favorable attention for your small business.

▇ Trade Shows

Trade shows can be a very effective way to market your new business. Find the right one, and you have the opportunity to sell to people who have already defined themselves as interested in your product or service. Attend several shows before signing up and paying to be a vendor. See what other businesses in your industry are doing, and what's effective. Benefits of exhibiting at a trade show include meeting with users of your product or service and getting feedback, selling merchandise or services, developing sales leads, keeping current on trends in the industry, showing your new products, and building your company's image. However, exhibiting at a trade show is expensive, so be selective and keep the following ideas in mind:

- Keep your booth small especially in the beginning or consider a co-op booth with someone who sells a complementary product or service;

- Don't overprint your literature;

- Collect names and mail or email contact information so you can follow up leads immediately after the show;

- Offer a show special, hold a contest, and/or hand out something related to your product or service or a sample;

- Try to be memorable or stand out, i.e. wear a costume or T-shirt with a catchy phrase or eye-catching logo.

Find more ideas and advice on the Trade Show News Network at www.tsnn.com. Setting up a booth at a trade show is a great way to make contacts, find people, and even sell products or services, and this comprehensive site provides information on more than 15,000 trade shows that you can find by industry, month of the year, city, state, or country. Trade show planning is also featured.

Like the business plan, a marketing plan is essential for a successful small business. Develop a consistent look and message for your business and use it to market your business every day. Word-of-mouth marketing and public relations are inexpensive and effective methods of gaining visibility and credibility; use them to your advantage. Listed below are many resources to help you learn how to market and advertise your new business.

REFERENCES

(Starred titles discussed in the chapter)

▎ Print Resources

Addison, Doug. *Small Websites, Great Results: The Blueprint for Creating Websites That Really Work*. Paraglyph, Inc., 2004. 352p. ISBN 1-932111-90-5. $29.99.

If you want a simple, well-designed, highly focused website, Addison's approach will work for your small business. Design ideas and marketing techniques are showcased in profiles of 20 small businesses. Readers will discover new approaches to creating sites, find out what really makes small sites work, learn about strategies for getting, keeping, and satisfying customers, and pick up tips on how to work with professional designers to get the results they want and need. Learn how to create an editorial calendar and how to organize the files on your website so your business site is always different, current, and easy to change. Discover what to leave off your site to keep it simple and uncluttered. Addison will convince you that quality is much better than quantity.

Attard, Janet. *Business Know-How; An Operational Guide for Home-Based and Micro-Sized Businesses with Limited Budgets*. Adams Media Corp., 1999. 390p. ISBN 1-58062-206-2. $17.95.

A major section of this title covers the various ways to market inexpensively. Find chapters on getting free publicity, using the mail to gain new customers, how to use trade shows to your advantage, and using the web to market your business. Using telemarketing and trade associations is also discussed. Sales strategies such as referrals and business-to-business selling as well as tracking your results are covered. Discover new methods to promote and market your business.

Banks, David H., Jr. *Market Planning Guide*. 6th ed. Dearborn Trade, 2002. 256p. ISBN 0-7931-5971-7. $22.95.

This practical, hands-on workbook presents tools and information for developing marketing plans and focused marketing strategies for small businesses. Banks includes questionnaires and checklists to help readers develop a marketing plan that will enable their company to stand out from the competition. A list of print and web resources and a glossary complete the volume. Whether you are a beginner or a pro, use this guide to create a winning plan.

Barletta, Martha. *Marketing to Women: How to Understand, Reach, and Increase your Share of the World's Largest Market Segment*. Dearborn Trade Pub., 2003. 253p. ISBN 0-7931-5963-6. $23.00.

Learn how to use the GenderTrends model, which provides explicit strategies and tactics for assessing your market, understanding your customer, and creating brand identity. Specific chapters also target salespeople, detailing selling ideas to attract more customers and close sales more often, and CEOs. This book emphasizes a women-focused marketing agenda that will provide a better return on marketing and sales dollars. In today's competitive market, Barletta's engaging book demonstrates how to understand, reach, and capture this largely untapped market.

Berkley, Holly. *Low-Budget Online Marketing for Small Business*. 4th ed. Self-Counsel Press, Inc., 2004. 144p. ISBN 1-55180-427-1. $14.95.

If you're interested in online marketing, this brief guide will steer you through the process. Chapters cover attracting your target audience, designing email marketing, building an online community, and working with a web developer. Inexpensive and well organized, this title will help online newbies market their business in an inexpensive way.

Carter, Susan M. *SPLASH Marketing for Overworked Small Business Owners: The Easy, Create-It-Once Strategy You Can Profit from Forever!* Nasus Publishing, 2003. 240p. ISBN 0-9670291-1-2. $24.95.

Carter helps users identify no-cost, low-cost marketing tactics to market your business effectively and successfully. Over 100 marketing ideas and 40 sales tips are presented. Handy checklists and helpful resources are also provided. Create a marketing campaign that will boost your small business into profit.

Cohen, William A. *The Marketing Plan*. 4th ed. John Wiley & Sons, Inc., 2004. 368p. ISBN 0-471-23059-6. $41.95.

This new edition presents step-by-step procedures to help you produce a clear plan that defines your marketing goals and how you plan to achieve them. Tools and techniques help you scan your industry and local environment, establish goals and objectives, and develop marketing strategies and tactics to successfully sell your product or service. Also included are time-saving forms to help you accomplish a variety of marketing planning tasks. Three new sample marketing plans from readers who have used previous editions to develop them are included in this edition. This practical guide will help you understand how and why a good marketing plan is so essential to every business venture.

Crawford, Fred and Mathews, Ryan. *The Myth of Excellence: Why Great Companies Never Try to Be the Best at Everything*. Crown Pub., 2001. 320p. ISBN 0-60-9608-207. $27.50.

After surveying 5,000 consumers to research purchasing behavior, the authors developed a "consumer relevancy" model. After explaining the importance of price, service, quality, access, and experience for the consumer, they suggest that companies need dominate only one of these five factors; stand out or differentiate themselves from competitors on another; and only be at a par with others in the industry on the remaining three in order to be successful. They also found the "Values are more important than value in the eyes of today's consumer" (p. 17). Truly this book is an eye-opening experience for consumers and businesses.

Cyr, Donald and Gray, Douglas. *Marketing Your Product*. 4th ed. Self-Counsel Press, Inc., 2004. 200p. ISBN 1-55180-394-1. $18.95.

Covering all the essentials of marketing, this expanded edition of a marketing classic demonstrates how your business can carve a niche for its products or services. Learn about market researching, market positioning, planning a marketing strategy, product launching, and competitor awareness. One highlight in this edition is a chapter on the value of the Internet as a marketing tool. Good worksheets help entrepreneurs and new small business owners develop their own marketing plan.

D'Allessandro, David F. and Owens, Michele. *Brand Warfare: 10 Rules for Building the Killer Brand*. McGraw-Hill, 2001. 208p. ISBN 0-07-1362-932. $24.95.

While Orville Redenbacher taught D'Allessandro "the power of a good brand to trump all rhyme or reason in the marketplace" (p. xi), he teaches us that brands save consumers time, project a certain image to the rest of the world, and make consumers feel part of the group that uses the brand. He discusses the steps to building and sustaining a brand or image, why it's as important to market your brand to your employees as it is to your customers, and why every business decision should be filtered through the prism of the brand. Learn about strategy and leadership in the world of branding.

**Doman, Don and Dennison, Dell. *Market Research Made Easy*. 2nd ed. Self-Counsel Press, Inc., 2004. 160p. ISBN 1-55180-409-3. $14.95.

Market research is described by the authors as a process of asking questions or finding existing information about the market, the competition, and potential customers. Written for the first-time, do-it-yourself market researcher, the authors guide readers step-by-step through marketing your first business. Worksheets and explanations in non-technical language help you decide if you want to consult a professional, how much you want to spend, and help you gather and analyze data to create a marketing strategy. Learn how to write a questionnaire. Various real-life case studies scattered throughout bring the important of market research and doing it well home. The authors ascertain that the most difficult part of market research is that it can burst your bubble and demolish a cherished idea, but it will save you money and point you in the right direction.

**Editor and Publisher Marketing Guide. Editor & Publisher. Annual. $150.00.

Statistical data is arranged alphabetically by state and city for the United States and by province and city for Canada. Cities included publish one or more daily newspapers. Information collected is wide ranging and examples include passenger auto registrations, residence electric meters, number and sales of furniture and home furnishings stores, and principal industries, number of employees, and average wage. Many libraries cannot afford to purchase annually but it is very useful data even if a few years old.

Edmunds, Holly. *AMA Complete Guide to Marketing Research for Small Business*. McGraw-Hill, 1996. 192p. ISBN 0-8442-3584-9. $29.95.

Though getting dated, this clear, concise, and comprehensive classic is still outstanding in leading do-it-yourself researchers through conducting basic market research. The step-by-step approach presented here will enable any business to better understand the environment in which they are operating and help them know their customers and potential customers better. Users will find help in designing usable questionnaires and effective mail surveys, learning how to work with outside vendors or consultants, conducting a useful telephone survey, and developing cost-conscious budgets. Discover how to set up your own "Mystery Shopper" program. Worksheets and checklists accompany each of the 11 chapters. The final chapters present case studies to show how small businesses have used the techniques presented here successfully. A practical guide like this to conducting small business market research is hard to find though unfortunately it is pre-Internet.

Godin, Seth. *Purple Cow: Transform Your Business by Being Remarkable*. Portfolio, 2003. 145p. ISBN 1-59184-021-X. $19.95.

What do Starbucks, KrispyKreme, HBO, and JetBlue have in common? They've created new ways of doing old business, and like a Purple Cow in a field of Holsteins, they stand

113

out. Godin uses case studies of real businesses to illustrate his points in each chapter. Powerful, fun, and simple—look at your marketing strategies with new eyes.

Griffiths, Andrew. *101 Ways to Advertise Your Business: Building a Successful Business with Smart Advertising.* Allen & Unwin Pty., Ltd., 2004. 256p. ISBN 1-86508-982-6. $14.95.

This conversational business book presents practical tips on advertising products and services. Learn how to create an advertisement, buy advertising space, and ensure that your advertising is effective. Griffiths discusses advertising in newspapers, magazines, on the radio, television, and the Internet, and on billboards. A glossary of advertising terms and a guide to smart advertising words and phrases are included. Checklists and blank forms round out this well-organized title.

Grossnickle, Joshua and Raskin, Oliver. *Handbook of Online Marketing Research.* McGraw-Hill, 2001. 433p. ISBN 0-07-136114-6. $39.95.

This volume will provide e-commerce companies and those interested in marketing their businesses on the Internet with comprehensive information about understanding, using, acquiring, and conducting market and marketing research online. Important chapters thoroughly cover sampling, questionnaire design, target markets, and tracking (feedback systems). The second half of the book covers the process of applying online marketing research to all phases of online product development and marketing. Use this information to assist you in developing every stage of an online venture.

Hague, Paul. *Market Research: A Guide to Planning, Methodology, and Evaluation.* 3rd ed. Kogan Page, 2002. 278p. ISBN 0-7494-3730-8. $37.50 (with CD-ROM).

Hague presents clear, concise advice with real-life case studies on the topic of market research. Slightly distracting is the very British slant. Tools and techniques used by market researchers are described and explained. Important chapters include Planning Market Research, How to Get Information for Next to Nothing, and Customer Satisfaction Surveys. References for further information are included for each chapter.

Hiebing, Roman G. and Cooper, Scott W. *The One Day Marketing Plan: Organizing and Completing a Plan That Works.* 3rd ed. McGraw-Hill, 2004. 344p. ISBN 0-07-139522-9. $24.95.

Learn how to quickly design a marketing plan for any type of business with the authors' streamlined, 10-step process. Templates and helpful checklists lead new marketers to complete an effective plan. Learn how to use Internet marketing tactics and learn to accurately evaluate bottom line results.

**Horowitz, Shel. *Grassroots Marketing: Getting Noticed in a Noisy World.* Rev. ed. Chelsea Green Publishing, 2004. 320p. ISBN 0-890132-68-3. $22.95.

Horowitz maintains that the average small business, individual, or organization needs to market very inexpensively. Learn how to identify your target market, get the message to your market, and convince the customer to do business with your company. If you need help with choosing a company name, writing press releases, using Yellow Page ads and direct mail advertising effectively, and the Internet, learn the basics here. Case histories and examples illustrate the effectiveness or ineffectiveness of many marketing vehicles for different types of businesses. Nine chapters cover using the Incredible Internet in Part IV. Chapter 21, Getting Started in Cyberspace, is particularly useful for those unfamiliar with e-commerce. An appendix of useful resources is also included. Learn how to attract favorable attention for your small business.

Johnson, Winslow "Bud." *Powerhouse Marketing Plans*. AMACOM, 2004. 352p. ISBN 0-8144-7219-2. $29.95.

Learn how to maximize market research initiatives such as phone surveys, focus groups, online surveys, and test marketing. You can explore the details of new marketing ventures and the interrelationship among those details. Watch the process from name development to package creation and from researching the competitive environment to understanding consumer segments and their motivations and interests. Each chapter takes a real product or service and works through the process to produce a sample Marketing Plan Summary at the end. The comprehensive sample marketing plan concluding the book is outstanding and a real example of what can be pulled together by using the advice Johnson presents. Discover the creative thinking and problem-solving processes behind good marketing plans.

Kobliski, Kathy J. *Advertising Without an Agency*. 3rd ed. Entrepreneur Press, 2005. 240p. ISBN 1-932531-28-9. $19.95.

This thorough reference guide will inform small business owners about the ins and outs of advertising and how to use it effectively. Kobliski covers radio, television, print, direct mail, and outdoor advertising. She provides worksheets to take the guesswork out of buying ad space or time and defines advertising jargon in easy-to-understand language with descriptive analogies. She discusses methods for finding out who your customers are and how to keep tract of them on paper. This book will help you advertise more effectively.

Kotler, Philip. *Ten Deadly Marketing Sins: Signs and Solutions*. John Wiley & Sons, 2004. 132p. ISBN 0-471-66206-2. $19.95.

Well-known and respected marketing expert Kotler identifies and describes the 10 glaring deficiencies companies make in their marketing efforts. Each mistake is covered thoroughly in its own chapter. Kotler explains how to remain customer-driven, understand your customers, track the competition, find new opportunities, and develop effective marketing plans. He also includes using technology to the fullest in your marketing plan. Find out if you're making any of these marketing mistakes and how to avoid or reverse them.

Laermer, Richard and Prichinello, Michael. *Full Frontal PR. Getting People Talking about You, Your Business, or Your Product*. Bloomberg Press, 2003. 256p. ISBN 1-5766-0099-8. $24.95.

Using case studies, this title illustrates how to use the press productively. Learn to identify your unique news-making hook, build relationships with local and industry press, and gain media attention for your business without the help of a PR firm and without a large budget. Get people to talk about you, your business, your product, and/or your service.

Levine, Michael. *Guerrilla PR Wired: Waging a Successful Publicity Campaign Online, Offine, and Everywhere in Between*. McGraw-Hill, 2003. 288p. ISBN 0-07-138232-1. $15.95.

This collection of cutting-edge, low-cost publicity techniques includes sample press releases and attention-getting strategies targeted for the wired environment. Focused on the web or Internet, the chapters on Internet PR and The Web and How to Unweave It, are particularly informative to Internet newbies. Levine has many years of experience in PR and more entrepreneurs will benefit from this discussion and hints gathered from his experiences.

Levinson, Jay Conrad, Frishman, Rick and Lublin, Jill. *Guerrilla Publicity*. Adams Media Corp., 2002. 304p. ISBN 1-5806-3682-3. $12.95.

This thorough guide presents plenty of sample materials including press kit components and printed promotional goodies. Learn how to use PR tools such as press releases, email, radio, direct mail, and more. Find out how to build a publicity plan and put it to work for you. Hundreds of publicity ideas are summarized in an easy-to-understand and easy-to-read format.

Machado, R. and Cassim, S. *Marketing for Entrepreneurs*. Juta Academic, 2004. 224p. ISBN 0-7021-5544-6. $24.95.

Covering all aspects of marketing, this title is especially strong in the product-service mix, branding, trademarks, packaging, warranties, and developing new products. Also learn how to identify, collect, analyze, and use the information collected through market research. This practical handbook will help develop a good marketing plan for your small business.

**McDonald, Malcolm and Keegan, Warren J. *Marketing Plans That Work*. 2nd ed. Elsevier, 2001. 264p. ISBN 0-7506-7307-9. $27.95.

New chapters in this second edition emphasize e-commerce and technology in marketing strategies. Readers will learn how to prepare a marketing plan that ensures unique value is created for the market and competitive advantage for the business. Flow charts and graphs are used to illustrate mapping and strategic assessment tools. Well organized, the step-by-step approach leads readers through the marketing process.

McKeever, Mike. *How to Write a Business Plan*. 7th ed. Nolo Press, 2005. 256p. ISBN 1-4133-0092-8. $34.99.

This logically organized, thoughtfully presented book uses examples and worksheets to help entrepreneurs prepare a successful business plan. Included are business plans for a small service and a manufacturing business. The chapter on writing your marketing and personnel plans is particularly helpful for the marketing section of a business plan. Before proceeding with the marketing plan, McKeever suggests you return to your written business description to see if it is still an accurate statement of how you view your business or if the thinking and writing experiences between chapters have changed your current ideas. A business plan is a dynamic document that needs constant revision to keep you and your business current. This new edition has good new online and offline resources to help the new entrepreneur plan his or her business.

McKinney, Anne. *Real Business Plans and Marketing Tools: Including Samples to Use in Starting, Growing, Marketing, and Selling Your Business*. PREP Publishing, 2003. 224p. ISBN 1-885288-36-0. $24.95.

Designed to help entrepreneurs prepare paperwork relating to starting, marketing, and growing a business, McKinney presents real business plans for 17 different types of businesses including a hair salon, brew pub, auto body shop, home-based wholesale company, and janitorial supply company, for example. The section on Marketing Tools will help new small business owners understand the fine points of marketing. Readers will also find samples of financial statements and other documents used to obtain bank loans and equity financing. This title will help new business owners in their strategic planning.

Mitchell, Jack. *Hug Your Customers: The Proven Way to Personalize Sales and Achieve Astounding Results.* Hyperion, 2003. 304p. ISBN 1-4013-0034-0. $19.95.

Mitchell suggests an approach to customer service and marketing that personalizes and saturates every aspect of your business. Using anecdotes that illustrate exemplary customer service, Mitchell presents his successful and innovative approach to merchandising, marketing, and management. Learn how to adapt Mitchell's ideas to any business in order to lower marketing costs, attract more customers, and maintain higher gross margins and long-term revenues. Discover how to create customer loyalty and long-lasting business relationships.

Norman, Jan. *What No One Ever Tells You About Marketing Your Own Business.* Dearborn Trade, 2004. 256p. ISBN 0-7931-8572-6. $18.95.

Collected and presented in this guide are the marketing experiences, techniques, and strategies of 101 entrepreneurs. Suggestions include create business cards, packaging, and signage that attract attention, customize the marketing effort to suit the company's personality, and win business at trade shows even without a booth. Divided into 10 sections, each section ends with a checklist, quiz, or sample to help readers apply what has been covered. Learn how to market your small business from your peers.

O'Hara, Patrick D. *SBA Loans: A Step-by-Step Guide.* John Wiley & Sons, Inc., 2002. 384p. ISBN 0-471-20752-7. $27.95.

This thorough and very comprehensive guide includes every SBA loan, program, and service available to small businesses and also provides help in advertising for the new business owner. Step-by-step, O'Hara takes you through the process of preparing a successful loan request for both a new or established business and offers help on developing an outstanding business plan for your new business. As useful as the 11 chapters are the 11 appendixes; Appendix C covers the Ten Rules of Advertising; Appendix E, Advertising-to-Sales Ratios; Appendix F, How to Write a Successful Yellow Pages Ad; and Appendix G, Advertising Considerations. A complete explanation of the financial data needed for the Operating Plan Forecast is covered in detail. Even if you are not considering working with the SBA on financing your business, consult this book as it will help you figure out how much to spend on advertising.

Parasuraman, A. and Colby, Charles L. *Techno-Ready Marketing: How and Why Your Customers Adopt Technology.* The Free Press, 2001. 240p. ISBN 0-68-4864-945. $27.00.

Presented here is a compelling framework for measuring the propensity of customers to welcome and use technology-intensive products and services. Learn how to determine each customer's Technology Readiness, how to motivate customers to use new technology, why people either embrace or resist technology, and divide your consumers into five distinct groups. CEOs, small business owner/managers, and marketing professionals will learn how to succeed in the technology-driven future.

Phillips, Michael and Rasberry, Salli. *Marketing Without Advertising.* 4th ed. Nolo Press, 2003. 240p. ISBN 0-87337-930-6. $24.00.

This book takes readers on an in-depth, practical journey through marketing strategies. One valuable section illustrates how to design and implement a marketing plan. Other topics include the physical appearance of your business, educating and helping prospective customers find your business, and using the Internet to market your business. Sections on the importance of good relations with your employees and how they influence the perception of your business are interesting and informative. Questionnaires, checklists, and worksheets included help readers understand important points.

Schenck, Barbara. *Small Business Marketing for Dummies*. 2nd ed. John Wiley & Sons, Inc., 2005. 384p. ISBN 0-7645-7839-1. $19.99.

Schenck emphasizes affordable marketing plans and solutions using Internet marketing, direct mail, and do-it-yourself public relations. Practical and comprehensive, this guide includes tips on generating publicity by word of mouth, creating effective advertising campaigns, and organizing your marketing strategy. Refer to this work when you are low on advertising and marketing ideas.

**SRDS Media Solutions. *The Lifestyle Market Analyst*. Annual. $460.00.

Compiled from 12 million households, this annual market analysis tool provides demographic, lifestyle, and consumer segment profiles to help users locate where consumers live and how they spend their money and free time. This volume takes interests, hobbies, and activities such as bicycling, fishing, gambling, and reading and combines them with demographic and geographic data. Use it to help you find regional buying powers, your target audience(s), and analyze 40 demographic segments. Check their website for more information, www.srds.com.

Stevenson, Jim. *Ultimate Small Business Marketing Guide: 1,500 Great Marketing Tricks That Will Drive Your Business Through the Roof!* McGraw-Hill, 2003. 288p. ISBN 1-932156-10-0. $22.95.

Written with small businesses in mind, readers will find cost-effective but innovative and time-tested ways to market this business. Chapters cover research, planning, competition, customer service, advertising, networking, websites, and trade shows. Checklists and sample forms help readers understand concepts and put them into practice. Internet resources that provide more marketing ideas are listed. This small business marketing library of information will help most entrepreneurs think of new ways to sell their products or services and win new customers.

**Survey of Business Power.* Sales and Marketing Management Magazine. Annual. $52.00 (accompanies subscription to Sales and Marketing Management Magazine).

Published in September, this classic library resource provides regional and state summary data on retail sales, media statistics, and its own Effective Buying Income (EBI) of households. The EBI is defined as personal income less personal income tax and non-tax payments or disposable income. Well known in the marketing industry, this source is expensive and may not be available at all libraries.

Sweeney, Susan. *101 Ways to Promote Your Web Site: Filled with Proven Internet Marketing Tips, Tools, Techniques, and Resources to Increase Your Web Site Traffic*. 4th ed. Maximum Press, 2002. 528p. ISBN 1-88506-890-5. $29.95.

Sweeney's practical guide provides checklists, templates, and forms to help entrepreneurs make their website more successful and productive by enticing surfers to check out the site, absorb what it offers, and return at some time in the future. Using email, links, and various forms of online advertising, entrepreneurs can get more visitors and more repeat visitors to their site. Use audio or video, meta tags, and news groups to enhance your web design. Use these techniques to improve your small business website.

Thaler, Linda Kaplan, Koval, Robin and Marshall, Delia. *Bang! Getting Your Message Heard in a Noisy World*. Currency, 2003. 256p. ISBN 0-38-5508-166. $24.95.

Learn why we've all heard of AFLAC and the duck, raising our consciousness about that insurance company from zero to instantly recognizable. Proven strategies and "out-of-the-box" thinking discussed here will help entrepreneurs, marketers, and students create loud, clear, attention-grabbing messages about their own products and services. Using real-life examples, the authors discuss successes and failures and suggest specific ways to create an atmosphere conducive to innovative breakthroughs.

**Yudkin, Marcia. *6 Steps to Free Publicity*. Rev. ed. Career Press, 2003. 272p. ISBN 1-56414-675-8. $19.99.

This small guide is packed with inspirational ideas and tips to bring visibility to your new venture. Chapters explain how to create and distribute a news release, write "advertorials," cope with reports and information overload, concoct creative angles, images, and exploits, and make time to publicize. Well written with more than a touch of humor, learn how to get media attention at no cost to you.

Online Resources

About.com: marketing.about.com (Accessed Fall 2005).

This large site has many different parts but the Marketing section is particularly well done. The section on Marketing Basics for the Small Business includes ideas and articles on using blogs to market your business, how to find your target market, sponsoring events to increase your credibility and prestige in your target market, and how to set the right prices. Learn more about Internet and email marketing. Continually updated and well organized, this site will help your marketing efforts. Another section of the About.com site is called Advertising at advertising.about.com. This site contains interesting promotional ideas and materials. Public relations is covered thoroughly as well. Learn why and how you should use promotional products and giveaways to advertise your business effectively.

American FactFinder: http://factfinder.census.gov/home/saff/main.html?_lang=en (Accessed Fall 2005).

This federal government source for information on population, housing, economic, and geographic data is easy to use and well designed. You can get a Fact Sheet for your community by just entering town, county, or zip code. A quick link gets you to the Decennial Census of Housing and Population, American Community Survey, the Economic Census, or the Population Estimates program. A couple clicks will get you to County Business Patterns, information on the NAICS code, statistics about small business from the Census

Bureau, the characteristics of business owners' database, and more. A glossary, FAQs, and search function will also help you use this great, free resource.

American Marketing Association: www.marketingpower.com (Accessed Fall 2005).

This website has many articles that will help you start and continue learning how to market your small business. The section on a Marketing Plan asks users questions to help them start thinking about the plan, their target consumers, the product, etc. The structure of a marketing plan is discussed and more. Other areas of the site provide articles on Best Practices in marketing, trends in marketing, networking opportunities, and Practitioner Resources. Joining the association gives you access to additional member-only resources. A directory of marketing suppliers as well as excellent marketing tools and templates are also available for free.

Bplans.com: www.bplans.com (Accessed Fall 2005).

This well-established, frequently updated site, sponsored by Palo Alto Software, Inc., is the best for help in writing your business plan. The section entitled Write a Business Plan contains articles, calculators on cash flow, starting costs, breakeven and more, a business plan template, and executive summary and mission statement help plus access to Expert Advice. Currently 60 free plans are viewable online. Fully searchable, users can quickly find topics that they need. Other sections include Finance and Capital, Marketing & Advertising, Buying a Business, Market Research, and a monthly Newsletter. Sample marketing plans include SWOT Analysis and further explain how to use it in marketing your business. Closely examine a sample marketing plan to help you write a good marketing strategy. Bplans.com is a useful, practical site that also offers fee-based experts and assistance.

Business.gov: www.business.gov (Accessed Fall 2005).

Another government site developed to help businesses find the information they need and want. The Market Research section of this site is especially noteworthy. Links to information on major industries, population, and demographic resources, plus Rural America Facts provide users with a multitude of useful resources. International trade connections are useful for global or Internet businesses too. Also find information on interviewing, working environments, training, hiring procedures, and employing minors.

**Edward Lowe Peerspectives: peerspectives.org (Accessed Fall 2005).

This well-known small business site contains a large section on Defining and Serving a Market. One of the articles in this section is Gathering Market Research, and it walks users through identifying data sources, gathering customer and competitor information, and gathering information on suppliers plus provides real-life examples of successful marketing. Additional resources are often provided at the end of articles. Other parts of this section include brand issues, customer feedback, direct mail advertising, market strategy, press releases, pricing, and sales techniques. Use Peerspectives.org when you need help and guidance in running or marketing your small business.

**Entrepreneur.com: www.entrepreneur.com (Accessed Fall 2005).

Entrepreneur Magazine provides a wealth of information and assistance to the new entrepreneur. A thorough understanding of the need to find the right type of marketing plan to fit your business and your style of planning and working is very important, and this site guides you through the process. Learn how to determine your marketing goals and objectives and how a plan will help you achieve them. Under Marketing & Sales, you will also find tips on building buzz, branding, word-of-mouth advertising, and marketing materials. Learn about the 9 Tools for building Customer Loyalty, for example. Discover how to create an ad budget and create great ads and direct mail pieces. Use this outstanding site often during the planning and opening of your new business.

Entrepreneurs' Help Page: www.tannedfeet.com (Accessed Fall 2005).

Find here help with business plans, financial statements, legal structure and legal forms, marketing and public relations, human resources (HR), and strategy. Designed, created, and published by a group of young professionals in Chicago, Entrepreneurs Help page does not claim to substitute for professional advice and judgment but provides information to entrepreneurs to get them started in the right direction. Experts offer advice on finding the right customers, how to select and work with an advertising agency, and marketing budgets. The idea for a marketing database to trace bits of information about your customers such as purchase history, demographics, service history, etc. has been shown to work for companies such as Amazon.com among others. Articles are usually not lengthy but ask questions to help the new business person start thinking about what is needed and what questions will be asked of him or her. Down-to-earth advice from peers is often the most valuable.

Home Business Magazine: www.homebusinessmag.com (Accessed Fall 2005).

The Marketing and Sales category accessible through the frame on the left side of the screen provides a wealth of articles on marketing any type of small business. Short courses on marketing success, information on how you could be hurting your sales, and other articles as well as subcategories on Direct Marketing, Web Marketing, Publicity, and Selling provide more inexpensive but effective marketing ideas. Advice and ideas on Business Start-up, Management, and Money are also included.

Inc.com: www.inc.com (Accessed Fall 2005).

The publishers of *Inc* magazine present a large directory of articles by topic targeting many problems, concerns, and decisions confronting new business owner/managers. Their articles on marketing and advertising are informative and practical. Simple but effective advice is the hallmark of this outstanding, easy-to-use site.

MoreBusiness.com: www.morebusiness.com (Accessed Fall 2005).

Sections on this site include Startup, Market Your Product & Services, Running Small Biz, Templates, and Tools. The Templates section provides sample business contracts and agreements, business and marketing plans, press releases, and business checklists. A large collection of articles and advice on marketing can also be found here under Business "How-to's." The section on Build Your Own Website is very useful. Many of the articles are lengthy and thorough. Use this site to help improve your marketing and management skills.

Mplans.com: www.mplans.com (Accessed Fall 2005).

This site does want to sell you marketing software and more, but it also provides interesting and useful articles for free. Articles will help you understand your competition, learn about target marketing, and develop a market forecast for your business. Articles are timely and well written. The free newsletter may help you market your business.

Online Women's Business Center: www.onlinewbc.gov (Accessed Fall 2005).

This site of the SBA's Office of Women's Business Ownership strives to help women business owners but provides a great deal of information free to all. Under Business Basics on the left side of the home page, you will find the Marketing Mall. Numerous topics on marketing, public relations, and advertising are covered in articles, both old and new. Learn about your target market, competitor and issues analysis, marketing strategy, the 4 P's of marketing, and online marketing. A wealth of information and links will help you develop your marketing strategy and marketing plan.

PowerHomeBiz.com: www.powerhomebiz.com/Index/financing.htm (Accessed Fall 2005).

This large, small business site has an outstanding collection of marketing advice. Featured articles include Promotions That Build Profit, The 7 Commandments of Marketing, and Top Ten Steps to Tweak Your Business Image. If you are new to marketing, the article First Steps to Picking the Perfect Marketing Method for You should help you get started. Must-Have Books are listed with some articles and Recommended Tools and Software as well. Recommended Magazines include several marketing classics. This established, well-organized site will help new entrepreneurs with financing and other parts of starting a new business.

SmallBusinessTV.com: sbtv.com (Accessed Fall 2005).

This web-based network provides information and advice of interest to entrepreneurs and small business owners and managers. Various channels such as Money, Marketing, Legal, Real Business, Women, and Technology contain a list of short videos where experts present practical advice. Sign up for the newsletter to keep current on what's happening. A faster than telephone line connection to the Internet is a real bonus for viewing the videos.

Smartbiz.com Small Business Resource: www.smartbiz.com (Accessed Fall 2005).

This large site is organized into six major sections, including Smart Moves, Heads Up, Network, Tech Center, Form Fetcher, and Smart Links. Users will find business forms like Daily Cash Flow, Employee Disciplinary Action, Employee Time Sheets, Sample Business and Marketing Plans, and Collection Letters. Continually updated, new articles on PR and marketing appear with some regularity. Find articles on the positive and negative attributes of radio, expanding your PR program, make it easy for customers to buy, outdoor advertising media, and how to ask your customers for their opinions. Marketing is vital to any small business, and this site helps you find new methods to improve your marketing and thus, improve sales.

**Trade Show News Network: www.tsnn.com (Accessed Fall 2005).

Though the Internet definitely has had an impact on the trade show market, sometimes setting up a booth at a trade show is a great way to make contacts, find people, and even sell products or services. This comprehensive site provides information on more than 15,000 trade shows that you can find by industry, month of the year, city, state, or country. The Small Business Guide also provides short articles on franchising, incorporating,

Internet ads, temporary help, bartering, and home-based businesses. Also find advice on virtual trade shows, trade show planning, convention centers, online service providers, and more.

**WebSite MarketingPlan: www.websitemarketingplan.com (Accessed Fall 2005).

This large site contains a wealth of information for small businesses. A large assortment of articles and sample marketing plans are available as well as sample business plans, a newsletter, Internet marketing articles, marketing strategy articles, and more. Featured Directory Categories include articles grouped under Search Engine Marketing, Marketing Strategy, Marketing Plan, and Public Relations. Learn about the four seasons of public relations. Lengthy articles on advertising, using PR for communicating to customers and finding new ones, and customer retention are outstanding. Many commercial links but plenty of free help for the new entrepreneur, too. This site is especially helpful for those interested in e-commerce. Easy to navigate, this site will help you develop a marketing plan that you can use.

MANAGEMENT 8

CHAPTER HIGHLIGHTS:

- Principles of Management
- Action Plans
- Structuring Your Organization
- Organization Chart
- Accounting/Bookkeeping
- Technology
- Time Management and Organization

"Management is, above all, a practice where art, science, and craft meet."
—Henry Mintzberg
McGill University

Effective management necessarily begins with planning, which implies goal-setting. Planning is the essence and most important function of managing and maintaining a business. Management is responsible for the accomplishment of the mission of an organization. The manager directs and integrates all the components, e.g., equipment, techniques, people, and practices of the business. Management involves problem solving, decision making, speculating on the future, setting objectives, and considering alternatives. The importance of good management skills cannot be overemphasized. Poor management and poor planning can put you out of business very quickly. You must continually exercise one of the four functions of managing: planning, organizing, leading, and controlling.

Managers decide such matters as what and how much to produce, which markets to serve and pursue, how much to advertise, and what prices to charge. A manager is the person responsible for planning and directing the work of a group of people, checking their work, and taking corrective action if necessary. In a small business, sometimes one person, you, plans and directs work of outside sources or contractors in order to accomplish delivery of the product or service. Remember, keeping better track of your money, staff, and paperwork will result in a more successful business.

PRINCIPLES OF MANAGEMENT

As stated above, the four major principles or functions of management are planning, organizing, leading, and controlling. Good managers accomplish the entire management process efficiently and effectively. Remember that your business will be the accumulation of the management decisions you make. Your business will accomplish its work under the guidelines that you set up. You need a vision of what you want your business or organization to be and accomplish. Also, remember that your customers are the real judges of how good your management decisions are. Base your decisions on how you want your customers to view your products or services.

However, let's run through each principle of management to understand it a bit more:

1. *Planning* is the intellectual process that determines the anticipated use of resources, methodology, and projected outcome on a given time line. Based on an organization's mission, planning begins with setting goals and objectives. A small business develops and uses its business plan to begin the challenge of managing the business. Look at your goals and plan how to achieve them.

2. *Organizing* involves decisions concerning the best allocation and utilization of resources for implementing the business or strategic plan. Managers coordinate the use of capital, information, and physical resources as well as people as part of this process. Choosing an organizational model is important and can determine the success or failure of your business. Are you ready to go into business? Make lists and make sure everything is in place and ready to begin.

3. *Leading* involves directing the people of the organization or staff and therefore, is a complex function. Managers with leadership ability get employees to willingly follow in the achievement of the organization's goals. Motivation is extremely important. Building a team is one method of leading an organization effectively. Good managers lead by example, so organize your work and keep everyone involved in your business informed about your needs and decisions. Communication skills are vital to good leadership. Although leadership is sometimes considered an art, it involves skills that can be learned. If your leadership skills are less than top-notch, take time to learn and cultivate them.

4. *Controlling* involves monitoring, evaluating, and correcting whatever is necessary to achieve the established goals. Planning and controlling are closely linked; and controlling involves comparing accomplishments at different intervals of time against the set goals and taking corrective action if necessary. When things are not going according to your plan, you need to step back and adjust. Problems will occur. Supplies won't be delivered on time,

or someone will get sick. Learn to improvise and revise, continue monitoring your business functions, and make changes to improve how it works.

To learn more about management techniques, organization, managing technology and more, try the Management Channel of SmallBusinessTV.com website at sbtv.com. These short videos cover a wide range of topics and can get you started in the right direction. The following book is also a wonderful resource to help guide you through your management challenges.

Parks, Ronald K. and Parks, Judith Stolz. *Manager's Mentor: A Guide for Small Business*. Prairie Sky Publishing Co., 2003. 256p. ISBN 0-9729165-0-4. $19.95.

This complete guide to starting and running your small business emphasizes the importance of management principles and their practical applications. An entire chapter is devoted to Efficiency and finding and developing ways to work more efficiently. Discover how to develop a company culture, develop good communication skills, manage capital assets, manage customers, vendors, and consultants, and ways to improve your management skills.

ACTION PLANS

How do you, the entrepreneur, accomplish everything, and still do what you really need to do? Three action plans can help build a framework or strategy for you to operate and manage your business by organizing the necessary activities such as obtaining and working with suppliers and other vendors to get necessary supplies, materials and services, filling orders, providing customer support and service after the sale, and dealing with unexpected occurrences. These action plans are really "to-do" lists and can be just for your use or you can add them as Supporting Documents in your business plan package. Many of the large small business sites such as the SBA's site provide start-up to-do lists to help small businesses organize their openings.

These action plans explain what you, the owner, need to do to get your business open. As your business evolves, you will move from doing things yourself to doing things through others. The success of your business may depend on how well you can make this transition.

1. Set up an *Operations Plan*. Figure out how you will create and deliver your product or service to your customers. What materials, software, hardware, equipment, etc., do you need? Where will it be set up? Does it work? Do you need a phone line or more than one phone line? Do you need a fax machine or copier? What type and how many computers do you need? Do you or others need new skills or expertise? Locate and sign up for workshops or classes. More about managing technology will be presented later in this chapter.

    Make a sketch of the work area—whether it's an office or complex of offices, a factory, a restaurant, a mail order packaging line, whatever. As thoroughly as you can, plan every step of the operation from raw material to delivery to the customer.

2. The next action plan is your *Management Plan*. Part of this will be managing employees, which we'll discuss more thoroughly in the next chapter but consider what employees you need to start and what jobs they will perform. As we learned above, part of managing is organizing. Delivery of products or services must be kept on schedule or customers will not return, and business will decline instead of grow. A good manager monitors all the diverse activities of the business and intervenes if things aren't happening or aren't happening in a timely fashion. Set up processes for getting things from accounting, payroll, deliveries, etc. done. Recognize if some activities are a major drain on your time and resources, preventing you from getting more important things done. Value your time as your most valuable asset; you can always make more money but not more time. We'll talk more about time management later in this chapter.

3. The final action plan is your *Contingency Plan*. Though careful planning is necessary, Murphy's Law (If anything can go wrong, it will) may intervene. Your Contingency Plan will help you avoid disruptions in your operation when industry, economic, or business conditions change beyond what you are prepared to handle—perhaps you'll have more customers than you had dreamed possible or your supplier cannot provide the materials you need or goes out of business completely. Basically, here you try to identify the areas in your business that are susceptible to variable factors. Contingency planning is a prearranged method of changing the direction of your business or retrenching in the face of less than hoped for results. So if things go much better or worse than expected, you have considered your responses and are prepared to react, perhaps more quickly than your competitors, thus presenting you with an opportunity or competitive advantage.

Action plans can also be part of strategic planning or developing a strategy for your business to grow and develop. If you want to learn more about strategic planning, check out the Small Business Notes website at www.smallbusiness notes.com under Management on the left side of the screen.

In the Planning section of Management, you will find many articles that can help you develop ways to continue planning your business moves after your initial business plan; for example, long-term strategic planning and action plans to implement your strategy are discussed. Planning should not consume the business owner's time, but it is a necessary element in developing a successful business.

STRUCTURING YOUR ORGANIZATION

How you design your organization plays a big part in your success in making your business plan work. Whether you have two or 2,000 employees, you need to under-

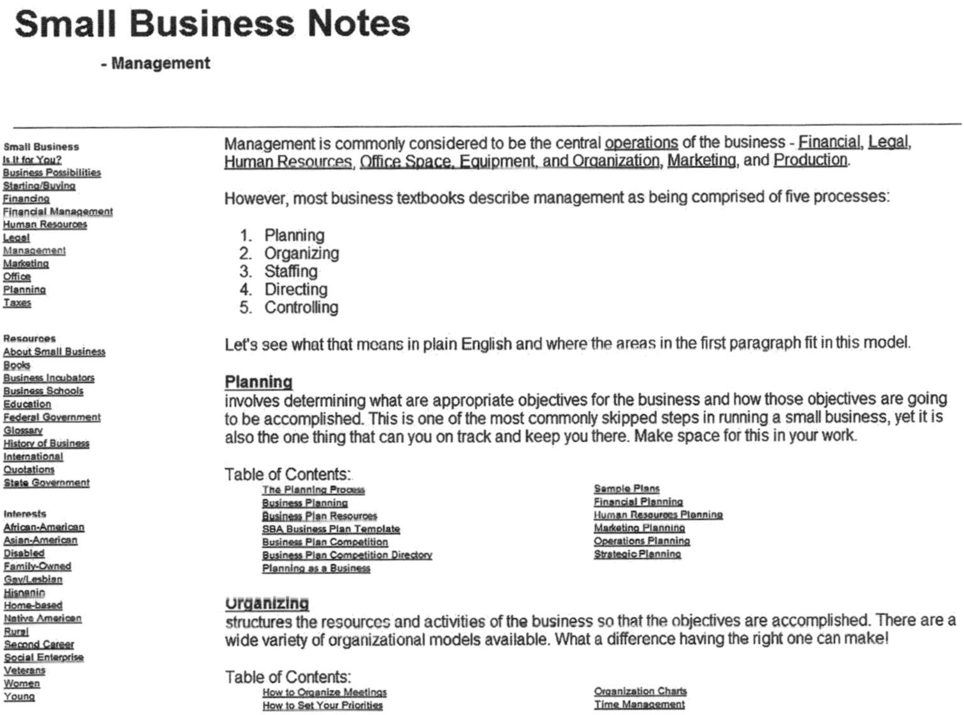

Small Business Notes

- Management

Small Business
Is It for You?
Business Possibilities
Starting/Buying
Financing
Financial Management
Human Resources
Legal
Management
Marketing
Office
Planning
Taxes

Resources
About Small Business
Books
Business Incubators
Business Schools
Education
Federal Government
Glossary
History of Business
International
Quotations
State Government

Interests
African-American
Asian-American
Disabled
Family-Owned
Gay/Lesbian
Hispanic
Home-based
Native American
Rural
Second Career
Social Enterprise
Veterans
Women
Young

Management is commonly considered to be the central operations of the business - Financial, Legal, Human Resources, Office Space, Equipment, and Organization, Marketing, and Production.

However, most business textbooks describe management as being comprised of five processes:

1. Planning
2. Organizing
3. Staffing
4. Directing
5. Controlling

Let's see what that means in plain English and where the areas in the first paragraph fit in this model.

Planning
involves determining what are appropriate objectives for the business and how those objectives are going to be accomplished. This is one of the most commonly skipped steps in running a small business, yet it is also the one thing that can you on track and keep you there. Make space for this in your work.

Table of Contents:
The Planning Process
Business Planning
Business Plan Resources
SBA Business Plan Template
Business Plan Competition
Business Plan Competition Directory
Planning as a Business
Sample Plans
Financial Planning
Human Resources Planning
Marketing Planning
Operations Planning
Strategic Planning

Organizing
structures the resources and activities of the business so that the objectives are accomplished. There are a wide variety of organizational models available. What a difference having the right one can make!

Table of Contents:
How to Organize Meetings
How to Set Your Priorities
Organization Charts
Time Management

Figure 8.1 Screenshot of Small Business Notes: Management (www.smallbusinessnotes.com/operating/management.html)

stand your employees' roles in carrying out the business plan and achieving company goals and objectives. In the beginning, your organizational chart will probably have you at the top as owner, and everyone/anyone else below, doing all the jobs that have to be done. This model works until you have over 20 employees. As your business grows, remember that the core of any organization is its people and their functions. Duties, tasks, and responsibilities often evolve in an expedient manner. As the firm develops, others are hired to fill specific roles, often on a functional basis. Roles that were handled by consultants and specialists outside the firm now are handled internally. As new needs emerge, new roles develop.

At this time, you want to consider investigating a functional model where different functions such as financial, customer service, and production are in subgroups or teams, a divisional model where divisions are based on products, or markets, or whatever; or a matrix model where everyone wears two hats, maybe one function group and one special project group. These models call for different management skills and often work well based on management training and leadership skills. Keep in mind that a simple organizational structure keeps costs under control and is more flexible. Be willing to change your organizational structure as your business grows, and keep exploring options as you go about creating and recreating your organization. To explore more ideas on organizational structure, check out the Edward Lowe PeerSpectives website at peerSpectives.org.

ORGANIZATION CHART

The management process is a key ingredient throughout the business life cycle, and related to the organizational structure is another management tool used to further the organization's goals, the organization chart, or org chart for short. Org charts illustrate the intended structure of the organization or company and reflect the power structure of the company. The entrepreneur may need to incorporate strong working relationships with outside consultants into the structure of everyday operations to form a management team for his or her organization or business. This team should be shown on your org chart and might consist of an accountant, lawyer, banker, and other consultants who provide needed expertise to assist in running the business. Develop an org chart that reflects where you want the organization to go and how it will grow rather than simply reflecting how it is now. For more help on building an org chart, take a look at Organization Charts as a Management Tool on the website management.about.com. Here you will find advice and examples representing different types of small and larger businesses.

Along with the org chart, develop a list of key personnel with a job description listing responsibilities and authority level. Planning in advance will help you grow your business in an organized manner resulting in less last-minute decision making. When an organization has structure, employees feel they know where the company is going and what their role is in getting there. A structured organization has a better chance at success.

ACCOUNTING/BOOKKEEPING

Even if you have no intention of keeping your own books, you need to have a basic knowledge of accounting to monitor your accountant or bookkeeper and determine if she or he is doing a good job. Accounting is the method by which financial information is gathered, processed, and summarized into useful financial statements and reports like cash flow, balance sheets, and income statements; simply put, it monitors how much money is being paid out and how much is coming in. To learn many of the basics of accounting and financial management, check out BusinessTown.com at www.businesstown.com. Besides an entire section on Accounting, you will find a section on Finance and Managing a Business. Use this site to increase your knowledge of financial statements in general.

Right from the start, you need to set up a system to track, record, and store your source documents for internal management and external taxation purposes. You need to track things including supplier invoices, customer sales orders, as well as pay taxes, develop capital and operating budgets, and manage and value product inventory. The best advice is probably to hire an accountant to set up an efficient, cost-effective bookkeeping system that you can follow. In today's business world, that system will probably be software on a computer. Software options today are varied in function and cost, including many designed for small businesses. If your accountant suggests using a software package, use that package because your information will be organized so that the accountant can work directly from your electronic files, saving her or him time and you money.

If you are able to manage your personal finances, you can probably learn to work with a small business accounting software package to enter and store your important financial data. To learn more about bookkeeping and accounting, try Angie Mohr's book, *Bookkeepers' Boot Camp: Get a Grip on Accounting Basics*. The advice in her guide will help you understand budgeting, accounting, and taxes. Also find help here on finding a good accountant to help your business grow.

Mohr, Angie. *Bookkeepers' Boot Camp: Get a Grip on Accounting Basics*. Self-Counsel Press, Ltd., 2003. 198p. ISBN 1-55180-449-2. $14.95.

This handy title will walk users through the essentials of record keeping for a small business and explain why it's so necessary to track this information. Learn how to sort through paperwork, how to record and file what is important for your business, and how to use that information to help your business succeed. The basics of balance sheets, income statements, cash flow statements, inventory management, and monitoring budgets and cash flow are thoroughly explained. Also covered is tax planning as well as choosing an accountant and the role of an accountant in running your small business. Learn how to manage the financial part of your business and personal life.

In Chapter 2, we talked a bit about industry ratios. Industry ratios are used to help you see what the financial condition of your business is compared to the averages of other businesses in your industry. You need to know the financial ratios of your business in order to compare yourself with the industry. Ratios also help you spot financial patterns that might threaten the health of your business. The AmericanExpress.com Small Business Network at www.americanexpress.com, under Financial Management, provides information on calculating and learning more about 11 key financial ratios. Even if you hire an accountant, you will want to know as much as you can about operational and profitability ratios as well as liquidity, efficiency, and solvency ratios. Another good site for learning about ratio analysis is Edward Lowe PeerSpectives at peerSpectives.org under Acquiring and Managing Finances. Check out these two sites to improve your knowledge of these important management tools.

TECHNOLOGY

A website today often functions much like a business card. In many industries, it is virtually impossible for entrepreneurs to function without a web presence. To many young people, using the Internet is as natural as using the telephone or cell phone. For some entrepreneurs, conducting business using the Internet is also taken for granted, while others are new to cyberspace. At the least, as a small business owner you will want to use the Internet to gather information about your industry and competitors and exchange email to facilitate networking with customers perhaps or suppliers or mentors. Decide how using the Internet will benefit your particular business.

The personal computer (PC) hardware sits at the center of this technology. Purchase the best desk-top computer that you can afford and some software will be available with the purchase or at reduced cost. Purchase software that can help you with your managerial duties such as word processing, possibly a spreadsheet or bookkeeping or accounting package recommended by your accountant, a fast modem, and software to manage the communications connection to the server computer. Your telephone company, cable or satellite television company, or a local Internet company can explain ways to connect and costs. Be sure to read the small print as there are many restrictions in the services offered by any company and talking to other business owners who have used the service is as important here as in other areas of doing business. With a computer, you can manage your inventory, track customer accounts, monitor your competition, and keep in touch with business associates and customers. If you are new to the Internet and the web, you might want to read a very good article on the Small Business Administration's website, www.sba.gov. Under Growing and Managing Your Business//Technology, where you will find an article entitled Understanding the Internet. Another article Getting on the Web is also very informative, with a link to Ecommerce Resources.

Website

Many entrepreneurs today are developing websites to enlarge their customer base and boost profits. Clearly define why you want or need a website and determine if you can afford it. Study websites of businesses similar to yours and make note of what you like and don't like about them. Are they well organized, how do you contact someone with a question, can you place an order quickly, and are you planning to offer that service on your site? Then, you will want to research locally and on the Internet different companies that can help in its design, development, and implementation. As in other phases of starting a business, research and preparation will help make your website project a success. Use the same criteria for hiring a professional website developer, if you go that route, as you did when hiring an accountant or lawyer. Study their work, check references, talk to colleagues, ask for bids, and shop around for the best price without sacrificing quality. Remember that you only have one chance on the Internet to make a good first impression. In your contract with a web designer, be sure to specify a work schedule, desired results, and payment terms as well as a termination clause.

A good print resource on a business website and its design is Doug Addison's *Small Websites, Great Results.*

Addison, Doug. *Small Websites, Great Results: The Blueprint for Creating Websites that Really Work.* Paraglyph, Inc., 2004. 352p. ISBN 1-932111-90-5. $29.99.

If you want a simple, well-designed, highly focused website, Addison's approach will work for your small business. Design ideas and marketing techniques are show-cased in profiles of 20 small businesses. Readers will discover new approaches to creating sites, find out what really makes small sites work, learn about strategies for getting, keeping, and satisfying customers, and pick up tips on how to work with professional designers to get the results they want and need. Learn how to create an update or editorial calendar and how to organize the files on your website so your business site is always different, current, and easy to change. Discover what to leave off your site to keep it simple and uncluttered. Addison will convince you that quality is much better than quantity.

Now that you have a website, you will need a web-hosting service. Some issues to consider when choosing a web host include:

1. Ask what uptime they will guarantee in writing and shoot for 95%. Ask them to sign an agreement to the effect that if the site is not up 95% of the time, they will lower your monthly fee.

2. Ask about their connection to the Internet and insist on T3 lines directly to the Internet, not through someone else's network. Ask about their servers to see that they are fast and reliable.

3. Check on what type of technical support is provided. Call at various evening and weekend hours to be sure there's a person to help you and not an answering machine. Send their customer service an email and see how fast they respond.

4. Of course, you will want to find out the costs and compare them with com-petitors. A simple site with one domain name might cost $50 per month while those taking up lots of disk space and large amounts of data transfer will drive the costs up. A very simple brochure online type website may only cost $10–15 per month.

5. Ask if they can handle the software used to design your site. This question may narrow your choices.

6. Be sure the web host uses special programs to conduct online transactions safely and protect the privacy and security of customers and their credit cards.

Work with your web designer to find a web host that works for you. Again, this will probably be a long-term relationship, and you will want to keep that in mind too. Another good book for helping you learn the basics about websites and e-commerce is:

> Holden, Greg. *Starting an Online Business for Dummies*. 3rd ed. For Dummies, 2002. 384p. ISBN 0-7645-1655-8. $24.99.
>
> As in other books of this series, readers find the basics of starting a business on the Internet. E-commerce survival stories, best practices, and other resources to help you develop your new business are provided. Good tips on selecting an online host, understanding website design, establishing a graphic identity, providing customer service, and providing various payment options. Some coverage of legal matters, trademarks, copyrighting, and taxes is included.

TIME MANAGEMENT AND ORGANIZATION

If you don't manage your time, time will manage you. There are never enough hours in the day to complete all the work associated with your small business, so learn some time management solutions. Efficiency is vital to any business and especially if it is a one-person operation. The following rules are general precepts that will help you save time and use it wisely:

1. *Track your time usage.* Make a copy of a page from your day planner and record the time you spend doing things for a week. Now you will see the pattern of how you are spending your time.

2. *Allocate and prioritize your time.* This step is very personal. Identify your most productive time. If you are a morning person, you may want to start the day with the most difficult or worrisome task and then mix in easy tasks as breaks. Or if it takes you awhile to get going in the morning, you may not want to return phone calls, check email, etc. until you are wide awake and ready to tackle difficult tasks. Whenever possible, complete projects with deadlines first for this will please your customer, win you repeat business, and get you positive reinforcement.

3. *Stick to the schedule and control your agenda.* Take time each afternoon to write a prioritized list of the next day's tasks and projects so you can start your day in a productive manner. Often by lunch time, your plans may be shattered, but try to complete as many tasks on the list as possible, and then move what can't be finished to the next day's list. Also make To-Do lists for the week and one for things to do during the month. As you accomplish these goals, cross them off for a feeling of accomplishment and moving forward.

   If you are constantly interrupted, you must make it clear that you can only be interrupted by dire emergencies—which you define. Turn on the answering machine; don't answer the door; do whatever it takes. If you are unable to do this in your workplace, take a day or an afternoon away from the workplace each week to catch up on whatever is being pushed aside or what needs your entire concentration to finish. If you are still having trouble, investigate day timer software to help you organize and manage your time.

4. *Stay or get organized*. This item is extremely important. Keep your desk and work space tidy. Completed projects should be filed. Answered phone messages filed or tossed. New orders filed. A neat space allows you to concentrate on the task at hand. A good filing system allows you to retrieve information you need quickly, without wasting time looking for things. Set aside time for planning and when planning, also schedule time for organizing.

5. *Delegate what you can*. You should delegate work to others in your organization (if there are others), particularly to those who may have more time or more skill in a particular area. Delegate routine administrative tasks, special projects, and tasks that an employee has a special talent for accomplishing. Explain fully what is expected of the employee and encourage him or her to ask questions at any time. Once the task or project has been completed, don't forget to evaluate the final product and discuss the results with the employee. As your business grows, you'll spend more time strategizing and less time on the daily components of running a business.

Remember to avoid the big "day wasters." Talking on the telephone, surfing the web, and email are all great things when used in moderation, but you can seriously lose hours and hours of your day with all of them. Limit your "day wasters" to your least productive hour or so each day. Also, don't forget that saying "no" can help you from being overburdened.

Managing paperwork is another daunting task. Every day it accumulates, but try to handle each piece of paper only once. File paperwork as diligently as you schedule meetings and appointments. Buy a weekly or daily planner and write things down. Have an address book or contact management software on your PC where you record contact information and toss piles of business cards. Buy different color folders for different topics, subjects, and segments of your business. Retire files as soon as possible but separate and retain any information needed for tax purposes or other financial matters. Remember there is no statute of limitations for reviewing business tax forms. Most importantly, purge files at the end of every year. Barbara Hemphill's book, *Taming the Paper Tiger at Work*, provides many ideas for helping you keep your desk and your office organized and ready to do business.

Hemphill, Barbara. *Taming the Paper Tiger at Work*. 3rd ed. Kiplinger Books, 2002. 170p. ISBN 0-9387-2198-4. $14.95.

If you need help in getting organized, Hemphill will help you. She clearly states the principles involved in organizing the mounds of paperwork and files filling most offices. Learn how to use action and reference files as well as to prepare and use To-Do lists effectively. In this new edition, readers will find website links, advice on how to work efficiently and effectively in virtual offices, and expanded information on computer-safety tips, email etiquette, and other electronic timesavers. Also learn how long you need to keep your files. Get organized and use your computer to help.

If you need more help with time management skills or organizing your work and workplace, check out the Business Know-how website at www.business knowhow.com. Some of the resources below will also provide more help in all the areas covered in this chapter.

REFERENCES

(Starred titles discussed in the chapter)

▎Print Resources

**Addison, Doug. *Small Websites, Great Results*. Paraglyph Press, Inc., 2005. 279p. ISBN 1-932111-90-5. $29.99.

Web designer Addison presents the latest trends of simplicity, ease-of-use, and efficiency to entrepreneurs and small business persons. He helps readers apply effective methods of design to encourage customer interaction and sell products or services. Learn how to work with a designer to create a simple, quality website. Featured here are a set of small sites that work for businesses representing professional services, artists, entertainers, writers, consultants, and speakers. Discover how to select winning themes and formats. Chapters cover issues including turning visitors into customers, keeping your site up-to-date, and creating a focus for your site. Learn why and when to employ a web designer. If you're new to websites, this book will help you get up to speed quickly.

Atchison, Michael D. *Managing a Successful Small Business: Thoughts and Experiences of an Entrepreneurial Consultant*. Resource Partners, LLC, 2001. 166p. ISBN 0-9708755-0-9. $29.94.

This practical guide to starting and running a successful business includes dozens of humorous stories gathered during the 25 years Atchison has worked with and for entrepreneurs in all types of small businesses. Atchison divides the book into a section on starting a new business and a second on managing the growth of an existing business. He includes models for financial statements, cash flow management tools, a practical filing system, business plans, financial resource plans, and marketing programs. Learn from his experiences or as he states, "the most painful way to lose a business is through poor administrative details."

De Beer, A. A., Kritzinger, A. A. C., Venter, C. H., Steyn, J. M. C., Labuschage, M., Ferreira, E., Groeneward, D., Stapelberg. J., E. *Management for Entrepreneurs*. 2nd ed. Juta Academic, 2004. 224p. ISBN 0-7021-5543-8. $24.95.

The authors focus on eight business functions including management, finance, marketing, operations, purchasing, human resources (HR), administration, and public relations. Each of these functions is described in terms of increasing profitability and ensuring the success of your business or company. Many activities and examples including self-evaluation quizzes are included with each chapter. Learn how to apply management ideas, techniques, and theories to your business.

Eisenberg, Ronni. *Organize Your Office! Simple Routines for Managing Your Workspace*. Rev. ed. Hyperion, 1999. 192p. ISBN 0-7868-8381-2. $9.96.

Eisenberg presents 10 rules to adhere to when filing and 14 ways to make meetings run smoothly and accomplish what you want to accomplish. Step-by-step methods for organizing and managing your workspace, from briefcase to bulletin board, and even help in managing your email and co-worker interruptions are provided.

Ezor, Jonathan I. *Clicking Through: A Survival Guide for Bringing Your Company Online*. Bloomberg Press, 1999. 253p. ISBN 1-57660-073-4. $19.95.

Ezor thoroughly describes how to manage the unique hazards of being in business online. He addresses questions on what to consider when selecting a site host and when and how to collect sales tax. Learn how to comply with international regulations and laws and structure online partnerships with other companies. Protect your business from e-sabotage and how to maintain privacy and security of consumer data. A new edition is needed but this comprehensive resource is well worth a look for e-commerce entrepreneurs.

Harvard Business School Staff, ed. *Harvard Business Essentials: Entrepreneur's Toolkit: Tools and Techniques to Launch and Grow Your New Business*. Harvard Business School Publishing, 2004. 256p. ISBN 1-59139-436-8. $19.95.

Presented here is background information and guidance to help readers from the initial question of should they start a business to the exit strategies needed for selling the business, retiring, or whatever option is chosen. The chapter on Organizing the Enterprise helps readers understand the legal structure of a business and each one's benefits and drawbacks. Chapters on Financing the Business and Angels and Venture Capitalists are particularly thorough. Five appendices cover financial statements, breakeven analysis, valuation concepts, help online, and Rule 144 (IPO restrictions). Well written and well organized, this practical guide will help new business owners or managers.

Hatten, Timothy S. *Small Business Management: Text with GoVenture CD-ROM*. 2nd ed. Houghton Mifflin, 2004. 660p. ISBN 0-618-25815-9. $90.27.

GoVenture—Live the Life of an Entrepreneur is a management simulation program on CD-ROM that is packaged with this copy of *Small Business Management*. Over 6,000 graphics, audio, and video clips immerse users in the day-to-day challenges of being an entrepreneur. Each chapter contains What Would You Do scenarios to allow users to make decisions and solve problems from real-life situations. The book includes a full chapter on business plans with sample plans for a service business and one for a retail business. Other chapters or sections cover Franchising, including selecting an international franchise, Marketing, Human Resources, and Management. The section on Financial and Legal Management is outstanding. Additionally, e-commerce is thoroughly covered including online marketing. It's expensive, but this package is definitely a useful tool for the new entrepreneur.

Helfert, Erich A. *Financial Analysis Tools and Techniques: A Guide for Managers*. McGraw-Hill, 2001. 480p. ISBN 0-0713-7834-0. $54.95.

Helfert simplifies the process of financial analysis by explaining how to interpret financial statements, develop financial projects, and assess the implications of financing choices. Read discussions of cash-flow trade-offs and time-value analysis of investments. Learn more about *pro forma* financial statements, cash management, cost of capital, and ratio analysis. Financial management expertise will help your business become more successful.

**Hemphill, Barbara. *Taming the Paper Tiger at Work*. 3rd ed. Kiplinger Books, 2002. 170p. ISBN 0-9387-2198-4. $14.95.

If you need help in getting organized, Hemphill will help you. She clearly states the principles involved in organizing the mounds of paperwork and files filling most offices. Learn how to use action and reference files as well as preparing and using To-Do lists effectively. In this new edition, readers will find website links, advice on how to work efficiently and effectively in virtual offices, and expanded information on computer-safety tips, email etiquette, and other electronic timesavers. Also learn how long you need to keep your files. Get organized and use your computer to help.

**Holden, Greg. *Starting an Online Business for Dummies*. 3rd ed. For Dummies, 2002. 384p. ISBN 0-7645-1655-8. $24.99.

As in other books of this series, readers find the basics of starting a business on the Internet. E-commerce survival stories, best practices, and other resources to help you develop your new business are provided. Good tips on selecting an online host, understanding website design, establishing a graphic identity, providing customer service, and providing various payment options. Some coverage of legal matters, trademarks, copyrighting, and taxes are included.

Little, Steven S. *The 7 Irrefutable Rules of Small Business Growth*. John Wiley & Sons, 2005. 256p. ISBN 0-471-70760-0. $18.95.

Find out Little's real and powerful principles for helping a small business expand and develop new business. Little acknowledges the difficulties small businesses have in today's global economy where competition comes from the Internet as well as the business down the street. Learn more about topics like technology, planning, hiring and firing, and globalization as they relate to small business today. An entire chapter is devoted to each of his seven rules. For example, he explains why it is essential to have a thorough understanding of the marketplace, why processes must be customer-driven, and how to attract and keep the best and brightest. Practical solutions and strategies are presented to achieve and sustain a competitive advantage. Simply but effectively written, Little teaches entrepreneurs to have a realistic view of the marketplace and their place in it.

Maxwell, John C. *Thinking for a Change: 11 Ways Highly Successful People Approach Life and Work*. Warner Books, 2003. 304p. ISBN 0-4465-2957-5. $22.95.

Maxwell's step-by-step format guides readers down the path of mastering what he calls "good thinking," which will help them achieve personal and professional goals. The various types of thinking he encourages are, for example, big-picture thinking, shared thinking, unselfish thinking, and bottom-line thinking. With an engaging writing style, Maxwell's book is easy to read and digest so readers will come away with new skills for finding solutions and workable ideas for a variety of personal and professional situations.

**Mohr, Angie. *Bookkeepers' Boot Camp: Get a Grip on Accounting Basics*. Self-Counsel Press, Ltd., 2003. 198p. ISBN 1-55180-449-2. $14.95.

This handy title will walk users through the essentials of record keeping for a small business and explain why it's so necessary to track this information. Learn how to sort through paperwork, how to record and file what is important for your business, and how to use that information to help your business succeed. The basics of balance sheets, income statements, cash flow statements, inventory management, and monitoring budgets and cash flow are thoroughly explained so readers can understand what the accountant is telling them. Brief case studies illustrate the use of financial data in your business. Also covered is tax planning as well as choosing an accountant and the role of an accountant in running your small business. Chapter summaries highlight important concepts in each chapter. Learn how to manage the financial part of your business and personal life.

**Parks, Ronald K. and Parks, Judith Stolz. *Manager's Mentor: A Guide for Small Business.* Prairie Sky Publishing Co., 2003. 256p. ISBN 0-9729165-0-4. $19.95.

This complete guide to starting and running your small business emphasizes the importance of management principles and their practical applications. Each chapter begins with a real-life story from Ron's childhood on a farm in Nebraska to illustrate his values, thought processes, and strategies used to run his successful business. An entire chapter is devoted to Efficiency and finding and developing ways to work more efficiently. Two chapters are devoted to Creating a Workforce and Taking Care of Employees, since hiring and keeping good employees are so essential to a small business. Discover how to develop a company culture, develop good communication skills, manage capital assets, manage customers, vendors, and consultants, and improve your management skills. As the title says, if you need a mentor to help in managing your small business, the Parkses can help you.

Scarborough, Norman M. and Zimmerer, Thomas. *Effective Small Business Management: An Entrepreneurial Approach.* 8th ed. Prentice Hall, 2005. 848p. ISBN 0-13-146984-3. $125.00.

One of the highlights of this volume is the use of numerous real-life examples; concepts covered include illustrations of how entrepreneurs are using them. Learn about e-commerce, strategic management, guerrilla marketing techniques, finding sources of equity and debt financing, and how to conduct business internationally. Learn how to build a customer database, how to determine the value of an existing business, and cash management techniques. Purchasing, layout, and inventory decisions are discussed. A boxed feature, Gaining the Competitive Edge, is designed to provide practical advice on a particular topic so readers can develop a competitive edge in their business or industry.

Shores, Randall. *Starting and Managing a Small Business.* Shores Publishing Co., 2003. 404p. ISBN 0-9746846-0-0. $39.99.

Based on a series of courses Shores taught at a community college, this practical guide covers all the basics including marketing, financing, budgeting, home-based businesses, and HR. Shores has also founded several small businesses himself, which has provided him with many practical examples and case studies. Well written and organized, use this book to start your own new business.

The Ultimate Small Business Guide: A Resource for Startups and Growing Businesses. Basic Books, 2004. 501p. ISBN 0-7382-0913-9. $19.95.

This large collection of how-to's, step-by-step objective lists, and enlightening FAQs covers all aspects of planning, launching, managing, and growing your small business.

Sections cover Refining and Protecting Your Idea, Communicating with Your Customers, Selling Online, and Managing Yourself and Others. Financing, pricing, cash flow, ratios, and assets are thoroughly and carefully covered in a section called Figuring It Out.

Yerkes, Leslie and Decker, Charles. *Beans: Four Principles for Running a Business in Good Times and Bad*. John Wiley & Sons, Inc., 2003. 176p. ISBN 0-7879-6764-5. $19.95.

From the true story of a small Seattle coffee bar, the authors distill universal business truths like maintain a consistent, quality product, view both customers and employees as friends, and be passionate about what you do. Each chapter is divided into scenes and contains lots of dialogue. Also stressed is the importance of intention in striving for and achieving success: you have achieved success when your results match your intentions. Learn good management skills by example.

Online Resources

About.com: management.about.com (Accessed Fall 2005).

Clearly management and management skills are huge topics and vitally important to a successful business. This site provides a treasure trove of information, links, books, and other assorted help in learning new management skills and improving those an entrepreneur has already developed. Sections cover Management 101, Management Tips, How to Manage, and more. Learn best business practices and leadership skills from experts. A related area of the site is Human Resources, which helps users learn about HR issues and managing employees.

American Express Small Business Exchange: http://www133.americanexpress. com/osbn/Landing/informyourdecisions.asp?us_nu=subtab (Accessed Fall 2005).

Small business owners will find help here on management, finding money, and marketing. This outstanding site has information on managing debt, business plans, fraud protection, and SBA loans. The article under Financial Management entitled Business Valuation Methods explains the various common methods used to come up with a value for a small business. The Starting a Business section tells users about structuring their business as well as some information on types of insurance.

Business.gov: www.business.gov (Accessed Fall 2005).

Another government site developed to help businesses find the information they need and want. Under the Managing section, you'll find articles on business laws, finances, research and resources, and making decisions. Also, under Managing Employees, find information on interviewing, working environments, training, hiring procedures, and employing minors. The search box helps users find what they need quickly and easily.

BusinessKnow-How.com: www.businessknowhow.com (Accessed Fall 2005).

This large site has an abundance of articles on starting and managing a small business. Different areas cover incorporating online, business loans, HR training and tools, and web design and tools. Users will find many articles on job descriptions, cash management and accounting, a breakeven calculator, and a job or product pricing system. Franchising and marketing strategies are also covered. Find basic business information here on a wide range of topics.

**BusinessTown.com: www.businesstown.com (Accessed Fall 2005).

This extensive business information site has sections on Managing a Business, Home Businesses, Internet Businesses, Accounting, Selling a Business, and more. The articles are not lengthy but quite thoroughly cover their subject. Under Home Business, you will find ideas for home businesses, how to set one up, and articles on getting started right. Under Accounting, you will learn basic concepts, how to budget, how to plan and project, and more. Also has links to a variety of Financial Calculators at www.dinkytown.net. Useful site and not commercial, use it to help you in any area where you need more information.

BusinessWeek Online: www.businessweek.com/smallbiz (Accessed Fall 2005).

This large timely site includes a large section on Technology, accessed from a tab at the top of the home page. Users will find tools and services needed to understand and manage all aspects of technology useful in running their own business as well as how it affects the business world in general. Also find Business and Government forms, legal training courses, and information on business structure laws. The SmallBiz Resource Center provides articles on business plans, target market research, and health insurance basics. Also available are articles on other specific areas of business development including HR, Finance, Technology, and Sales. Keep current on all areas of business and economic news here.

**Edward Lowe PEERSPECTIVES: PeerSpectives.org (Accessed Fall 2005).

This nonprofit organization promotes entrepreneurship by providing information, research, and education. The Acquiring and Managing Finances section will help new entrepreneurs learn more about all aspects related to their business's financial situation. The section of this useful site entitled Building and Inspiring an Organization will lead you to articles on crisis management, communication skills, management development, organizational structure, and more. Use this site also to find practical articles on marketing, finances, HR management, and legal issues and taxes. Networking possibilities include conferences and educational seminars listed here.

Entrepreneur.com: www.entrepreneurmag.com (Accessed Fall 2005).

Maintained by *Entrepreneur Magazine*, this site supports new businesses and growing companies. Two important areas of this page are listed at the top, Management and Business Coaches. Here you'll find lists of articles covering various topics in management such as trends in management, time management, managing employees, and more. Business Coaches can help you through difficult times in your business life. Start Up Topics include organization and managing, finding a location, naming your biz, and business structure. Find ready-made business forms here, too. Use this site whenever you need help in determining what to do next.

Entrepreneur's Guidebook Series: www.smbtn.com/businessplanguides/ (Accessed Fall 2005).

Defining real entrepreneurs as managers who adopt key behaviors developed by understanding key market concepts and theories and who are successful because of their planning and researching skills, this site covers a wide variety of subjects in its Small Business Plan Guides. Here you will discover articles on managerial and leadership skills and time management. Explore this website for more good ideas.

Internal Revenue Service: www.irs.ustreas.gov (Accessed Fall 2005).

Find good information about keeping good records here. Learn about what kinds of records to keep and how long to keep them. A sample record system is presented. A great deal of information on small business taxes of all kinds can be found here. Also available through a link is the IRS's site for Small Business/Self-Employed at www.irs.gov/businesses/small. This site provides information and links on many issues such as employment taxes, paperwork reduction for employers, changes to IRS Schedule C-EZ, small business forms and publications, and more. Tax scams and tax education information is also included.

MoreBusiness.com: www.morebusiness.com (Accessed Fall 2005).

Sections on this site include Startup, Running SmallBiz, Templates, and Tools. The Templates section provides sample business contracts and agreements, business and marketing plans, press releases, and business checklists. A large collection of articles and advice under Business Technology will help you understand the Internet, online shopping, website technology, hacking, and even laptop issues. The section on Build Your Own Website is very useful. Many of the articles are lengthy and thorough. Use this site to help improve your marketing and management skills.

Online Women's Business Center: www.onlinewbc.gov (Accessed Fall 2005).

This site of the SBA's Office of Women's Business Ownership strives to help women business owners but provides a great deal of information free to all. Under Business Basics on the left side of the home page, you will find the Financing Your Business. Numerous topics in the Finance Center on types of loans, how to qualify for a loan, links to SBA loans, and more can be located here. Bookkeeping and Accounting are explained as well as information on insurance and leases. Good articles on time management are also provided for new managers or managers having trouble controlling their time. A wealth of information and links will help you keep records and learn more about most management issues involved in running your own business.

SBDCNET: sbdcnet.utsa.edu (Accessed Fall 2005).

The Small Business Development Center National Information Clearinghouse provides timely, web-based information to entrepreneurs. Small Business Development Centers are located in all 50 states. This website provides information on business start-up, e-commerce, industry research, marketing, trends, and more. Entrepreneurs will find plenty of links and information here to help them plan and run their new business.

**Small Business Notes: www.smallbusinessnotes.com (Accessed Fall 2005).

Here you will find articles on starting or buying your first business as well as merging, planning, management, and legal issues. Explore articles on business Management and Planning. Under Management are articles on the planning process, sample plans, business plan resources, strategic planning, and more. Basic articles contain links to fuller explanatory articles on a wide variety of topics like business models, recordkeeping, etc. The articles on

Why Merge and Merge Wisely are enlightening and provide the owner with information and food for thought when considering a merger. A useful site for many topics related to small business and entrepreneurship come here for answers to basic and more complex questions.

**SmallBusinessTV.com: sbtv.com (Accessed Fall 2005).

This web-based network provides information and advice of interest to entrepreneurs and small business owners and managers. Various channels such as Money, Marketing, Legal, Real Business, Women, and Technology contain a list of short videos where experts present practical advice. Sign up for the newsletter to keep current on what's happening. A faster than telephone line connection to the Internet is a real bonus for viewing the videos.

Small Business Administration: www.sba.gov (Accessed Fall 2005).

This official government site offers a wealth of resources and programs for starting and growing a small business. In the library of the SBA site, the Small Business Management Series contains a group of publications such as planning and goal setting for small business, inventory management, etc. Also the Emerging Business Series covers topics including strategic planning, management issues, and human resource management. Other major sections of the site cover business planning, financing, managing, marketing, employees, taxes, legal aspects, and business opportunities. Under Financing you will find articles on Breakeven Analysis, Estimating Costs, and Cash Management. Also, find here online forms, business plans, and loan information. Some contents are available in Spanish.

GS1 US http://www.gs1us.org/gs1us.html (Accessed Fall 2005).

This site was formerly called the Uniform Code Council and its mission remains the same. The new name encompasses the family of subsidiaries and partnerships it now represents. Still the bar code, or 12-digit all-numeric Universal Product Code, is essential for anyone selling a product in today's global marketplace. The UPC identifies each product, the company that makes it, and where it is warehoused, sold, delivered, and billed either through wholesale or retail channels. In order to obtain a UPC, you must become a member of the Uniform Code Council, Inc.; it's a two-step process. First you have your numbers and then you go to one of the UCC's Solution Partners to produce the bar code symbols themselves. On the left side of the home page, under EAN.UCC System, you will find I Need a Bar Code where you can quickly get to the explanation. Cost is based on how many products you have and your annual sales. This site is easy to navigate and thoroughly explains the process of obtaining a bar code.

PERSONNEL/HUMAN RESOURCES 9

CHAPTER HIGHLIGHTS:

- Determining What Your Needs Are

- Hiring Employees

- Good Hiring Practices

- Unsatisfactory Employee Performance

- Keeping Good Employees

- Employee Retirement Income Security Act (ERISA)

- Firing an Employee

Not every small business needs or should hire employees. According to recent surveys, nearly 80% of sole proprietorships do not have more than one employee, the owner. However, maybe during your setup phase, you find yourself overwhelmed with work, or as your business grows, it's impossible to manage it efficiently by yourself; then it's time to add staff. It's important to make decisions and have policies and procedures in place before you hire anyone in order to avoid personnel problems later. In this chapter, various types of employees available will be considered and described. Also, you will find out how you can learn how to write and establish job descriptions to enable you to find and hire the right people. Your expectations must be realistic, and you must be able to communicate them to prospective employees.

DETERMINING WHAT YOUR NEEDS ARE

Before taking the step of hiring anyone, carefully consider creative solutions to staffing that might work for the short term. Try to project into the future and determine if current demand and workload will keep outstripping your personal ability to cope.

Make a list of what you would like another person or persons to do, and then add a second section of what the person might do in the future after mastering the first list. Look beyond your immediate needs. Consider which tasks can easily be taught to someone else; or think about skills you don't have that someone else could provide to help build your business. Take into account what qualifications a person would need to be able to complete your list of job duties. With those lists in mind, consider whether any of the following types of employees could fill your need:

1. *Independent contractors.* These workers complete projects for you as well as other clients on their own terms; you just specify what you want them to do, the quality required, and when delivery is due. This worker is not someone who works on your site 9 to 5 to greet visitors and answer the telephone. Usually contract employees are used for specific projects or consulting services. A couple of caveats must be mentioned. First, independent contractors are not bound by the contract they sign to complete the job; and second, if you treat an independent contractor like an employee and fail to pay employment taxes, you could face a tax bill that might bankrupt your business. The IRS has very specific guidelines for identifying Independent Contractors, and these can be found at their website www.irs.ustreas.gov.

2. *Leased employees.* This type of worker is employed by another company that does the payroll and administers benefits, etc., and you pay the company a fee plus expenses to do so. Employment-leasing companies remove many employee problems from the owner's shoulders as the owner does not have to understand and pay Workers' Compensation, State and Federal Unemployment Taxes, FICA and Medicare, Pension Plan, Health Care, and other benefits. Because this employment-leasing company has many workers leased to different companies, it can often offer better benefits at a lower cost than your small business can offer. This arrangement may be cheaper for your company even if you need several employees.

3. *Temporary help.* Especially useful if you can't determine that you need an employee or employees for the long term, it may be prudent and less costly to hire someone through a temporary help agency that takes care of the payroll administration and fringe benefits. The agency will also recruit and send you qualified applicants saving you time as well as possibly money. However, if your needs continue, you may have to train a stream of workers who leave at unpredictable times. On the other hand, you may find a good temp who can work for you permanently and save recruiting time and expenses.

For more thorough coverage of all these topics, Dennis L. DeMey's book, *25 Essential Lessons for Employee Management* is an excellent resource. DeMey details the ins and outs of all types of employees, and how to manage each type. Practical and concise, Demey's advice will help you make the important decisions about employees.

DeMey, Dennis L. *25 Essential Lessons for Employee Management: How to Protect Your Business.* Facts on Demand Press, 2001. 307p. ISBN 1-889150-25-8. $22.95.

This very practical, down-to-earth, and easy-to-understand resource provides small business owners with the information they need to avoid costly employment pitfalls, reduce costs, and maintain a productive workforce. Learn to understand employment-related laws and legislation and develop employment policies that work. Four main sections cover The Hiring Process, Bringing the New Employee On Board, When Problems Arise, and Abiding by the Law. Each chapter ends with Recommended Resources, which list several websites to check for more information. Appendix III includes 22 sample employment forms that you can tailor to use in your business. Learn to find and retain good employees, what should be in your employee hand-book, and how to protect your business from litigation.

HIRING EMPLOYEES

Once you have looked at your needs, created a job description and qualifications, and determined that you need a full- or half-time employee, take some time to scru-tinize the issue. Be sure to consider and investigate all the costs involved, not just salary but insurance, worker's compensation, withholding taxes, equipment, office furniture and supplies, etc. You also have to decide what kind of salary or hourly wage to offer. Check want ads in the local paper to see what other companies are offering. If you can't afford to pay as much as others, think of low-cost or no-cost benefits you might offer, such as flexible working hours, job sharing, time off for classes, telecommuting, or working part time from home. As you can probably already tell, hiring employees takes your time and attention away from core business activities. This investment of your time is an ongoing commitment to hiring, train-ing, compensating, and motivating good employees to help your business succeed.

It's not always easy to find qualified employees. Placing a want ad is a start. Also, try contacting your state's Department of Employment or Labor to see if you can place your help-wanted position on an online site or office bulletin boards or whatever mechanism they use. You might want to try local colleges or schools to get recent graduates or part-time or summer help. Asking friends, fam-ily, former co-workers, and business associates to refer potential employees is still the hands-down best source of employees.

GOOD HIRING PRACTICES

Though not required by law, it's good business practice to develop a written job description and application form. Since you've already decided what the position involves and have identified the skills and qualifications needed to do the job, write a job description that blends these two elements. List each essential func-tion, rank the functions in order of importance, list the activities involved with completing each function, and list the skills and abilities needed to perform the activities. For example, for a receptionist, the number one function or task might be greeting customers; activities would include in-person and telephone greet-ings and answering questions; and skills would include good speaking skills, pleasant dress and manner, and working knowledge of good customer service skills. Also, be sure to state where this job fits in your organization's structure and to whom the employee reports. Have a salary range in mind for the position. For more information on job titles and duties as well as wages, check out the *Occupational Outlook Handbook* from the U.S. Department of Labor at www.bls.gov/oco/home.htm.

The job application form helps you gather the same essential information from all applicants and allows you to make a fair decision. A basic application should contain applicant's name, address, and Social Security number, education, previous employment (past 10 years is standard), and signature with date. Next, you should verify some of the information presented to check its accuracy. Speak with former employers and other references listed.

Once you have a pool of applicants, you must select the interviewees. Remember that not only are you interviewing the job applicant, but also the applicant will interview you. You both need to agree to work together before a solid working relationship can develop.

Before beginning the interviews, develop a list of interview questions focused on the position that you are trying to fill, on the applicant's previous job experiences, and/or on your company or industry. Some commonly asked interview questions include:

1. Why did you apply for this position and where did you hear about the opening?

2. Why did you leave your last job?

3. What are your strengths? Weaknesses?

4. Describe a situation where you made a mistake and how you resolved it.

5. Why should I hire you?

6. What motivates you?

7. Do you have any questions for me?

Take notes and retain your notes for your records, whether the individual is hired or not. People often bring lawsuits. Retaining complete records on everyone will protect you, and give you a defensive position. Also be aware of body language and other nonverbal cues when interviewing. Consider dress, eye contact, posture, facial expressions, and tone of voice as clues to the applicant's character, attitudes, and emotions.

Depending on the current job market in your area, you may have many qualified applicants or you may not. If a nearly qualified candidate comes along who isn't quite what you had in mind but who is enthusiastic and appears to be a quick learner, perhaps you can negotiate a slightly lower pay, hire on a probationary basis, and challenge him or her to discover if he or she is right for the job. Follow your instincts on picking the right person for your business and to work with you.

Speaking of probationary employment, it's probably a good idea for all employees to work as a probationary employee for the first 60 to 90 working days. A probationary employment policy must be in writing and should state the length of time of the probationary period. Probationary employees may be terminated without explanation. A probationary period gives you—the employer—time to observe and evaluate the new employee. The probationary employment policy statement should be included on the application form that every applicant signs. At the end of the probationary period, review the employee's performance with him or her. Annual performance reviews are a good time for both parties to share concerns. This annual discussion is an opportunity to review the employee's personal and career goals and to discuss possible opportunities for promotion and expansion of responsibilities.

UNSATISFACTORY EMPLOYEE PERFORMANCE

When there is a problem with an employee's performance, it's best to try and find the root cause. If they've been performing well and suddenly there's a noticeable change, like calling in sick once a week or arriving late every day, a discussion with the employee about why this change happened may work toward solving the problem. Communication with employees will go a long way towards solving many problems. Listen to employees when problems occur.

It never hurts to be prepared. Common disciplinary problems include absenteeism, alcohol or drugs on the job, inability to get along with others, lack of productivity, tardiness, sloppy or inappropriate dress, etc. Consider when you would give a "warning," verbal or written, about these behaviors, when and what action you might take, and finally when you would terminate or fire for not changing behaviors or conforming to expectations.

Try to use discipline as an opportunity to motivate your employee or employees to better performance. Never correct or discipline an employee in a public or even semi-public place. Try never to be angry when disciplining an employee, but realize that the sooner you bring the problem or behavior to the employee's attention, the sooner the improper behavior will be stopped. Conduct the corrective meeting in private, stay on topic, remain calm, and try to be as positive as possible. Remember it's a dialog or discussion, not a speech. Concentrate on the behavior you want to change, not the person or personality. End on a positive note and be sure to schedule a follow-up meeting.

It's important to recognize good work, and improvement is definitely worthy of praise and acknowledgment. When you hire employees, you must work with a variety of personalities and cultures different from your own. It's always useful to get another perspective, and Pincus in her book, *Managing Difficult People*, provides advice and techniques for working with a wide range of employees. Read her book to find help in dealing with different personality types.

> Pincus, Marilyn. *Managing Difficult People*. Adams Media Corp., 2004. 224p. ISBN 1-59337-186-1. $9.95.

> Discover and identify the 10 most common types of difficult people including sneaky slackers, resident workplace tormentors, whiners, social butterflies, and manipulators. Pincus details positive, proactive measures to target these behaviors and put an end to the workplace tension and stress they cause. Employees with negative attitudes can disrupt and bring down the morale of the entire staff. Understand your employees and deal with bad behavior in creative ways.

KEEPING GOOD EMPLOYEES

Employee motivation is a key management skill. Whether you have one employee or one hundred, it is important to work to create a motivating workplace. Employees who feel valued and rewarded naturally have fewer performance problems and issues. Recognizing good work at a staff meeting can help build morale. Keeping lines of communication open throughout the organization is also important to encourage new ideas. A competitive salary is a key ingredient for keeping and building morale. Remember benefits are optional and not required by law, but benefits packages that include paid vacation and sick time, conference attendance, paid education or training, bonuses, flex-time, and surprise small rewards can increase job satisfaction. Make employees feel important and recognized. Focus on the individual's strengths to motivate them to do better work. Be creative and find out what works for your employees. For many good articles on the subject of motivating employees, use the Motivation Center at URL: humanresources.about.com. For an excellent book on employee reward ideas, look at *The 1001 Rewards and Recognition Field Book* by Bob Nelson and Dean Spitzer for excellent plans, ideas, and checklists for implementing your program.

> Nelson, Bob and Spitzer, Dean R. *The 1001 Rewards and Recognition Fieldbook*. Workman Pub. Co., 2003. 384p. ISBN 0-7611-2139-0. $17.95.

> Using the basics of motivation, learn how to develop and manage a rewards or recognition program in your workplace. Topics covered include how to recognize an individual or group, and how to develop and implement a low-cost recognition program. Discover how to improve attendance, increase retention, and improve morale. The case studies, from companies like Starbucks, IBM, FedEx, Pizza Hut, and Southwest Airlines, illustrate important points made by the authors. Unique ideas for employee rewards like the secret Happiness Committee and asking each employee to write down 10 things that motivate them so you have an individualized motivation checklist for each employee are presented. The 1001 low-cost/no-cost recognition ideas are sure to be of interest to any small employer.

EMPLOYEE RETIREMENT INCOME SECURITY ACT (ERISA)

ERISA protects employees' rights to employer-provided pension and health and welfare plans. It is often easier to keep employees if you can offer some benefits. Neither the federal government nor ERISA requires that employers provide such benefits, but when benefits are provided, ERISA outlines the rules employers must follow. Enforced by both the IRS and the Department of Labor, see one or both of the following websites for more information www.benefitslink.com/erisa/index.shtml or the Department of Labor site at www.dol.gov/dol/topic/retirement/erisa.htm. In order for your business to receive a tax deduction for benefit plan contributions, you must comply with the tax code provisions under ERISA. Small businesses are sometimes discouraged from offering qualified retirement plans because of the administrative costs related to ERISA.

FIRING AN EMPLOYEE

Needless to say, when an employee just doesn't work out, following the correct procedures is critical. This situation is difficult and uncomfortable to handle for even the most experienced manager/owner. However, it is sometimes unavoidable. It's not fair to the employee, the other employees, your business, or yourself to keep an employee who's not performing up to your standards. Muster up your courage; be sensitive and kind, but be honest. Be sure you have a legitimate and unbiased reason and explain it thoroughly and calmly to the employee in a private termination meeting. Be sure you have paper documentation to show previously discussed warnings, meetings, and/or actions. If you'd like more information on how to terminate, check out the Business Town website at www.businesstown.com/people/firing.asp.

The following references and resources will further explain and amplify employment management issues and procedures.

REFERENCES

(Starred titles discussed in the chapter)

▓ Print Resources

American Bar Association. *Legal Guide for Small Business*. Three Rivers Press, 2000. 523p. ISBN 0-8129-3015-0. $17.00.

This handy little guide will help small businesses understand their legal responsibilities and options. It thoroughly covers the legal aspects of topics like employees, franchising, contracts, taxes, and start-up basics. Highlights of the employee section include a short course on law in the workplace, terminating employees, maintaining a safe place of business as well as dealing with customers and customer credit.

Arthur, Diane. *The Employee Recruitment and Retention Handbook*. AMACOM, 2001. 402p. ISBN 0-8144-0552-5. $75.00.

This handbook thoroughly covers the topic of human resources (HR) in a changing business world. Key chapters cover what workers want, why workers leave their jobs, and what many companies are doing to attract and retain the best employees. Though not aimed at small business, tips and techniques can be applied creatively by a small employer.

Daily, Frederick W. *Tax Savvy for Small Business: Year-Round Tax Strategies to Save You Money.* 8th ed. Nolo Press, 2004. 352p. ISBN 1-4133-0061-8. $36.99.

One section covers Fringe Benefits very thoroughly, and another discusses Retirement Plans and ERISA. Learn how to manage employee benefits. Discover how to pay payroll taxes on time, use retirement funds as a tax break, and negotiate payment for late taxes. If you are faced with an audit for any reason, Daily will help you prepare in advance. This handy reference guide will help you plan employee benefits and work with your accountant or lawyer.

DelPo, Amy and Guerin, Lisa. *Create Your Own Employee Handbook: A Legal and Practical Guide.* Nolo Press, 2003. 290p. ISBN 0-87337-916-0. $49.99 includes CD-ROM.

Lawyers DelPo and Guerin provide information on at-will employment, hours, pay, vacation and sick leave, benefits, performance, workplace behavior, termination, privacy, trade secrets, complaints, and employee classification. Each chapter explains the legal and practical considerations and includes sample policies. The CD-ROM presents the policies so they can be mixed and matched as needed by the business owner or HR manager.

**DeMey, Dennis L. *25 Essential Lessons for Employee Management: How to Protect Your Business.* Facts on Demand Press, 2001. 307p. ISBN 1-889150-25-8. $22.95.

This very practical, down-to-earth, and easy-to-understand resource provides small business owners with the information they need to avoid costly employment pitfalls, reduce costs, and maintain a productive workforce. Learn to understand employment-related laws and legislation and develop employment policies that work. Four main sections cover The Hiring Process, Bringing the New Employee On Board, When Problems Arise, and Abiding by the Law. Each chapter ends with Recommended Resources, which list several websites to check for more information. Appendix III includes 22 sample employment forms that you can tailor to use in your business. Learn to find and retain good employees, what should be in your employee handbook, and how to protect your business from litigation.

Fleischer, Charles H. *HR for Small Business.* Sphinx Pub., 2005. 416p. ISBN 1-572-48504-3. $14.95.

This handy guide explains in concise language what employers need to know in order to comply with the law when dealing with their employees. It covers employment law from federal statutes and the general principles of state law. Useful appendices include Employee Handbook Outline, Legal Holidays, and Required Postings in the Workplace. Useful Internet resources are also provided and a complete glossary.

Grensing-Pophal, Lin. *The HR Book: Human Resources Management for Small Business.* Self-Counsel Press, Inc., 2004. 265p. ISBN 1-55180-241-4. $22.95.

Small businesses especially must select and nurture employees who mirror the company's culture and performance objectives. Included here are checklists and samples of all the forms necessary to maintain an efficient, productive workforce. Find hints on developing interview and questioning skills, selecting the best candidate, conducting performance reviews, motivating your employees, and managing dismissals and departures.

The basics of employment law are also thoroughly covered. This title is a one-stop manual for hiring, firing, and keeping employees for your small business.

Grensing-Pophal, Lin. *Telecommuting: Managing Off-Site Staff for Small Business*. Self-Counsel Press, Inc., 2004. 216p. ISBN 1-55180-308-9. $16.95.

Not housing all the workers you need in your small business space may save you money and provide your employees with a flexible work environment. Be innovative and creative in finding the employees that you need to meet your business goals and objectives. Grensing-Pophal helps you determine if telecommuting is right for your company, assess current and new telework candidates, train teleworkers, communicate with off-site employees effectively and routinely, and measure the success of this idea for your company. The history of telecommuting presented here is also fascinating, and it's not really a new idea at all. Grensing-Pophal also covers the legal aspects of distance workers. Comprehensive and well written, this title teaches readers how to manage telecommuters.

Holzschu, Michael. *Complete Employee Handbook: A Step-by-Step Guide to Create a Custom Handbook That Protects Both the Employer and the Employee*. 2nd ed. Moyer Bell, 2003. 320p. ISBN 1-55921-256-X. $39.95.

This comprehensive resource guides employers in the development of a cohesive personnel program to fit their business's unique needs and goals. Discover how to deal with personnel issues before they become problems. Policy areas covered include hiring, benefits, standards, terminations, job descriptions, and personnel files. Sample forms are also included. A key piece of wisdom is to remind employers to have a lawyer review their handbook before implementing it in their workplace.

Hornsby, Jeffrey S. and Kuratko, Donald F. *The Human Resource Function in Emerging Enterprises*. Dryden Press, 2001. 369p. $116.95.

Besides covering all the basics like job descriptions, recruiting, performance appraisals, discipline, and administering salaries and benefits, this guide will help you develop and implement a human resource management strategy. If you are thinking of adding employees to your growing business, this work will help you deal with attracting and retaining good employees and employment legal issues. Questionnaires and practical examples help explain good human resource management.

Maister, David H. *Practice What You Preach: What Managers Must Do to Create a High Achievement Culture*. Free Press, 2003. 272p. ISBN 0-7432-2320-9. $14.99.

Offering employees a fun, fast-paced, creative work environment will help a company retain the best. Case studies reveal what techniques top managers use to motivate and inspire employees to perform at their peak. Maister ascertains that good character and integrity of management correlates with financial success. Learn how to create good morale and build an energized workplace.

**Nelson, Bob and Spitzer, Dean R. *The 1001 Rewards and Recognition Fieldbook*. Workman Pub. Co., 2003. 384p. ISBN 0-7611-2139-0. $17.95.

Using the basics of motivation, learn how to develop and manage a rewards or recognition program in your workplace. Topics covered include how to recognize an individual or group, and how to develop and implement a low-cost recognition program.

Discover how to improve attendance, increase retention, and improve morale. The case studies, from companies like Land's End, FedEx, and Southwest Airlines, illustrate important points made by the authors. Unique ideas for employee rewards like the secret Happiness Committee and asking each employee to write down 10 things that motivate them so you have an individualized motivation checklist for each employee are explained. Learn how to use Recognition Technique Reminder Cards and Recognition Planning Worksheets, for example. The 1001 low-cost/no-cost recognition ideas are sure to be of interest to any small employer.

Parks, Ronald K. and Parks, Judith Stolz. *Manager's Mentor: A Guide for Small Business.* Prairie Sky Publishing Co., 2003. 256p. ISBN 0-9729165-0-4. $19.95.

This complete guide to starting and running your small business emphasizes the importance of management principles and their practical applications. An entire chapter is devoted to Efficiency and finding and developing ways to work more efficiently. Two chapters are devoted to Creating a Workforce and Taking Care of Employees, since hiring and keeping good employees are so essential to a small business. Discover how to develop a company culture, develop good communication skills, manage capital assets, manage customers, vendors, and consultants, and improve your management skills. As the title says, if you need a mentor to help in managing your small business and/or your employees, the Parkses can help you.

**Pincus, Marilyn. *Managing Difficult People.* Adams Media Corp., 2004. 224p. ISBN 1-59337-186-1. $9.95.

Discover and identify the 10 most common types of difficult people including sneaky slackers, resident workplace tormentors, whiners, social butterflies, and manipulators. Pincus details positive, proactive measures to target these behaviors and put an end to the workplace tension and stress they cause. Employees with negative attitudes can disrupt and bring down the morale of the entire staff. Understand your employees and deal with bad behavior in creative ways.

Podmoroff, Dianna. *How to Hire, Train, and Keep the Best Employees for Your Small Business.* Atlantic Publishing Co., 2004. 284p. ISBN 0-910627-37-1. $29.95 with CD-ROM.

Employee turnover can cost your business lots of money; currently, it's estimated that to replace an employee, the costs amount to 150% of that individual's base salary. Learn to create a motivated workplace. Learn to spot high-performance applicants as well as evasions and half-truths on applications and in the interview. Podmoroff presents innovative, low-cost, and fun training ideas. Discover how to keep employees interested and involved. Case studies illustrate how other companies have created an environment where employees feel passionate about their work. The companion CD-ROM contains over 100 customized forms and checklists for your use. Additionally, you'll find "rules to live by," confidentiality agreements, and extensive human resource audit forms. You'll refer to this book frequently.

Steingold, Fred S. *Legal Guide for Starting and Running a Small Business.* 7th ed. Nolo Press, 2003. 275p. ISBN 0-87337-910-1. $34.99.

This helpful approach to the start-up process is written in a clear, practical manner that most small business owners can understand. Learn to negotiate a favorable lease, hire and fire employees, understand the tax laws, create contracts and agreements, and cope with financial problems. Appendix A also lists State Offices That Provide Small Business Start-Up Help for every state.

Stredwick, John. *Managing People in a Small Business*. Kogan Page, 2002. 280p. ISBN 0-74-943622-0. $27.50.

Stredwick deals with all the essential areas of personnel management including recruitment, selection, training, improving performance, communication, and disciplinary issues. This clear, thorough guide will help owners prevent personnel problems and quickly correct performance when necessary.

Weiss, Donald H. *Fair, Square, and Legal*. 4th ed. AMACOM, 2000. 384p. ISBN 0-8144-0813-3. $35.00.

This title is your key if you are serious about understanding employment law and protecting your company and yourself from legal problems and treating your employees fairly. Find out how to deal with both everyday and extraordinary situations that confront you when dealing with employees. Crucial information is presented on sexual harassment, affirmative action, proper discipline and termination procedures, the Family and Medical Leave Act, age-based discrimination, and workplace rights.

Yerkes, Leslie and Decker, Charles. *Beans: Four Principles for Running a Business in Good Times or Bad*. John Wiley & Sons, Inc., 2003. 176p. ISBN 0-7879-67-64-5. $19.95.

This charming business fable presents the simple rules for business success as the four P's: passion, people, personnel, and product. The rules apply to everyone, owners and employees alike. Each chapter is divided into scenes and is largely dialogue. Discussion questions and exercises are also provided. Brief, entertaining, and well written, this small book can create a jolt, inspire action, and renew energy in yourself and your employees.

Yerkes, Leslie. *Fun Works: Creating Places Where People Love to Work*. Berrett-Koehler Pub., Inc., 2001. 215p. ISBN 1-57675-154-6. $17.95.

Many managers have not yet learned that fun as a value of the company's culture and as a set of daily behaviors can mean success both financially and personally. Yerkes details how 11 successful companies, such as Pike Place Fish, Southwest Airlines, and Prudential, have brought fun into the workplace and demonstrates how this has improved the company's results. Using these stories, Yerkes demonstrates the 11 principles of what she has called the Fun/Work Fusion. These principles include ideas including give permission to perform, challenge your bias, capitalize on spontaneous, and hire good people and get out of the way. Though Yerkes used large companies in general, the strategies, resources, tools, tips, and techniques presented by Yerkes will motivate you to unleash the power of fun in your workplace so your company will be a success.

Online Resources

About.com: humanresources.about.com (Accessed Fall 2005).

The Motivation Center is a highlight of the large HR section. This large website provides articles and resources on policies with samples, managing performance, salary and benefits, training and education, team building, work relationships, employment law, coaching and mentoring, and recruiting and staffing. Employee recognition ideas are presented as well as empowerment suggestions. Outsourcing is also thoroughly covered. Refer to this site often for new ideas on managing employees.

**BenefitsLink: benefitslink.com/index.html (Accessed Fall 2005).

This site provides users with everything they want to know about employee benefits. Benefits Buzz finds links on the Web to employee benefit plan compliance matters like 401(k) plans, COBRA, deferred compensation, ERISA, and more. The Q&A columns answer everyone's questions on benefits, and links to laws and regulations are also provided. Articles provide links to other sites with information on benefits. This large site will help answer questions and solve problems related to employee benefits.

**Bureau of Labor Statistics (BLS): www.bls.gov/oco/home.htm (Accessed Fall 2005).

Find here publications like the *Dictionary of Occupational Titles* and the *Occupational Outlook Handbook* online. The Handbook provides training and education needed, earnings, and expected job prospects for a wide range of jobs. Use this site to locate information on all aspects of the legalities of employees. If you follow the federal guidelines, you're likely to be in compliance with state regulations as well.

Business.gov: www.business.gov (Accessed Fall 2005).

Another government site developed to help businesses find the information they need and want. Here under Hiring Employees FAQs, you will find links to IRS forms and the U.S. Department of Labor's Employment Law Guide, both of which you can download to your PC and printer. Also find information on interviewing, working environments, training, hiring procedures, and employing minors.

Edward Lowe Peerspectives: peerspectives.org (Accessed Fall 2005).

This nonprofit organization promotes entrepreneurship by providing information, research, and education. Use this site to find practical articles on marketing, finances, HR management, and legal issues and taxes. The Human Resources Management section contains articles and resources on interviewing, employee retention, benefits, diversity, morale, motivation, and performance appraisals. Networking possibilities include conferences and educational seminars listed here.

Employers of America: www.employerhelp.org (Accessed Fall 2005).

This large website can help you work together with your employees toward common goals. Find information on writing job descriptions, HR manuals, employee reviews, how to coach and train new employees, safety tips, and more. If you have concerns about sexual harassment, you'll find tools to help you here. Top stories keep you up-to-date on HR trends like ways to motivate your employees. The well-organized, easy-to-navigate site can help you with personnel issues.

FindLaw for Small Business: smallbusiness.findlaw.com (Accessed Fall 2005).

Chock full of articles and guides on all aspects of business development, the Employment & HR section is particularly outstanding. Find out how to write good job descriptions and advertisements, avoid discrimination during hiring, and good interviewing techniques. Safety for employees and termination procedures are also presented. Links to relevant regulatory agencies are also provided. Forms and contracts are also discussed and samples provided. An entire section is devoted to Workers' Compensation. Taxes and immigration sections also provide help for the new employer. If you have legal questions, check this site for advice and discussion.

HRTools.com: www.hrtools.com (Accessed Fall 2005).

Good information and articles are presented in sections like Staffing, Legal Compliance, Training and Performance, and Benefits and Compensation. Free registration is required, and free newsletter is available with registration. Legal Updates and HR News are also highlighted. An eTools section provides especially good information on workers' compensation, federal and state coverage.

**Internal Revenue Service: www.irs.ustreas.gov (Accessed Fall 2005).

Find here a detailed description of independent contractors and how they differ from employees of a business. Before you hire your first employee, read the section on Businesses with Employees for advice and assistance. Also find information on self-employment and employment taxes. The IRS publication *Employer's Supplemental Tax Guide* is also available from their site. Common employment tax forms for small businesses can also be accessed. A great deal of information on small business taxes of all kinds can be found here.

MoreBusiness.com: www.morebusiness.com (Accessed Fall 2005).

Basic sections on this site include Startup, Running SmallBiz, Templates, and Tools. The Templates section provides sample business contracts and agreements, business and marketing plans, press releases, and business checklists. A large collection of articles and advice on employees can also be found here under Running SmallBiz. Learn how to motivate employees and how good coaching can improve attitudes. Articles on technology and your employees are very useful. Learn about customer service training for your employees too. Many of the articles are lengthy and thorough. Use this site to help improve your people management skills.

Nolo Press: www.nolo.com (Accessed Fall 2005).

This commercial site provides a good collection of free articles written by lawyers generally. The Business and Human Resources section has many interesting articles on things like Abiding by Wage and Hour Laws, Ensuring Privacy in the Workplace, and Firing Employees. The main article on Employers' Rights and Responsibilities is very thorough and easy to understand. You'll also find help on writing your own Employee Handbook. Nolo's legal self help books, now often accompanied by CD-ROMs, are outstanding, and you will find useful information and advice on the site as well as invitations to buy their products.

Smartbiz.com Small Business Resource: www.smartbiz.com (Accessed Fall 2005).

This large site is organized into six major sections, including Smart Moves, Heads Up, Network, Tech Center, Form Fetcher, and Smart Links. Users will find business forms like Daily Cash Flow, Employee Disciplinary Action, Employee Time Sheets, Sample Business and Marketing Plans, and Collection Letters. Interesting articles cover Secrets to Organizational Greatness, and Keeping a Staff Motivated through Training and Development. One exceptional article is entitled Minimize Negativity. Sample policies like Drug Test, Smoking, Safety, Time Off, and Workplace AIDS are also provided. The Network section will prove useful to many new entrepreneurs.

LEGAL/TAXES

10

CHAPTER HIGHLIGHTS:

- Know the Law
- Complying with the Law
- Legalities of Business Names
- Tax Basics
- How and When to Use a Lawyer
- Finding an Accountant and/or a Lawyer

It might send shivers up your spine or make your head spin, but running a business involves many legal and financial decisions, and your business's performance depends on your ability and expertise to make those decisions. Some areas we've already discussed and we'll just recap or connect those decisions to other legal implications such as taxes. Much of this chapter will deal with various taxes that you, as a small business owner, must be aware of and be careful to understand. If at any time, you are confused or can't grasp the legal implications, please seek the advice of a lawyer. As we all know, "ignorance of the law is no excuse" and "knowledge is power." Every unique situation cannot be covered here, just the basics. Understanding your legal rights and responsibilities and being aware of your options is one of the key factors in business success. Doing it right the first time will save you and your business time and money.

KNOW THE LAW

Knowledge is power and as a small business owner, you need to understand some basic legal issues to avoid legal problems. Listed below are the citations for a couple of good basic small business legal resources. Read and understand the sections that apply to your small business.

American Bar Association. *Legal Guide for Small Business.* Three Rivers Press, 2000. 523p. ISBN 0-8129-3015-0. $17.00.

This handy little guide will help small businesses understand their legal responsibilities and options. It thoroughly covers the legal aspects of topics such as financing, employees, franchising, contracts, taxes, and start-up basics. Highlights include chapters on home-based businesses, franchises, insurance, and maintaining a safe place of business as well as dealing with customers and customer credit. If you are still in doubt about which legal structure, sole proprietorship, corporation, or LLC, is best for your business, this book has a chapter on each form and then a chapter, So What's the Best Business Form for You?, that discusses the options using real-life examples to help you consider all the options with more information. The chapters on when you need a lawyer and how to choose a lawyer are also very useful.

Steingold, Fred S. *Legal Guide for Starting and Running a Small Business*. 7th ed. Nolo Press, 2003. 275p. ISBN 0-87337-910-1. $34.99.

This helpful approach to the start-up process is written in a clear, practical manner, which most small business owners can understand. Learn to negotiate a favorable lease, hire and fire employees, understand the tax laws, create contracts and agreements, and cope with financial problems. Representing Yourself in Small Claims Court is a unique and thorough chapter if that situation arises. Appendix A also lists State Offices that Provide Small Business Start-Up Help for every state.

Some of the areas that were discussed earlier include selecting a name and deciding on a legal structure for your business. Both of the above resources list ways to register your name, trademarks and copyright, and cover the legal implications of selecting each of the different legal structures (refer to Chapter 3 for more discussion on these topics as well as later in this chapter).

COMPLYING WITH THE LAW

Regulations vary by state and locality and depend on the type of business you start. For a local tax registration certificate or business license, check with your city or county clerk. In most states, any business that sells any type of tangible goods to the public needs a seller's permit. In some states, businesses that only sell services are exempt from obtaining a seller's permit. Even if you don't need to collect sales tax, you may need a seller's permit. Check with local authorities.

If you're starting a home-based business, don't assume that licensing and zoning laws or regulations don't apply to your small business. Check first and avoid unpleasant surprises. Be flexible, use common sense, and negotiate with neighbors or local authorities if necessary. For more information on home-based businesses, check with the American Association of Home-Based Businesses at their website, www.jbsba.com.

If your business is open to the public, get information from your city's or state's economic development office on the Americans with Disabilities Act (ADA). Environmental regulations affect some businesses with rules on water and air pollution, toxic chemical disposal, etc., so check with local officials. A website that also may help you is the U.S. Environmental Protection Agency at www.epa.gov/smallbusiness/. Also check on local building codes and zoning ordinances. As you can see, many agencies get involved with small businesses. Be as thorough as you can and obtain all necessary licenses, permits, and permissions. Also, keep records of who you contacted, on what date, and what you were told in case at a later date you are told something different. Regulations do change, and it's always good to document that you have tried to follow the rules.

LEGALITIES OF BUSINESS NAMES

As has been alluded to several times, naming your business may not be as simple as you might think. You want a short, easy-to-remember, somewhat descriptive, and attention-getting and/or appealing name. Do not be misleading in any way—this is a kiss of death to a small business. In order to register your name and receive approval from local and/or state government where you are located or organized, there are a few specific requirements to follow depending on the type of business structure you have chosen and you'll want to research them more thoroughly than can be covered here.

1. *Sole Proprietorships.* Usually, it is assumed that you operate under the owner's name, but if you choose a fictitious name, you must file a fictitious owner affidavit and indicate the assumed name and identify the owner. This affidavit notifies the public and the local government that you are the owner and that your company is operating under an "assumed" name. Contact the county recorder of deeds office to get specific information on proper filing procedures and the necessary forms. You will need a copy of this affidavit when you open your business bank account under the fictitious name. You will also want to get your business license in the fictitious name.

2. *Partnerships.* A general partnership follows the same procedure as a sole proprietorship. However, limited partnerships need to file a certificate of limited partnership with usually the secretary of state's office and a unique name is required. Call the secretary of state or use its website to see if your selected name has been used or reserved by someone else.

3. *Corporations.* Again, the name must be filed with the secretary of state's office and must not be used or reserved for another corporation. Be sure the name you choose does not closely resemble another name already in use as this can cause major problems for your business in the future. Also, the name must include one of the words "corporation," "incorporated," "limited," "company," or "chartered"; the abbreviations "Inc." or "Corp." or "Ltd."; or some other phrase indicating the entity is truly a corporation. S corporations do not have to indicate their status as such in their names, only when filing federal and possibly state income tax returns. Usually you can reserve an available name with the secretary of state's office in your state for at least 100 days if you are not yet ready to incorporate your business but are performing the name search.

4. *Limited Liability Company.* Laws governing LLCs differ in each state. Generally, this name must also be registered with the secretary of state's

office, usually when the articles of organization are registered, it must be unique, and it must include the words "limited liability company," or "limited liability partnership," the letters "L.L.C." or "L.L.P.," or some phrase indicating its status.

Performing the name search for your new company will necessarily be somewhat unique in each state. However, some general resources to search can be mentioned besides your secretary of state's listings. Check with your local public or college library to see if you can access Lexis/Nexis, a legal research database. Search its corporate name database for the state where you will incorporate or form an LLC. Try using several Web search engines such as Google, Yahoo!, and AltaVista to search the name, and see if it is being used elsewhere. Because you will probably want to register a domain name for your business, it's probably useful to search InterNIC.com, a large website established to provide public information regarding Internet domain names at www.internic.com. Another large public or university library resource that searches millions of business names in yellow pages across the country is *ReferenceUSA*. In this database, you can search just your state, several states, or across the nation to see if the business name you're thinking about is used in the yellow pages. One final place to check is the United States Patent & Trademark Office website at portal.uspto.gov. If you turn up a very similar or even identical name, you probably want to think of something else. Remember if your business name diminishes or disparages the reputation of a famous trademark, the owners of the famous trademark, which is probably a larger and wealthier business, may stop you from using the name, even if it's highly unlikely that your company and theirs would be confused.

Before you begin your naming process and search, a good resource to consult is the chapter Picking Winning Business Names That Won't Land You in Court, in Peri H. Pakroo's book, *The Small Business Start-Up Kit*.

Pakroo, Peri. *The Small Business Start-Up Kit*. 2nd ed. Nolo Press, 2003. 250p. ISBN 0-87337-924-1. $29.99.

Besides covering the basics, the chapter on Financial Statements is also very useful. Chapters on federal, state, and local start-up requirements, on insurance and risk management, and on taxes are also treasure troves of practical, useful information for every new business owner. Additionally, a CD-ROM is included with the book and contains useful tax forms and a partnership agreement.

TAX BASICS

For some entrepreneurs, the laws governing taxation of business and personal income can be difficult to understand. If you have a solid recordkeeping system, a good accountant, and a basic awareness of tax law, taxes just become a part of doing business. Remember that there is no statute of limitations on business taxes. Keep all tax records as long as the business is in existence. As with bookkeeping, never abandon your responsibility even when you hire a professional to assist you in accounting and preparing your tax returns. You are ultimately responsible for your tax obligations and should have a basic knowledge of the tax system. Tax laws change constantly so keep in touch with your accountant to learn if changes affect your business. If you are in doubt at any time, check with your local IRS office for advice; they'll be more than happy to tell you what you owe.

Your federal and state tax requirements include, but are not limited to, the following:

1. *Federal Tax Identification Number.* If you are a sole proprietor with no employees, you can use your Social Security number, but it's best to get a Federal Employer Tax Identification Number (EIN) from the IRS to keep business finances separate from personal finances. You file an IRS Form SS4 obtained either from your local IRS office or online at www.irs.ustreas.gov to get your EIN. At this time, you might also request the IRS's packet of forms and publications entitled Your Business Tax Kit, which contains a great deal of information about federal business taxes.

2. *State Sales Tax Registration.* You are required to collect sales tax, if your state has sales tax, and must register with the appropriate state agency in your state, even if you are running an e-commerce business. Also obtain a resale tax certificate if you buy materials or products from wholesalers. Each state has its own filing requirements and deadlines, but usually you submit sales tax monthly.

3. *Withholding Requirements.* If you have employees, you need to withhold federal and state income taxes from their wages, as well as Social Security and Medicare (also known as FICA from the Federal Insurance Contributions Act) taxes and remit these funds regularly to the IRS and appropriate state agency.

4. *Unemployment Insurance Tax.* Again, this tax is required for all businesses with employees and has a state and federal component. Check with your accountant.

5. *Self-Employment Tax.* If you operate as a sole proprietorship or partnership and earn at least $400 per year from your business, you will need to pay self-employment taxes. This tax is imposed on your net self-employment income and reported on Schedule SE of Form 1040.

6. *Federal and State Income Tax.* Of course, we all know about personal income tax, but based on your legal structure, you will also be obligated to file an annual federal business income tax return and possibly a state form.

   a. *Sole Proprietor* files taxes as an individual, using a Schedule C or C-EZ. Here you figure net profit or loss by entering gross receipts minus returns and allowances, then subtract deductible expenses and the cost of inventory, supplies, and labor other than your own. Profit or loss is reported on your 1040.

b. *Partnership* files a Form 1065 with Schedule K-1. The K-1 divides the income (or loss) of the partnership between you and your partners. It is then included on your Form 1040.

c. *C corporation* is a separate legal entity and it files a Form 1120 Corporate Income Tax Return and also pays corporate income taxes on its income. Shareholders then pay tax on their dividends so the income is double taxed. Federal corporate tax brackets are different from individual ones and are not adjusted each year for inflation.

d. *S corporation* is a tax status similar to a partnership and is computed in a similar fashion. It reports its income on Form 1120S but does not pay tax. Shareholders must pay taxes on their share of the income.

e. *Limited Liability Company (LLC)* combines the best of partnerships and corporations, and it can choose to be taxed as a partnership or a C corporation. As a member of an LLC, you are a partner, not an employee, and as such, are not subject to self-employment tax.

Obviously, this has been a very brief, minimal coverage of basic taxes that small businesses are faced with when they begin their business. An excellent source for a more thorough explanation of taxes is Barbara Weltman's *J.K. Lasser's Small Business Taxes* (John Wiley & Sons, 2004). Weltman is an expert in taxation for small businesses and details coverage of new tax laws and IRS rules, including deductible expenses, employment taxes, and tax planning strategies.

Weltman, Barbara. *J.K. Lasser's Small Business Taxes*. 6th ed. John Wiley & Sons, Ltd., 2004. 528p. ISBN 0-471-45472-9. $16.95.

Discover how to take advantage of every tax break you are entitled to by reading Weltman's complete explanation and using the tax advice and strategies she suggests. A chapter is dedicated to each deductible expense and includes dollar limits and documentation requirements. She includes sample forms and checklists to help you prepare for tax time. The guide to informational returns you may need to file is very comprehensive. Well organized and well indexed, use this book to lower your tax bill.

Since taxes may be one of the most challenging parts of starting and running a small business and you'll certainly want to try and avoid an IRS audit, consult a tax adviser or accountant early in your start-up phase. Maintain a well-annotated set of books in which you document your income, losses, gains, expenses, and other information required by your tax preparer. Remember that you can deduct many start-up costs, so keep accurate records concerning your investigation of your new business or business ideas. Keep all records that document information on your tax returns organized and in a safe place. Document all business deduction expenses by saving receipts and canceled checks.

HOW AND WHEN TO USE A LAWYER

Do you need a lawyer when you first organize your small business? Here are some considerations when you are concerned about legal issues. If your business started out with just you as sole proprietor and begins growing and expanding, and if you want or need other investors, you'll likely want to change your legal structure. Discussing the various forms in relation to your situation with a lawyer would probably be prudent. One way to save some money is to ask your attorney to suggest how work on a legal matter could be divided between him or her and you. Instead of the lawyer handling the legal matter from beginning to end, you would gather some information, fill out some forms, write some letters, and the lawyer would coach you, offer suggestions, and check to be sure everything is completed legally. This procedure is called "unbundling" and it could save you some money. When more money and risk are involved in a business transaction, it's best to get legal advice and help to make good decisions.

An annual legal audit, a time to sit down with your lawyer and review the legal side of your business, can pinpoint omissions or changes in documents brought about by new laws or regulations and changes in the business. This meeting provides an opportunity for the business owner to discuss potential problems concerning him or her. Year-end tax planning issues could also be discussed. Legal help is important before problems occur and before you sign that big contract.

FINDING AN ACCOUNTANT AND/OR A LAWYER

As discussed earlier, hiring a professional is like hiring any other employee for your business. Look for someone who has experience in organizing and representing small businesses. Find someone who is intelligent, competent, and trustworthy. Use referrals from other business people, perhaps through the local chamber of commerce, or insurance agent or again friends. State and national certification programs can also provide a list of lawyers experienced in commercial and corporate law or tax law, etc. For an accountant, contact the American Institute of Certified Public Accountants (AICPA) main office at 1211 Avenue of the Americas, New York, NY 10035-8775 or at their website: www.aicpa.org. State or local CPA groups or the Better Business Bureau may also provide information. Prepare a list of questions to ask as if it were an interview to see if the lawyer or accountant you call may fit your needs and budget. Call several lawyers and accountants and ask the same questions about previous experience, availability, and fees. Whenever you meet with a professional, it's always good to prepare a list of questions you have regarding the current situation. It will save you time and money. Don't forget to consider your comfort level when hiring a lawyer or accountant. Does his or her personality, office location and environment, and staff make you feel at ease and that you will receive the time and attention you need? Remember that lawyers charge for their time so you can reduce the necessary time spent on your legal matters by preparing in advance. Find a lawyer who will let you unbundle some of the legal services you need.

The Business.gov site at www.business.gov contains a Business Laws section. Here you will find a good article about Hiring a Lawyer, as well as links to the American Bar Association (ABA), your state bar association, and the Martindale-Hubbell Law Directory for more information on lawyers in your state. The ABA also provides a page on Fees and Expenses.

Fees should be negotiated with accountants in advance so that there are no surprises. An accountant is instrumental in establishing good recordkeeping practices for your small business and to provide you with the information you need for taxes and many business decisions; a lawyer can help you make good management decisions before you open your business, and provide important legal counsel if some unforeseen situation arises. By clearly organizing your business and the needs of your business, you will make it easier and quicker for professionals to provide the services you need.

The resources listed below will help you make business decisions that are legal and expedient. Good management skills are necessary to run a successful business, and developing better skills is a long-term task of education and practice.

REFERENCES

(Starred titles are mentioned in the chapter)

■ Print Resources

**American Bar Association. *Legal Guide for Small Business*. Three Rivers Press, 2000. 523p. ISBN 0-8129-3015-0. $17.00.

This handy little guide will help small businesses understand their legal responsibilities and options. It thoroughly covers the legal aspects of topics such as employees, franchising, contracts, taxes, and start-up basics. Learn about types of business organizations/structures, business taxes, state and city taxes, and knowing your rights and responsibilities as an employer. Contract law is covered as well as protecting your intellectual property rights. Home-based businesses, extending credit, and getting help from a lawyer when you need it are also discussed. Exit strategies such as retirement, selling, or a death are described with the various legal ramifications. Learn how to spot problems before they become major legal issues, minimize the time and expense you spend on legal problems, and learn how to protect your business. Refer to this handbook whenever you are faced with legal decisions.

Carter, Gary W. *Savvy Savings Guide for Home and Business: Small Business Tax Secrets*. John Wiley & Sons, Inc., 2003. 178p. ISBN 0-471-460-60-5. $14.99.

Learn how to organize and run your small business for maximum tax benefits and avoid tax mistakes and missed opportunities. Carter will apprise you of current deductible expenses and how to keep your records up to IRS standards. Sample tax forms will help you understand the new tax laws and IRS rules, too. Clearly presented and nicely organized, Carter's book will help readers organize their receipts and statements in files instead of a shoebox and always be ready for the "tax man."

Crouch, Holmes F., ed. *Small C & S Corporations*. Allyear Tax Guides, 2000. 224p. ISBN 0-9448-1760-2. $24.95.

Crouch discusses the various tax situations and deductions that apply to C corporations and S corporations and examines the characteristics of a corporation with annual gross receipts under $5 million. Chapters cover accounting consistency and methods, signs of undercapitalization, C versus S treatment of retained earnings, and more. Explanations of tax code pertaining to C and S corporations and the rules of the Securities and Exchange Commission are very detailed. Well organized and well written, entrepreneurs will learn a great deal about these legal business structures through this book.

Daily, Frederick W. *Tax Savvy for Small Business: Year-Round Tax Strategies to Save You Money*. 8th ed. Nolo Press, 2004. 352p. ISBN 1-4133-0061-8. $36.99.

Learn the ins and outs of the tax code and avoid trouble with the IRS from Daily, who translates the tax code into plain English. Discover how to write off up to $24,000 long-term assets each year, compare the tax advantages of different legal structures, pay payroll taxes on time, use retirement funds as a tax break, and negotiate payment for late taxes. Understand how your legal structure affects your tax bill. What do you do if you can't pay the taxes you owe? If you are faced with an audit, Daily will help you prepare in advance. Understand penalties, interest notices, and how to get penalties reduced. The last chapter, Answers to 25 Frequently Asked Tax Questions, will answer many questions you have or will have in the future. A Glossary, Appendix, and Index provide more access and information to business tax issues. This handy reference guide will help you work with your accountant or lawyer.

Damman, Gregory C. *How to Form and Operate a Limited Liability Company*. Self-Counsel Press, 2003. 160p. ISBN 1-551-8040-3-4. $19.95.

Discover exactly what a limited liability company is and how to set one up and maintain it. Damman explains the financial and tax benefits and the advantages and disadvantages of turning an existing business into an LLC. Laws differ in each state so more investigation will be necessary to understand how your state handles LLCs.

Duboff, Leonard. *The Law (in Plain English) for Small Business*. 3rd ed. Sphinx Publishing, Inc., 2004. 288p. ISBN 1-572-48377-6. $19.95.

Duboff covers all the areas of concern when an entrepreneur begins his or her first business venture. He explains choosing a legal structure and the steps to take to legally structure the business and how to write a business plan. Insurance options and tax deductions are discussed. Also included are legal issues involved with product liability and how to protect your trademarks and patents. Very complete and easy to understand, this title will help you navigate the complex world of laws relating to small businesses.

Elias, Stephen. *Trademark: Legal Care for Your Business and Product Name*. 6th ed. Nolo Press, 2003. 336p. ISBN 0-8733-7945-4. $39.99.

Learn the correct procedures to register your name or other mark with the U.S. Patent and Trademark Office (USPTO), and find here all necessary forms and step-by-step instructions. Discover how to protect your marks from use by others and maintain their legal strength. Changes to the USPTO's electronic trademark programs and new electronic forms for various marks are also included. Uniquely and especially important to online businesses, Elias also explains how to apply trademark law to domain names and web pages.

Ezor, Jonathan I. *Clicking Through: A Survival Guide for Bringing Your Company Online.* Bloomberg Press, 1999. 253p. ISBN 1-57660-073-4. $19.95.

Ezor describes how to manage the unique hazards of being in business online. Learn how to comply with international regulations and laws and structure online partnerships with other companies. Protect your business from e-sabotage and learn how to maintain privacy and security of consumer data. A new edition is needed but this comprehensive resource is well worth a look for e-commerce entrepreneurs.

Fishman, Stephen. *Deduct It: Lower Your Small Business Taxes.* Nolo Press, 2004. 250p. ISBN 1-4133-0020-0. $34.99.

Help your small business make more money by paying less in taxes. Maximize all the business deductions that you and your business are entitled to legally. Fishman describes how different business structures are taxed and how tax deductions work. He explains how to keep audit-proof records and avoid most common mistakes made by entrepreneurs and small businesses. The information on deductions is organized by category and utilizes all the latest tax laws through the beginning of 2004.

Gilbert, Jill. *The Entrepreneur's Guide to Patents, Copyrights, Trademarks, Trade Secrets, and Licensing.* Berkley Pub. Group, 2004. 323p. ISBN 0-425-19409-4. $14.00.

Discover how to protect your intellectual property through all the legal protections listed in the title of this book and even on the Internet. Find out what your ideas are really worth and why trade secrets are often not protected. Examples from lessons learned by Amazon.com, AOL, and Microsoft are presented. Learn to protect your ideas and trademarks.

Hupalo, Peter I. *How to Start and Run Your Own Corporation: S-Corporations for Small Business Owners.* HCM Pub., 2003. 208p. ISBN 0-9671-624-4-0. $22.95.

This thorough, instructional explanation of S corporations explains why this business structure may be right for your business. He also employs dozens of examples to illustrate the key issues involved in choosing a business structure and how to manage it later. Learn the role of bylaws and how to minimize taxes and issue shares. Hupalo explains how to fill out the 1120S Corporate Income Tax form as well as Social Security and Unemployment Insurance for officer salaries. A chapter on Attracting Angel Investors for Your Corporation is also included. Well written and informative, this guide will help you shape your new business.

Jester, Michael H. *Patents and Trademarks Plain and Simple.* Career Press, 2004. 256p. ISBN 1-564-1472-8-2. $16.99.

If you need to obtain a patent, and in this book you will learn what can be patented, Jester explains what needs to be included in a patent application, how to do a patent search, and how to select a patent attorney. Learn how the IRS is involved with an invention, how to market your invention, and how to license your invention. The U.S. patent and trademark legal system is not always easy to understand and use but this guide will help you through it.

Kamoroff, Bernard B. *422 Tax Deductions for Businesses and Self-Employed Individuals.* 5th ed. Bell Springs Pub., 2004. 224p. ISBN 0-917-510-3-2. $18.95.

Arranged alphabetically, this book walks you through this collection of legal deductions, not tax avoidance schemes or questionable areas of law. Kamoroff uses layman's language, not accounting jargon, to discuss deductions from the cost of buying, feeding, and maintaining a watch dog and the depreciation of athletic facilities to the creation of Medical Savings Accounts. Inspiring quotes, cartoons, and little-known facts are interspersed throughout the book to make the subject less intimidating.

Mancuso, Anthony. *Nolo's Quick LLC: All You Need to Know About Limited Liability Companies.* 3rd ed. Nolo Press, 2003. 200p. ISBN 0-87337-929-2. $29.99.

This easy reference guide describes the advantages and drawbacks of forming an LLC. The Articles of Organization are filed with the state and must conform to state regulations. Mancuso thoroughly explains the Operating Agreement, tax options, and paperwork and how an LLC differs from corporations, partnerships, and sole proprietorships. Thorough and easy to understand, another good reference from Nolo.

Nathan, Karen B. and Magos, Alice. *Incorporate!: An Easy Step-by-Step Plan for Entrepreneurs.* McGraw-Hill, 2003. 272p. ISBN 0-07140-983-1. $17.95.

The nuts-and-bolts of incorporating your business are presented in this comprehensive guidebook. Organized chronologically, chapters cover whether you should incorporate, C or S corporations, protecting your corporate name, preparing articles of incorporation with examples, creating corporate bylaws, and how to get money out of the corporation. The necessary forms and instructions plus rules and laws for each state are also included. An index provides more access points and a glossary explains unfamiliar terms.

*Pakroo, Peri. *The Small Business Start-Up Kit.* 2nd ed. Nolo Press, 2003. 250p. ISBN 0-87337-924-1. $29.99.

Besides covering the basics, Chapter 3, Picking Winning Business Names That Won't Land You in Court, is an outstanding collection of information and advice on trademarks, names, and domain names. His chapter on Financial Statements is also very useful. Chapters on federal, state, and local start-up requirements, on insurance and risk management, and on taxes are also treasure troves of practical, useful information for every new business owner. Additionally, a CD-ROM is included with the book and contains useful tax forms and a partnership agreement.

Pinson, Linda. *Keeping the Books: Basic Recordkeeping and Accounting for the Successful Small Business.* 6th ed. Dearborn Trade Pub., 2004. 210p. ISBN 0-7931-7929-7. $22.95.

Pinson, an expert on business planning and financial management, explains how to set up an effective bookkeeping system and how to keep good records. She walks readers through preparing projected and historical financial statements to show where your business is headed. Use her system to maintain required records and prevent tax disasters.

Numerous samples and worksheets are included. Good records will enable you to examine trends, make decisions, and implement changes to help your business prosper and grow.

Rosenberg, Eva. *Small Business Taxes Made Easy: How to Increase Your Deductions, Reduce What You Owe, and Boost Your Profits.* McGraw-Hill, 2004. 282p. ISBN 0-07-144168-9. $16.95.

This guide will help you understand the taxes your small business must pay. Rosenberg walks you through the process and shows you how to reduce the amount of taxes you pay each year. Find out the tax benefits of various forms of financing your business. Her analysis of the home-office deduction enables taxpayers to take full advantage of this tax break with a clear conscience. Learn about the tax benefits of various forms of financing and how to spot errors in 1099s. The chapter Special Considerations for Online Businesses covers Internet sales tax issues, sales tax case law, and legal issues on the Internet. What special tax breaks do independent truckers have? What are Mixed-Use Assets and are they deductible? Learn how to keep good records and how long you should keep them on file. Chapters are concluded with a list of web resources for more information on the topic covered in the chapter. Comprehensive information on tax notices, audits, and collection notes is also provided. Useful checklists are also included to help you organize your many responsibilities as a small business owner.

Sitarz, Daniel. *Small Business Legal Forms Simplified* (with CD-ROM). Nova Publishing Co., 2004. 256p. ISBN 0-935755-98-5. $29.95.

This comprehensive resource not only provides the forms to handle a multitude of legal situations but straightforward instructions explain what forms are necessary, how to prepare them, and what the legal effect of each form is. The enclosed CD-ROM contains the forms with Adobe Acrobat Reader software. Over 130 forms including contracts, deeds, leases, receipts, employment forms, and releases are provided. Most of the forms are valid in all 50 states and Washington, D.C.

*Steingold, Fred S. *Legal Guide for Starting and Running a Small Business.* 7th ed. Nolo Press, 2003. 275p. ISBN 0-87337-910-1. $34.99.

This helpful approach to the start-up process is written in a clear, practical manner which most small business owners can understand. Understand how your business's legal structure can help you and your business. Find answers to questions about naming your business or naming your products. Learn to negotiate a favorable lease, hire and fire employees, understand the tax laws, create contracts and agreements, and cope with financial problems. Let Steingold walk you through the process of buying a business or a franchise. Discover how to save money on insurance. Find out how to extend credit and solve collection problems. Representing Yourself in Small Claims Court is a unique and thorough chapter if that situation arises. Appendix A also lists State Offices That Provide Small Business Start-Up Help for every state. Steingold wants to put the power of the law in your hands.

Steingold, Fred S. *How to Get Your Business on the Web: A Legal Guide to E-Commerce.* Nolo Press, 2002. 352p. ISBN 0-87337-753-2. $29.99.

Whether you are an entrepreneur starting a new business or a brick-and-mortar business adding a website, Steingold translates the legal jargon to help you get off on the right foot. Learn how to choose the best legal structure, register your domain name, create a good privacy policy, and learn the rules and regulations of selling online. If you're new to e-commerce, this book will help you understand its complications.

Stephenson, James. *Ultimate Homebased Business Handbook: How to Start, Run and Grow Your Own Profitable Business*. Entrepreneur Press, 2004. 404p. ISBN 1-932-5310-2-5. $23.95.

This handy guide will help you start your own venture in your kitchen or spare room. Every stage of business creation is covered but the chapter on setting up your business legally is especially noteworthy. Stephenson provides how-to tips, ideas, and tools to organize and develop a winning business strategy. Operations, collections, taxes, licenses, and increasing sales are presented thoroughly and in layperson's language. And, if you haven't determined what kind of business to start, good ideas are also available here. This useful book will help many new entrepreneurs.

Thaler, John. *The Elements of Small Business: A Lay Person's Guide to the Financial Terms, Marketing Concepts, and Legal Forms That Every Entrepreneur Needs*. Silver Lake Publishing, 2005. 354p. ISBN 1-56343-784-4. $24.95.

Specializing in small business law, this lawyer and small business owner presents tools, tips, and advice to help you get your business off to a smooth and legal start. Chapters are thorough and cover topics like Business Formation, Franchises, Business Plans, Insurance, Computers and E-Commerce, and Marriage and Divorce. Each chapter concludes with a list of resources. Over 20 appendices provide forms and sample reports such as registration for a fictitious business name, operating agreement for an LLC, financial statements, etc. This well-written book will help entrepreneurs.

**Weltman, Barbara. *J.K. Lasser's Small Business Taxes*. 6th ed. John Wiley & Sons, Ltd., 2004. 528p. ISBN 0-471-45472-9. $16.95.

Discover how to take advantage of every tax break you are entitled to by reading Weltman's complete explanation and using the tax advice and strategies she suggests. A chapter is dedicated to each deductible expense and includes dollar limits and documentation requirements. She includes sample forms and checklists to help you prepare for tax time. The guide to informational returns you may need to file is very comprehensive. Also included are reporting farm expenses and losses, home office deductions, deductions for insurance premiums, and capital gains and losses. Find out the tax advantages to C and S corporations and more. Well organized and well indexed, use this book to lower your tax bill.

▓ Online Resources

About.com: entrepreneurs.about.com (Accessed Fall 2005).

This large website provides articles and resources on business legal structures, business plans, naming your business, e-commerce, and more. Taxes are covered, including ideas for recordkeeping. Legal issues affecting small businesses are discussed in several sections. A section on Home-Based Businesses is very useful. Articles on creating a business name and filing your trade name are especially noteworthy. Refer to this site often for new ideas on managing employees too.

All Business: www.allbusiness.com (Accessed Fall 2005).

This huge site contains articles and advice on any area of the law including legal structure, property leases, patents, trademarks, employment law, taxes, and even how to work with your lawyer. Links to many directories are also provided as well as news and business information sites. Forms and agreements are also covered in detail. The checklists, including contract checklist, issuing stock checklist, and more, are very thorough. The tax articles discuss things like barter tax and accounting issues and tax strategies for keeping the family business in the family. Use this well-organized, functional website often.

**American Association of Home-Based Businesses (AAHBB): www.jbsba.com (Accessed Fall 2005).

The AAHBB's official website is part of Jim Blasingame's large website now. Here you will find articles on starting a home-based business, what's hot in home-based businesses, zoning information, insurance, etc. Articles are grouped into categories such as Financial Planning, Futurists and Trend Trackers, Human Resources, and Sales and Sales Management, for example. Learn about managing and growing your home-based business here.

American Express Business Resources: http://www133.americanexpress.com/osbn/Landing/informyourdecisions.asp?us_nu=subtab (Accessed Fall 2005).

Small business owners will find help here on management, finding money, and marketing. This outstanding site has information on managing debt, business plans, fraud protection, and SBA loans. The article under Financial Management entitled Business Valuation Methods explains the various common methods used to come up with a value for a small business. The Starting a Business section tells users about structuring their business as well as some information on types of insurance.

American Institute of Certified Public Accountants (AICPA): www.aicpa.org (Accessed Fall 2005).

This site is geared toward CPAs but does provide some information on accreditation and finding a good CPA for your business. Business valuation and auditing are also covered. The FAQ section provides information on local chapters, charges for the services of a CPA, etc.

BFI Business Filings Inc.: www.bizfilings.com (Accessed Fall 2005).

This large site provides detailed information on incorporating, listing advantages and disadvantages, forms needed, advice on where to incorporate, and publication requirements. LLCs are also discussed in detail. Learn why many corporations file their incorporation papers in Delaware and each state's requirements for incorporating. The Small Business Information section covers many subjects related to start-up, taxes, and legal issues. Business Tools provide sample forms and agreements from CCH Incorporated. Ask Alice! is a series of columns where small business owners ask questions about issues they've encountered from computer encryption to finding a business incubator. Learn how to select an accountant and an attorney.

**Business.gov: www.business.gov (Accessed Fall 2005).

Another government site developed to help businesses find the information they need and want. Under Business Law, find resources on Hiring a Lawyer. Links to information on major industries, population and demographic resources, plus Rural America Facts provide users with a multitude of useful resources. International trade connections are useful for global or Internet businesses too. Major categories include Laws & Regulations, Buying & Selling, Financial Assistance, Taxes, etc. Also find workplace issue information on interviewing, working environments, training, hiring procedures, and employing minors. The Site Map works like a Table of Contents and gets you where you want to go quickly and easily.

Business Owner's Toolkit: csi.toolkit.cch.com (Accessed Fall 2005).

Commerce Clearinghouse's Small Business Guide provides pages of information and tools to help individuals start, run, and grow a successful small business. Business tools provided include sample letters, contracts, forms, and agreements ready for you to customize for your business and use. Financial spreadsheet templates are available as well as checklists to help you stay organized in completing necessary tasks. IRS tax forms, state tax forms, employee management forms, and more are all linked to this site. Also find articles on how tax law changes could affect your business.

BusinessWeek Online: www.businessweek.com/smallbiz (Accessed Fall 2005).

This large timely site includes a large section on Legal Solutions, accessed from a tab at the top of the home page. Users will find tools and services needed to understand all legal aspects of running their own business. Also find business and government forms, legal training courses, and information on business structure laws. Find out how to incorporate your business. Also available are articles on other areas of business development such as human resources (HR), Finance, Technology, and Sales. Keep current on all areas of business and economic news here.

Entrepreneurs' Help Page: www.tannedfeet.com (Accessed Fall 2005).

Find here help with business plans, financial statements, legal structure and legal forms, marketing and public relations (PR), HR, and strategy. Designed, created, and published by a group of young professionals in Chicago, Entrepreneurs' Help Page does not claim to substitute for professional advice and judgment but provides information to entrepreneurs to get them started in the right direction. Legal and Legal Forms are found on buttons at the top of the home page that lead you to information on LLCs, incorporating, and partnerships as well as sole proprietorships. Experts offer advice on finding the right customers, how to select and work with an advertising agency, and marketing budgets. Articles are usually not lengthy but ask questions to help the new business person start thinking about what is needed and what questions will be asked of him or her. Down-to-earth advice from peers is often the most valuable.

FindLaw for Small Business: smallbusiness.findlaw.com (Accessed Fall 2005).

Chock full of articles and guides on all aspects of business development, the Employment & HR section is particularly outstanding. However, legal information on business structure, finance, and intellectual property is also covered thoroughly. The article entitled Ten Things to Think About—Picking a Business Form is very thought provoking. Information on a wide variety of small business legal issues is covered including forms and contracts and starting a business. Tax issues including help in preparing for an audit are also covered. A directory of lawyers by zip code is also available. Links to relevant regulatory agencies are also provided.

Home Business Magazine: www.homebusinessmag.com (Accessed Fall 2005).

Legal issues concerning home-based businesses are covered in the Business Startup category. Learn about direct marketing, franchises, the Internet, and personal service businesses. The Money category accessible through the frame on the left side of the screen provides a wealth of articles on money management for any type of small business. Advice and ideas on Home Office, Management, and Marketing and Sales is also included. If you want to give up the daily commute and work at home, here's the site to use to explore the issues involved.

**Internal Revenue Service: www.irs.ustreas.gov (Accessed Fall 2005).

Find here a detailed description of independent contractors and how they differ from employees of a business. The Employer ID Number (EIN) and its importance is fully explained. Also find information on self-employment and employment taxes. Publication 583, What New Business Owners Need to Know, is available on this site and will help you get started right. Other publications online include *Tax Guide for Small Business, Partnerships, Corporations,* and *Business Use of Your Home.* A great deal of information on small business taxes of all kinds can be found here. Also available through a link is the IRS's site for Small Business/Self-Employed at www.irs.gov/businesses/small. This site provides information and links on many issues such as employment taxes, paperwork reduction for employers, changes to IRS Schedule C-EZ, small business forms and publications, and more.

**InterNIC.com: www.internic.com (Accessed Fall 2005).

This website was established to provide public information in regard to Internet domain name registration services and is updated frequently. A directory lists the ICANN-accredited (Internet Corporation for Assigned Names and Numbers) registrars; for more information on ICANN, go to their website at www.icann.org. InterNIC's FAQs will answer many of your questions about registering a domain name and the competitive registration environment.

National Association of Home Based Businesses (NAHBB): www.usahomebusiness.com (Accessed Fall 2005).

NAHBB offers information about marketing your home business and sharing the expense and learning how to design your own web pages and/or create links to other sites on the Internet. Learn how to start and manage your own home office. International connections to home-based businesses around the world are also included.

Nolo Press: www.nolo.com (Accessed Fall 2005).

This commercial site provides a good collection of free articles written by lawyers generally. Three particularly good sections are Choosing a Business Name, Doing Business Online, and Business Taxes. Nolo's legal self-help books, now often accompanied by CD-ROMs, are outstanding, and you will find useful information and advice on the site as well as invitations to buy their products.

Small Business Advisor: www.isquare.com (Accessed Fall 2005).

This large site has lots of articles and advice for entrepreneurs just getting started in business. The Small Biz FAQs answer many of the basic questions like should I incorporate in Delaware and why so many businesses do, do I need a Federal ID number, and do

I need a business license? Tax Advice is another major section as well as Checklists for Success. Find articles on pricing your product or service, steps to improve sales, and how to build customer loyalty. Books, Business Services, and a Glossary add value. The U.S. Government and State Information are also very helpful. Use this site to help you get started right.

**United States Environmental Protection Agency (EPA): www.epa.gov/smallbusiness (Accessed Fall 2005).

The Small Business Gateway does more than inform small businesses about environmental information and assistance. The section entitled The Bottom Line: Saving and Finding Money provides information on grant writing, environmental accounting, doing business with the EPA, and more. The Small Business Ombudsman provides documents on EPA Small Business Initiatives, a source book on environmental auditing, a directory of small business environmental assistance providers, etc.

**United States Patent & Trademark Office: portal.uspto.gov (Accessed Fall 2005).

If you need or think you need to obtain a patent or trademark for your business, this site can help you. An online guide for Trademark Guidance as well as the searchable databases for patents and trademarks is available here. FAQs as well as a tutorial, How to Use USPTO.GOV, are easy to find too. You can apply for patents and trademarks online, too, but seeing an attorney first is probably advisable.

Wall Street Journal **Center for Entrepreneurs:** www.startupjournal.com/ (Accessed Fall 2005).

WSJ's Startup Journal is an authoritative site that has a section entitled Running a Business. Collected here are many articles about different aspects of running a business. The Tax and Legal Advice part includes articles like Large Tax Blunders for Small Businesses, and Tax-Law Changes Will Help the Self-Employed. Jane Attard's article Should You Hire an Accountant? will help you answer that question once and for all. Continually updated and well written, this site is useful to all entrepreneurs.

WORKING WITH THE GOVERNMENT

11

CHAPTER HIGHLIGHTS:

- Small Business Administration
- FedBizOpps.gov
- Central Contractor Registration
- Business.gov
- Networking
- Request for Proposals (RFPs) or Negotiated Procurement
- Writing Bids and Proposals
- State Governments

Qualifying to sell to the federal government can be complicated and time-consuming given the amount of paperwork and large number of potential agencies to approach. Any contracts falling between $2,500 and $100,000 are reserved for small, small disadvantaged, small women-owned, and small veteran-owned businesses, which, in fiscal year 2002, meant 8 million contracts. In reality, the same basic business principles and strategies apply in selling your products or services to commercial customers and selling them to government entities. You need to know your customers' needs/wants, how they buy, and who buys what. It's market research, but for a different market. So, how do you begin?

SMALL BUSINESS ADMINISTRATION

The simplest place to start is at the SBA's website, the Government Contracting area: www.sba.gov/GC. The Frequently Asked Questions (FAQs) will answer many of your initial questions. How do I find the person in the government who purchases my product or service? How can I get a DUNS number? DUNS stands for Data Universal Numbering System and is used to identify contractors and their locations for all procurement-related activities. Assigned and maintained solely by Dun and Bradstreet (D&B), this unique nine-digit identification code has been assigned to over 84 million businesses worldwide. It is also used to register with the Central Contractor Register (CCR) and the Electronic Commerce/Electronic

Data interchange system (EC/EDI) called FACNET. FACNET, the Federal Acquisition Computer Network, enables the entire procurement process from solicitation through award and payment, to be done electronically.

If this all sounds complicated, just step back and understand that if you're dealing with 8 million contracts, there will be some complications, but you can move through them one at a time. A small business can obtain a DUNS number from D&B at no cost by calling 866-705-5711 or more quickly on the Web at https://eupdate.dnb.com/requestoptions/government/ccrreg/. Also under Government Contracting, the Resources and Opportunities section will lead you to PowerPoint presentations on Selling to the Federal Government and Government Contracting. A wide variety of other links are provided to Contract Opportunities, Outside Resources for Government Contracting, and Federal Acquisition and Procurement Opportunities. The SBA has also created SUBNet, a tool to help small firms search and find subcontracting opportunities from prime contractors.

FEDBIZOPPS.GOV

Under Federal Acquisition and Procurement Opportunities is the link to FedBizOpps.gov (FBO), which is the single most important point of entry for federal government procurement opportunities over $25,000. FedBizOpps.gov replaces *Commerce Business Daily* and the SBA's PRO-Net online system if you are familiar with either of those methods of learning about government contracts. Vendors use FBO to search, monitor, and retrieve opportunities to sell to the federal government, and agency procurement officers use it to identify potential contractors for open bids and to publicize their business opportunities to private companies. The FBO portal site has a great list of FAQs to help businesses new to working with the federal government. Various questions are answered, including how to reach the FBO help desk, what are Procurement Classification Codes, how to obtain a user's manual for FBO, and how to access the demo training site.

To further help facilitate your entry into the world of selling to the federal government, seek out a Small Business Development Center at the SBDC National Information Clearinghouse website sbdcnet.utsa.edu. The SBDC can help facilitate this process by showing you how to contact agencies, get on bid lists, understand solicitations, and explain other parts of the process that you do not understand. Using the FBO is the best way to get involved in doing business with the government so be sure to understand its processes and procedures.

CENTRAL CONTRACTOR REGISTRATION

Another entry point for selling to the federal government can be gained when you register with the Central Contractor Registration (CCR) website, at www.ccr.gov. This site provides information to small businesses and vendors as well as federal agency buyers. Several different government programs use CCR data, so you are adding more agencies and programs to the customer base for your business. The CCR registration form contains both mandatory and optional fields, but fill in as much information as possible so more government buying offices will identify your business as one that can provide the products and services they need. Be sure to have your DUNS number, SIC and NAICS codes, information about electronic funds transfer, and point of contact information ready to fill in the form completely.

BUSINESS.GOV

Yet another website to gather data to enrich your selling to the government experience is the Business.gov (www.business.gov) site. On the right-hand side of the home page, click on Government Contracting. Click on Where to Start, and you will find a list of articles and links that will help you learn how to begin to procure contracts with the government.

Getting Your Share of the Federal Government Business is an article that lists things like visiting the nearest SBA office, or SBDC (Small Business Development Center) or locating and visiting your nearest Procurement Technical Assistance Center (PTAC). The PTACs assist small businesses in marketing and selling products and services to federal, state, and local government agencies. They also recommend visiting the contracting agencies that you want to do business with and networking with other business owners. The CCR Handbook, in both PDF and HTML formats, is also available through a link from this site. Under the Contracting Overview section of Business.gov, you will find articles on How the Government Buys and Preparing Bids and Proposals plus Government Contracting FAQs. Learn to use the SBA.gov or the Business.gov site to help you in your bids to sell to the government. A great print resource on selling and working with the federal government is Scott Stanberry's *Federal Contracting Made Easy*, where you will learn about the CCR process, invitation for bids (IFBs), RFPs, and more.

Stanberry, Scott A. *Federal Contracting Made Easy*. 2nd ed. Management Concepts, Inc., 2004. 408p. ISBN 1-56726-150-7. $29.00.

This practical guide explains the process of selling to the government in easy-to-understand language that is simple to follow. Learn how to identify new contracting opportunities, how to find the 2,500 buying offices in the nation, enhance your efficiency in preparing bids and RFPs, and improve your profitability by doing business with the government. Stanberry includes sample government forms, rate calculations, sample cost formulas, and bid formulas. Also described is the SBA's subcontracting program that pairs small businesses with prime contractors. Proven marketing strategies used to obtain government business are outlined in a lengthy chapter. This book is a good investment if you're trying to sell to the government.

Figure 11.1 Screenshot of Business.gov (business.gov)

NETWORKING

Besides using the web, you can take other steps to make contact with purchasing representatives:

1. Attend procurement conferences, trade shows, and workshops.

2. Set up appointments to meet with purchasing agents in your area.

3. Advertise in trade journals read by purchasing agents.

4. Find a procurement officer trade association and join or attend industry expos and professional meetings.

5. Seek out a mentor, someone who has successfully worked with the federal government as a supplier or contractor.

Personal contacts and networking are always important methods for gaining access to the right people and good information.

REQUEST FOR PROPOSALS (RFPs) OR NEGOTIATED PROCUREMENT

When a government entity identifies a product or service it needs, it often issues an RFP or Request for Proposal, sometimes now referred to as Negotiated Procurement. RFPs are issued to companies on the agency's bid list and advertised in the FBO. Remember the FBO website is the public notification medium that U.S. government agencies now use to identify proposed contract actions and contract awards. To learn more about agency requirements, you can also request a copy of the entire RFP. All RFPs have a due date, and be absolutely sure to submit all necessary materials by the deadline. If you decide not to bid on an RFP, send a "no bid" letter to the contracting officer before the deadline that you will not be submitting a proposal as a courtesy. If you don't withdraw your bid, your company will be deleted from the bid list. On the other hand, you, the bidder, can withdraw a proposal at any time before an award is made.

The sealed bid process requires that IFBs be issued by the purchasing officer or office. IFBs usually include a copy of the specifications for the particular proposed purchase, instructions for preparation of bids, and the conditions of purchase, delivery, and payment schedule. The IFB indicates the date and time of bid opening. Each sealed bid is opened in public at the purchasing office at the time designated in the invitation. Facts about each bid are read aloud and recorded. The lowest bidder, whose bid meets with all the IFB's requirements and is most advantageous to the government, is then awarded.

WRITING BIDS AND PROPOSALS

Generally there are two types of offers. Bids and proposals. Bids are part of the sealed bidding purchases process, while proposals involve awards to be made following negotiation.

Some general guidelines for writing bids or proposals are listed below:

1. Before preparing a bid offer, closely study the specifications to understand the requirements and pay special attention to the instructions to offerers

and to conditions of purchase, delivery, and payment. Also, read the complete RFP several times to fully understand what is required.

2. For bids, be careful to include all costs of material, labor, overhead, packaging, and transportation. Always follow the requirements of the bid solicitation or the RFP instructions as closely as possible. If you don't understand some of the information in the RFP, submit written questions to the Contracting Officer.

3. Be sure to professionally package your RFP or bid using a quality cover and good paper. You want your business and your bid or proposal to exceed expectations.

4. Always, always mail your offer in sufficient time to reach the purchasing office before the closing date, with all materials properly tagged and marked. Also mail any samples well in advance of the opening date. Bids or proposals received even one minute after the deadline are considered non-responsive. On the other hand, if you want to change or withdraw a sealed bid, send a letter or telegram to that effect to the purchasing office, and it must reach the office prior to the time set for opening the bids.

The RFP or negotiated procurement proposal process is a bit more flexible than the sealed bid process, because there is greater opportunity to seek modification of specifications, conditions of purchase, or delivery and payment. If the contracting officer will negotiate on a firm's proposal, he or she will require a complete cost analysis so be prepared to support your quotation with facts and figures.

If the above information has aroused your curiosity and you want to know more about RFP writing, try Deborah Kluge's website at www.proposalwriter.com. She gives visitors many pointers on writing proposals with tips on what to include, a checklist of things to do and include, and other hints on how to do business with the government. Or, depending on how large and important to your business the RFP is, you could also hire her to write the RFP. If you're interested in a good book on writing proposals, want to learn how to do it yourself, or want to make sure whoever prepares it does a good job, see the citation below:

Porter-Roth, Bud and Young, Ralph. *Request for Proposal: A Guide to Effective RFP Development*. Addison-Wesley Professional, 2001. 288p. ISBN 0-201-7757-5-1. $44.99.

Offering several templates that you can adapt for your own organization's RFP efforts, the authors provide pointers and advice to help you avoid common pitfalls and explain RFP best practices. Learn how to plan and organize each and every section of an RFP and develop, write, and review all the requirements. Walk through the entire life cycle of the RFP process. A variety of checklists and illustrations reinforce concepts and advice. Vendors who understand a buyer's requirements will win awards from their well-constructed RFPs.

More resources at the end of this chapter can help you in your attempts to market and sell to the federal government.

STATE GOVERNMENTS

All the federal rules and regulations may seem a bit overwhelming to you as a new business owner. Why not start with selling to your own state government? To find a directory of purchasing or procurement officers for your state, start at the website of the National Association of State Procurement Officials at www.naspo.org. Listed alphabetically, each state provides the name of someone to contact and a link to the state's website for purchasing or procurement. The MasterCard Small Business website also has a good article on selling to state governments under Procurement Guide. Visit their website at www.mastercardbusiness.com.

Many of the resources listed below will help you get started in selling to federal, state, or local governments. Face-to-face meetings and contacts are often the best way to find out what services or products you can sell.

REFERENCES

(Starred titles discussed in the chapter)

■ Print Resources

21ˢᵗ Century Essential Guide to Federal Business Opportunities: Doing Business with the Government, Selling Products and Services, Vendor and Contractor Information, Government Contracting and Acquisition, Vendor Solicitations, Easy-to-Use Reference Sources. Progressive Management, 2003. 4 CD-ROMs. ISBN 1-592-4829-5-3. $39.95.

Using Adobe Acrobat PDF software, the government files and documents can be viewed with Windows or Apple Macintosh systems. Reader software is included on the CD. This collection of public domain government information contains data on what products and services agencies such as the Department of Transportation, Department of Defense, EPA, USDA, FAA, FEMA, SBA, Department of State, Department of the Treasury, and USGS have purchased in the past. Most of the information is available on the web, but this resource pulls it together in one place.

Attard, Janet. *Business Know-How. An Operational Guide for Home-Based and Micro-Sized Businesses with Limited Budgets.* Adams Media Corp., 1999. 390p. ISBN 1-58062-206-2. $17.95.

Attard's Chapter 11 on Selling to the Government is very thorough and covers ways that small businesses can sell their products and services to governments and larger corporations. Federal, state, city, and county government agencies should be good sales prospects. Learn how to break into the government market, plot your attack, and get free help from small business specialists. Learn about attending free or low-cost procurement conferences and training sessions to meet the people who buy for government entities. Find out how to use Procurement Technical Assistance Centers. Discover how selling to the government can make your small business more profitable.

**Porter-Roth, Bud and Young, Ralph. *Request for Proposal: A Guide to Effective RFP Development*. Addison-Wesley Professional, 2001. 288p. ISBN 0-201-7757-5-1. $44.99.

Offering several templates that you can adapt for your own organization's RFP efforts, the authors provide pointers and advice to help you avoid common pitfalls and explain RFP best practices. Learn how to plan and organize each and every section of an RFP and develop, write, and review all the requirements. Walk through the entire life cycle of the RFP process. A variety of checklists and illustrations reinforce concepts and advice. Vendors who understand a buyer's requirements will win awards from their well-constructed RFPs.

Sant, Tom. *Persuasive Business Proposals: Writing to Win More Customers, Clients, and Contracts*. 2nd ed. AMACOM, 2004. 224p. ISBN 0-81447-153-6. $17.95.

Sant scrutinizes the entire proposal development process and brings possible pitfalls to the reader's attention. He presents tips, tricks, and techniques to improve anyone's business proposal writing expertise and art of persuasion. Learn to organize your thoughts and your proposals. Real-life examples are a bonus. He reminds writers to keep the focus on what the customer needs. The chapter on word choice will particularly delight wordsmiths and help those constantly searching for a better word. This unique and useful book on business writing will help everyone write more effectively.

**Stanberry, Scott A. *Federal Contracting Made Easy*. 2nd ed. Management Concepts, Inc., 2004. 408p. ISBN 1-56726-150-7. $29.00.

This practical guide explains the process of selling to the government in easy-to-understand language that is easy to follow. Learn how to identify new contracting opportunities, how to find the 2,500 buying offices in the nation, enhance your efficiency in preparing bids and RFPs, and improve your profitability by doing business with the government. Stanberry includes sample government forms, rate calculations, sample cost formulas, and bid formulas. Also described is the SBA's subcontracting program that pairs small businesses with prime contractors. Websites are provided to help you learn more about selling to a particular agency or area of the government. Proven marketing strategies used to obtain government business are also included. This book is a good investment if you're trying to sell to the government.

Online Resources

Business.gov: www.business.gov (Accessed Fall 2005).

This site provides a long list of articles under the heading of Government Contracting; sub-sections include Contracting Overview and Where to Start. A guide in plain English explains government contracting and information on the Federal Register and Federal Government Contract Center is provided also. Find out how much it costs to prepare a Request For Quotation (RFQ) and locate the CCR Handbook. This huge site will help you get started and be successful in your efforts to sell to the federal government.

Business Owner's Toolkit: csi.toolkit.cch.com (Accessed Fall 2005).

The section of this large site entitled Win Government Contracts tells small businesses what the government needs, defines the rules, and presents case studies of small businesses that have been successful in their efforts to sell to the federal government. One company began supplying fasteners to the military 16 years ago, and another precision machine shop makes tools for the aerospace and pharmaceutical industries. An artist in Oregon was awarded an indefinite federal contract for wildlife artist services, paintings portraying a variety of subjects. Government Contracting Forms, such as a sample Request for Quotation and the Central Contractor Registration Form, are also available here. If you think the government doesn't need or want your products or services, you might want to think again.

Central Contractor Registration (CCR): www.ccr.gov (Accessed Fall 2005).

This website provides another entry point for selling to the federal government. This site provides information to both small businesses and vendors and federal agency buyers. Several different government programs use CCR data so you are adding more agencies and programs to the customer base for your business. The CCR registration form contains both mandatory and optional fields but fill in as much information as possible so more government buying offices will identify your business as one that can provide the products and services they need. Be sure to have your DUNS number, SIC and NAICS codes, information about electronic funds transfer, and point of contact information ready to fill in the form completely.

FedBizOpps.gov: fedbizopps.gov (Accessed Fall 2005).

FedBizOpps.gov (FBO) is the single most important point-of-entry for federal government procurement opportunities over $25,000. FedBizOpps.gov replaces *Commerce Business Daily* and the SBA's PRO-Net online system if you are familiar with either of those methods of learning about government contracts. Vendors use FBO to search, monitor, and retrieve opportunities to sell to the federal government, and agency procurement officers use it to identify potential contractors for open bids and to publicize their business opportunities to private companies. The FBO portal site has a great list of FAQs to help businesses new to working with the federal government. Questions are answered such as how to reach the FBO help desk, what are Procurement Classification Codes, how to obtain a user's manual for FBO, and how to access the demo training site.

GovPro.com: www.govpro.com (Accessed Fall 2005).

This website provides news, articles, and other information about state and local government procurement. Designed to meet the needs of the government professional and featuring information from the publications, *Government Product News* and the *Government PROcurement Journal*, vendors will find information on what is being sold to the government. An article archive and supplier directory are available as well as a listing of events. Products for the office, homeland security, earth-friendly solutions, parks and recreation, and worker protection are showcased. Sign up to receive their free newsletter, too.

**MasterCard Small Business: www.mastercardbusiness.com (Accessed Fall 2005).

This large site has a good Procurement Guide listed under its Small Business section. Articles describe state government procurement methods, key steps in marketing to state governments, and more. The Business Center also has a Financial Resource Guide and White Papers/Research section.

**National Association of State Procurement Officials (NASPO): www.naspo.org (Accessed Fall 2005).

This non-profit association strengthens the procurement community through education, research, and communication. This group wants to improve the quality of purchasing and procurement, provide leadership in professional public purchasing, and exchange information and cooperate to attain greater efficiency and economy for the state governments. A directory provides links to the state procurement or purchasing offices and the names of procurement officers in each state. Many states do have publications such as Selling to the State of Arizona, for example.

Online Women's Business Center: www.onlinewbc.gov (Accessed Fall 2005).

This site of the SBA's Office of Women's Business Ownership strives to help women business owners but provides a great deal of information free to all. Under Business Basics on the left side of the home page, you will find Procurement. Numerous topics on selling, especially to the federal government, are covered in several articles. Also learn about subcontracting with a prime contractor and where to go for more information. The Appendix has a long list of references in the Resource Bibliography. This collection of information and links will help you sell your products or services to the government.

**Proposal Writer: www.proposalwriter.com (Accessed Fall 2005).

Deborah Kluge has prepared and maintains an outstanding website designed to help visitors write proposals for government contracting: both the U.S. government and international governments. She provides RFP tips, the proposal outline, and a Proposal Preparation Checklist. She includes long lists of links to different government agencies, sources of government loans and grants, and more.

Small Business Advisor: www.isquare.com (Accessed Fall 2005).

This large site has lots of articles and advice for entrepreneurs just getting started in business. The Small Biz FAQs answer many of the basic start-up questions. The U.S. Gov Biz section discusses Doing Business with the U.S. Government and provides links to many government sites. A useful guide on the site is entitled United States Government—New Customer! State-specific information provides data on procurement offices and state fiscal years. Tax Advice is another major section as well as Checklists for Success. Use this site to help you get started selling your products or services to the government.

**Small Business Development Center National Information Clearinghouse: sbdcnet.utsa.edu (Accessed Fall 2005).

The Small Business Development Centers are partners with the SBA in providing education and assistance to small businesses in the United States. This large site tries to meet the information needs of the SBDC community and provides a great deal of information. Under Government Procurement, links are provided to federal government websites such as the Department of Defense Procurement Gateway, the Federal Acquisition Jumpstation, the SBA Office of Government Contracting, and the FedBizOpps.gov site. Also provided is a link to the State Procurement Office Directory with links to state procurement offices. Well organized and easy to use, this site will help you sell to the governments.

COMPETITIVE ANALYSIS

12

CHAPTER HIGHLIGHTS:

- Identify Your Competitors

- Data Gathering

- Monitor the Competition Constantly

- Analyze Competitive Intelligence

- SWOT Analysis

- Competitive Advantage

The world of business is one of competition and volatility. It is very important to know and understand your competition and keep track of their activities. Competitive intelligence (CI), also known as market intelligence and business intelligence, is the information a company accumulates and analyzes on another company. This information is systematically and ethically gathered from public sources and effective interviewing skills. Competitive analysis (CA) uses CI to make good business plans and decisions or strategy. As an entrepreneur, you must begin this process when you begin making your business plan. Competitive analysis is part of the business plan procedure, but it doesn't end once the business is open. Similar to planning and strategizing, CA is an ongoing process and continues while the business exists. Most businesses gather information about competitors and the external business environment informally. If a more formalized method for collecting, assimilating, and converting the competitive information into knowledge is developed, it can be used to increase the competitive advantage of the business and a successful business will result, thereby "beating the competition."

The most competitive businesses transfer data relating to competitors into insights for their business strategy. A critical element of the CI process is positioning or attempting to raise the position of your company's products or services to current and potential customers relative to competitors' offerings in the marketplace. To learn more about gathering and using CI, read Chris West's book, *Competitive Intelligence*.

West, Christopher. *Competitive Intelligence.* Palgrave, 2001. 236p. ISBN 0-3337-8669-6. $40.00.

This work provides the framework for understanding different kinds of CI and explains the methods of gathering these different kinds of intelligence. West breaks down CI into six different categories of intelligence: financial, technical, sales and marketing, pricing and discount, people, and operational. The goal of CI is to collect information from all of these areas and analyze how the competition is affecting your business. West provides The Competitive Intelligence Checklist to help organize the information collected. West also explores using market and consumer research as a source of CI going into some detail on using panels, retail audits, and customer satisfaction surveys to produce data on how a customer feels about your company and your competitors. He also provides guidance on hiring an intelligence firm. This overview of best practices in the field of CI is worth reading.

IDENTIFY YOUR COMPETITORS

By now, it is hoped you can list the answers to the following questions:

1. Who are your three or four nearest direct competitors?

2. Do you have and who are your indirect competitors?

3. How does your product or service differ from your direct competitors and any indirect ones?

4. What do you know about their operations or advertising that could improve your business?

5. List your strengths and weaknesses and their strengths and weaknesses.

By knowing what your competitors are doing, you will gain a better understanding of what products or services you should be offering, how to market your products or services effectively, and how you can position your business in the marketplace. Sometimes businesses devote too much attention to the current large market-share competitors and overlook smaller potential competitors. Critical insight can be gained in customers' buying behaviors by analyzing smaller rivals or the "substitute" rivals. Businesses with products or services that could be alternatives are "substitute" rivals.

DATA GATHERING

Start a file on each of those three or four competitors you named and a similar one for your company. Research your own company right along with all your competitors. CA can help you reflect on and learn about your own business and its vulnerabilities, limitations, and capabilities in relation to the competition. Develop a list of items it would be helpful to know about each competitor. This list might include how they're structured, their area of specialty or niche, their level of service or quality of their product, values and practices, their financial strength, market share, and what they are likely to do next. Increase your awareness of the market in general.

Watch your competitors and market for customers' perceptions and loyalty, promotional campaigns, product quality and service levels, and changes in products or services. Understand how your competitors provide value to the customer. The following resource will help you use the Internet to begin gathering data:

Vibert, Conor. *Competitive Intelligence: A Framework for Web-based Analysis and Decision Making.* South-Western, 2003. 264p. ISBN 0-324-20325-X. $39.95.

Vibert explains how to conduct competitive research using the Internet. Part I contains a chapter on Strategically Searching the Web and Differentiating Good Online Information from Bad. Part II has chapters on Analysis: Why It Is Important and Web-Based Research Mission—Incorporating the Internet into Analysis. Part III's best chapter is Using Web CI to Understand the Online Music Business, A Case Example. The contributors all focus on free, publicly available information sources rather than expensive commercial databases. Learn about Internet research on competitors and how it can be used to help your business.

Don't limit yourself to just using the free resources on the Internet, but consider all of the following, including the Internet:

1. *Advertising.* Collect competitors' product literature or business brochures. Closely read and analyze their ads. Make note of prices, the publication, frequency, special offers, product features, and style. What audience is it targeting? If you see a competitor's ad in an industry publication neither of you is currently selling to, it indicates they're trying to expand their customer base or reach a new market segment. Take note of the design and tone of ads. Are their ads in black-and-white or color? Why does it attract attention? What do you like or dislike about it?

2. *The Internet.* This huge, powerful tool can help you find information on competitors, the industry, and your market. Use search engines, periodical databases, and government sources. Diverse types and sources of information on competitors are readily available on the Internet; use it to see what you can find or ask someone who's more familiar with searching to see what he or she can find. Besides the book mentioned above, check back to Chapter 2 on Research, Statistics, and Information Gathering for more ideas on industry and market resources. Don't forget government websites. Visit your competitors' website and take notes on what's included, how often it's updated, how they are advertising their products or services, and keep track of how often their website changes. Perhaps they have some type of annual report online. Don't forget to take an impartial look at your own website, too. Do you have too little or too much company information available?

3. *Direct Observation.* Buy one of their products, if that's feasible, and compare it with your own. Is something better about it? Is it a better price or does it give the customer better value for their money? Let friends or relatives try

it and collect opinions on it. Compare it to your own product. Can you draw any conclusions about your competitor's capabilities or technological innovations?

See how competitors present themselves at trade shows. If possible, listen to a sales presentation. Observe how they talk to prospective clients or customers. Are there new companies who will soon be competitors to your business? Do they have a print annual report available? If a competitor is speaking at the show, attend to hear what she or he has to say.

4. *Published Sources.* Read your industry's trade publications and see if your competitors are mentioned and what is said about them. Does the trade association have any published statistical sources or conducted surveys? Visit the library and search a large periodical database for newspaper and general business magazine articles on your competitor. Are there press releases indicating opening a new location or adding employees? Has a journalist done a favorable or unfavorable article about them? Can you find product reviews? Use the commercial sources to compare financial ratios (sources covered in Chapter 2).

5. *Customer Service.* If possible, visit your competitor's store or sales location. Observe how much stock is available, placement of products, or any special displays. Ask questions. How does their customer service compare with yours? Call or ask a friend to call their toll-free number with questions or problems to see how those are handled. Don't use an alias when collecting competitor intelligence as it may come back to haunt you. Do an informal survey of your customers to see what they think about your competitors. You might even consider holding a focus group to find out the impressions and experiences customers have had with your company and the competitors.

6. *Employees.* Probably one of the best sources for CI is your employees; they gather immense amounts of information through dealings with suppliers, customers, and other industry contacts. CI should be a regular topic in staff meetings, and all members of the organization are valuable intelligence agents. Also check your competitors' job postings; recruiting technical or maybe marketing specialist(s) might indicate where the company is heading in the future. Job competencies required will also indicate a company's abilities and intentions.

7. *Business Network.* Talk to mutual suppliers and industry experts. Don't forget trade shows and seminars. Training seminars are sometimes useful opportunities for ethical CI gathering. Perhaps you even see your competitors socially or at chamber of commerce events. Simple, everyday conversations can provide useful information about business successes or new customers. Listening is an important skill in any business interaction.

A good book to use to help you organize and start analyzing your CI gathering effort is called *The Manager's Guide to Competitive Intelligence*.

McGonagle, John J. and Vella, Carolyn M. *The Manager's Guide to Competitive Intelligence*. Greenwood Pub. Group, Inc., 2003. 272p. ISBN 1-56720-571-2. $74.95.

This practical resource covers basic topics including what CI means to a manager/owner, legal and ethical issues, an overview of managing data gathering, effectively communicating CI, and measuring the impact of CI on the company. Readers will find checklists and forms that can be used to gather and analyze CI. Also included is the best way to set up a CI unit including hiring, managing, salary scales, etc.

MONITOR THE COMPETITION CONSTANTLY

Why should you monitor the competition? Because by knowing your competitors, you can predict their next moves, exploit their weaknesses, and undermine their strengths. If you track your competition, you will see the big picture (or at least most of it), and you will recognize changes as they occur. Figure out what the changes in a competitor's strategy indicate about the current, emerging, and potential marketplace. Assess how well a competitor's performance is changing, gaining, or losing market share compared to your company or other competitors.

How does one continually monitor competitors? Frequently review the files you have on your competitors, and constantly compare your company to them. See how often your competitors have discount sales. Review and study any new advertising copy and promotional materials. Use this information to plan or change your own marketing efforts. Also, keep in mind and monitor the strength of your market: is it growing or shrinking? Are their enough customers for both you and your competitors to reach your sales targets? What's happening in the industry as a whole? Personal traits you will want to cultivate in order to become a good CI analyst include being a good listener, being creative and persistent, and being a good interviewer and writer. Communication and people skills are real assets in the business world. Also, you will want to read national, regional, and/or local business journals and newspapers to keep up with industry and economic news. The *Wall Street Journal* is an excellent source, and a subscription should be considered to keep up with trends and current events in the business world. *Business Week* is also an excellent source of business and economic trends and news. *Money* or *Smart Money* magazine are oriented toward investing but carry interesting articles on business. Don't forget to read the publications of the trade association you have chosen to join to help keep abreast of news in your industry.

Don't forget to keep an eye out for potential and emerging competitors—companies who may be moving into your market. Businesses that complement each other can also become competitors. For example, books provide content for magazines, and magazines print publicity and reviews for books. These businesses complement each other but can become competitors if they begin selling the same products or provide similar services. Perhaps you run a coffee shop and the convenience store across the street decides to offer "gourmet" coffee with lattes, espresso, etc.; try to think about whether this new competition is serious and how you can counter some of the effect. Should you change prices? Should you add new products or services? Could your product or service be offered on the Internet by a competitor? How would that affect your business? Conversely, if you're opening/running an Internet business, what happens if a bricks-and-mortar operation opens in your town? Always be aware of what's happening in your industry and market. Know the triggers that indicate you should step up or institute a CI project, including a lost contract bid, a competitor's new product launch, pending legislation, or supply shortages.

Every business has competitors. Even if your product or service is truly innovative, you need to determine what product or service customers are currently using to accomplish the task or fill their needs. Keep in mind that success breeds competition. Competitors often create new technologies or expand market opportunities. Competitors force you to constantly improve your business to get, satisfy, and keep your customers. Customers make market choices, deciding what to buy and where to spend their money based on needs and willingness to pay. Find out why customers buy from your competitors. Is it price or value, service or convenience? Focus on perceived strengths and weaknesses as well as real ones. Customer perception is sometimes more meaningful than reality. For help on Profiling Your Competitors, and researching your market and industry, read the marketing and working with customers chapters in *The Ultimate Small Business Guide*.

The Ultimate Small Business Guide: A Resource for Startups and Growing Businesses. Basic Books, 2004. 501p. ISBN 0-7382-0913-9. $19.95.

This large collection of how-to's, step-by-step objective lists, and enlightening FAQs covers all aspects of planning, launching, managing, and growing your small business. SWOT analysis is discussed in a chapter also. Sections cover Refining and Protecting Your Idea, Communicating with Your Customers, Selling Online, and Managing Yourself and Others. The Directory at the end of the book leads users to more resources.

ANALYZE COMPETITIVE INTELLIGENCE

Now it's time to analyze the data you've gathered. From the information, CI, build a grid, including your own company, so you can easily review and compare these four or five companies. List the name, product or service information, market share, strengths, and weaknesses. If you can, list expected strategies or what their next move is in the marketplace. What are the opportunities and threats in the industry or your locations?

SWOT ANALYSIS

A SWOT analysis—Strengths, Weaknesses, Opportunities, and Threats—is a marketing/management tool used to evaluate a company's competitive position. A SWOT analysis diagrams your present business situation. Market research works hand-in-hand with CA, so review Chapter 7 on Marketing and consult your marketing plan as you continue through your CA. This process focuses on the strengths and weaknesses of you, your products or services, your business, and your staff plus looks at the external opportunities and threats that impact your business such as market and consumer trends, changes in technology, government legislation, and financial issues. Let's define these terms further:

1. *Strengths.* Look at what your firm does well, what competitive advantages your firm has over competitors, what resources you have including staff, customer loyalty, products, location, packaging, hours, etc. Strengths are defined as your company's core competencies. However, if you and your major competitor both have very friendly staff, it can't be considered a strength for your company. If your delivery is friendlier and faster than your competitor's, then that is a strength. Your education, experience, and reputation in your area of expertise are strengths. As you list your strengths, be as honest and realistic as possible. The analysis of strengths provides ideas for future expansion for your business.

2. *Weaknesses.* Again being as objective as possible, describe what you could do better. What are your company's drawbacks? Could your product or service be improved in some way? How reliable is your customer service? Does your supplier deliver exactly when you want it and exactly what you want? Do you need more staff to provide better customer service? Look at your business from the customer's perspective. Look at the big picture of your company. You might survey your customers or several big or frequent customers.

3. *Opportunities.* These are favorable situations or characteristics within the larger marketplace that could create benefits or competitive advantage to

Figure 12.1 Strengths, Weaknesses, Opportunities, and Threats (SWOT) Analysis

Strengths	Weaknesses
1. New equipment	1. Poor location for public access
2. Plentiful capital	2. No PR staff
Opportunities	Threats
1. Growing market	1. New government regulations
2. Strong local economy	2.

your company if pursued. Examples would be competitors who are not performing very well, legislation favorable to your industry or affecting your customers, technological developments in hardware or software perhaps, or market trends or changes in consumer buying habits or even changes in the state or local economy. Quick action before your competitors could help you develop a niche market or expand your current market. Creative managers/owners are constantly looking for opportunities and trying to capitalize on them ahead of the competition. Think about ways to turn weaknesses into opportunities, too. An experienced staff member leaving for a better job or retiring is a loss creating a weakness, but if you can hire someone with new skills your company needs it becomes an opportunity.

4. *Threats.* Obstacles or conditions that prevent your company from achieving its objectives are threats. Similar to opportunities, competitors' actions, demographic changes, environmental issues, changing technology, legislation, or your own limited financial resources can all be threats to the success of your business. Often threats are intuitive guesses that never happen, but being vigilant means that you can react quickly if a threat does materialize. What happens if a new competitor moves into your market? What if a new product outperforms yours or can be sold cheaper through new technology? Consider how your company could respond.

An excellent website to help in your SWOT Analysis is at www.websitemarketing plan.com. The article SWOT Analysis—Beyond the Textbook by Bobette Kyle is enlightening, and other articles are also available. A SWOT analysis also is a method of presenting knowledge about your business to others who have a need to know and who can help advance the quality of the knowledge it imparts. This visual communication of key learning or business intelligence stimulates dialogue and promotes action. Another good site to learn more about SWOT analysis and how to perform and present it visually is the Bplans.com website at www.bplans.com. Use the SWOT analysis to identify potential and critical issues affecting your business on an ongoing basis.

As with your CA, you must learn from your SWOT analysis. Build on your strengths and use them to your full potential. Determine how financial resources, staff, and capacity should be allocated to create an exploitable advantage. Minimize the risk your weaknesses represent or overcome them if possible. If you find a weakness that undermines an opportunity, you can work toward correcting that situation or problem area. Now that you can see some opportunities, plan how to capitalize on them. Try to turn threats into opportunities, and counter any threats as they come up.

The SWOT analysis presents you with an overview of how your business is functioning and evaluates the external and internal forces that can help your business succeed and grow. Similar to other parts of running a business, a SWOT analysis is not a one-time event, but an ongoing good business practice. Plan to update it and refer to it on a regular basis as one of your management tools.

COMPETITIVE ADVANTAGE

Competitive advantage is found in the differences between competitors. In order to succeed, each must be different enough to have a unique advantage. Competitive advantage creates superior value above its rivals. A competitive advantage can be achieved through product, service, people, or image differentiation, and the foundations of competitive advantage are efficiency, quality, or innovation. If there are two small restaurants on the same street, the one that differentiates itself through price, product mix, customer service, or ambiance plus good food is more likely to survive and prosper. A competitive strategy means deliberately choosing a different set of activities to deliver a unique mix of value. Look at two airlines and see what distinguishes one from the other. Is it more frequent flights? Or lower fares or more leg room, for example? eBay created a unique way for users to sell and acquire used and new items. The company serves the same purpose as classified ads, flea markets, or formal auctions but made it global, simple, and efficient. Look at your competitors and learn from them through CA to create competitive advantage. Once you've identified your competitive advantage, work to convey it to your customers through advertising and promotions.

Listed below are many resources to help you expand your knowledge of CI, CA, and how to use them both to help your business prosper and grow in the competitive world of business.

REFERENCES

(Starred titles discussed in the chapter)

Print Resources

The Benjamin Group. *Introduction to Online Competitive Intelligence Research.* South-Western, 2004. 344p. ISBN 0-538-72680-6. $49.95.

This work provides a comprehensive introduction to online CI. One chapter outlines both sources and uses of CI. Others cover the invisible Web, vertical portals, and newsgroups and chat forums. Case studies are used to illustrate how to obtain CI. Learn how to collect information on markets, marketers, consumers, the media, and social issues. Data sources are evaluated in the final chapter. This step-by-step advice will help you analyze, interpret, and collect data for informed decision making.

Burwell, Helen P. *Online Competitive Intelligence: Increase Your Profits Using Cyber-Intelligence.* 2nd ed. Facts on Demand Press, 2004. 400p. ISBN 1-889150-41-X. $25.95.

This well-written guide to "where to find" and "how to use" the best commercial and Internet resources will help your small business remain profitable. Use the data Burwell helps you access to develop company strategies to beat your competitors in your market. Learn how to build and retain market share by targeting new and emerging markets and anticipating industry changes. Learn how to evaluate the information you find. Discover how to save money and maximize your profits. Her chapter on the Invisible Web is thorough and includes many choices for searching deeper for competitive information. Use the techniques Burwell explains to see what competitors can find out about your own business. Use the references described of over 1,500 websites to help your company keep ahead of the competition. Section four divides Burwell's list of Bookmarks and Favorites into categories such as Demographics, European Union, Financial Information Sites, Industry Research, Market Research, People Locators, and many, many more.

Carr, Margaret Metcalf. *Super Searchers on Competitive Intelligence: The Online and Offline Secrets of Top CI Researchers*. Information Today, Inc., 2003. 336p. ISBN 0-910965-64-1. $24.95.

Find out how to use CI resources, analytical techniques, and models from 15 leading CI researchers. Monitoring competitive companies and keeping on top of industry trends, opportunities, and threats is vital in business today, and Carr will help you learn how to do it. Each chapter ends with Super Searcher Power Tips, which will help novice and experienced CI researchers alike learn the tricks and tips of this useful skill.

Fleisher, Craig S. and Bensoussan, Babette. *Strategic and Competitive Analysis: Methods and Techniques for Analyzing Business Competition*. Prentice Hall, 2002. 457p. ISBN 0-13-088852-4. $84.00.

Fleisher and Bensoussan examine the wide variety of techniques used in analyzing business and competitive data, including environmental analysis, industry analysis, competitor analysis, and temporal analysis models. Over 20 analytical tools are discussed and evaluated with examples to illustrate the best application. This undergraduate text will help small business owners/managers learn the theory and application of competitive analysis.

Gilad, Ben. *Early Warning: Using Competitive Intelligence to Anticipate Market Shifts, Control Risk, and Create Powerful Strategies*. AMACOM, 2003. 272p. ISBN 0-8144-0786-2. $27.95.

Gilad explains and makes a case for his Competitive Early Warning (CEW) system. Discovering that other companies are ahead of yours is not a good thing in any industry. CEW combines strategic planning, CI, and management action to meet new realities. Each chapter ends with the Manager's Checklist of key points. Using wry humor and providing lots of charts, tables, and tools, Gilad reveals how to read the signs that indicate a change is coming. Case studies illustrate his important points. Learn to use your competitive analysis to help your business succeed.

Hussey, David E. and Jenster, Per V. *Competitor Intelligence: Turning Analysis into Success*. John Wiley & Sons, Inc., 1999. 292p. ISBN 0-471-98407-8. $85.00.

Learn how to legitimately obtain competitor information, analyze the information collected to better understand competitors and the industry, and develop ways to increase the competitive advantage of a company to move ahead of competitors. Using case studies and the practical experience of the authors, methods of using competitor information are presented in practical situations. Competition in various industries is examined.

Kahaner, Larry. *Competitive Intelligence: How to Gather, Analyze, and Use Information to Move Your Business to the Top*. Simon & Schuster, 1998. 304p. ISBN 0-684-84404-4. $14.00.

CI reveals where the market is going, who is leading it, and why. Kahaner, using case studies, shows how to collect CI information and how to protect your company from others. This book is basic and aimed at those who are new to the idea and practice of CI gathering.

**McGonagle, John J. and Vella, Carolyn M. *The Manager's Guide to Competitive Intelligence.* Greenwood Pub. Group, Inc., 2003. 272p. ISBN 1-56720-571-2. $74.95.

This practical resource covers basic topics including what CI means to a manager/owner, legal and ethical issues, an overview of managing data gathering, effectively communicating CI, and measuring the impact of CI on the company. Readers will find checklists and forms that can be used to gather and analyze CI. Also included is the best way to set up a CI unit including hiring, managing, salary scales, etc. The importance of CI is identified and ways to use it are presented in a clear, organized manner.

Miller, Jerry P. *Millennium Intelligence: Understanding and Conducting Competitive Intelligence in the Digital Age.* Cyberage Books, 2000. 276p. ISBN 0-9109-6528-5. $29.95.

Key issues in CI are covered here. From the technology marketplace to resources for CI, legal and ethical issues, and accounting models, the entire function is described and discussed. Find tips on gathering CI and learn about security issues related to your company. Every business needs to gather information on their competitors, and this title will help you do it effectively.

Porter, Michael. *Competitive Strategy: Techniques for Analyzing Industries and Competitors.* Free Press, 1998. 432p. ISBN 0-684-84148-7. $37.50.

Porter is a leading authority on competition and strategy, and this work is a standard classic in modern business education. Part I discusses the structural analysis of industries, competitive strategies, a framework for competitor analysis, and structural analysis within industries. Part II presents competitive strategy within various industry environments including emerging industries, mature industries, and global industries, for example. Part III discusses various strategic decisions such as vertical integration and expansion of companies in their industries. Particularly noteworthy and useful are Appendix A, Portfolio Techniques in Competitor Analysis, and Appendix B, How to Conduct an Industry Analysis. If you find you enjoy Michael Porter's writing, you might also read *Competitive Advantage: Creating and Sustaining Superior Performance* (Simon & Schuster, 1998, ISBN 0-684-84146-0).

Prescott, John E. and Miller, Stephen H. *Proven Strategies in Competitive Intelligence.* John Wiley & Sons, 2001. 288p. ISBN 0-471-4017-8-1. $24.95.

The highlight of this collection is the case studies. Learn how large companies collect competitive information. Discover and understand the philosophy, tactics, and concepts behind CI. Learn how CI techniques are used and applied in market research and forecasting and product development. Though not always applicable to a small business, the real-life examples will illustrate CI's importance to success.

Rothbert, Helen and Erickson, G. Scott. *From Knowledge to Intelligence: Creating Competitive Advantage in the Next Economy.* Elsevier Science and Technology Books, 2004. 368p. ISBN 0-7506-7762-7. $29.95.

Competitive intelligence or the strategic gathering of knowledge about competitors, climate, trends, and new products generates competitive advantage. Topics include how to develop a strategy for sharing and gathering information, best CI practices, and using internal and external intelligence to gain a competitive advantage. Real examples from the corporate world are also provided.

**The Ultimate Small Business Guide:A Resource for Startups and Growing Businesses.* Basic Books, 2004. 501p. ISBN 0-7382-0913-9. $19.95.

This large collection of how-to's, step-by-step objective lists, and enlightening FAQs covers all aspects of planning, launching, managing, and growing your small business. Sections cover Refining and Protecting Your Idea, Communicating with Your Customers, Selling Online, and Managing Yourself and Others. Financing, pricing, cash flow, ratios, and assets are thoroughly and carefully covered in a section called Figuring It Out. The Directory at the end of the book leads users to more resources. Simple and effectively written, in a few short pages, readers will understand how important a competitive advantage is to their business.

**Vibert, Conor. *Competitive Intelligence: A Framework for Web-based Analysis and Decision Making*. South-Western, 2003. 264p. ISBN 0-324-20325-X. $39.95.

Vibert explains how to conduct competitive research using the Internet. Part I contains a chapter on Strategically Searching the Web and Differentiating Good Online Information from Bad. Part II has chapters on Analysis: Why It Is Important and Web-Based Research Mission—Incorporating the Internet into Analysis. Part III's best chapter is Using Web CI to Understand the Online Music Business, A Case Example. The contributors all focus on free, publicly available information sources rather than expensive commercial databases. Learn about Internet research on competitors and how it can be used to help your business.

**West, Christopher. *Competitive Intelligence*. Palgrave, 2001. 236p. ISBN 0-3337-8669-6. $40.00.

This work provides the framework for understanding different kinds of CI and explains the methods of gathering these different kinds of intelligence. West breaks down CI into six different categories of intelligence: financial, technical, sales and marketing, pricing and discount, people, and operational. The goal of CI is to collect information from all of these areas and analyze how the competition is affecting your business. West describes many secondary sources found in libraries and devotes an entire chapter to using the Internet as a secondary source. West also explores using market and consumer research as a source of CI going into some detail on using panels, retail audits, and customer satisfaction surveys to produce data on how a customer feels about your company and your competitors. He also provides guidance on hiring an intelligence firm. This overview of best practices in the field of CI is worth reading.

Online Resources

About.com: management.about.com (Accessed Fall 2005).

Under Business Strategy on the Management section of the huge About.com site, you will find several good articles on gathering CI. In addition to suggestions about public or commercial sources of information, you will find links to companies that will track a company or industry for you and provide periodic updates. Also, you will find articles on competitive analysis in the Small Business, Writing a Business Plan section of this site. Analyzing the competition is important when you prepare your business plan but it is essential to continue monitoring the competition as long as you are in business.

American Express Small Business http://www10.americanexpress.com/sif/cda/page/ 0,1641,15565,00.asp (Accessed Fall 2005).

Small business owners will find help here on day-to-day management, finding money, taxes, e-commerce, and in the Export/Import Center. The article entitled Effective Competitive Analysis is brief but thorough, and leads you through the basics of a SWOT analysis of the data you have gathered on your competitors. Marketing and Market Research articles also help explain a competitive advantage. This outstanding site has unique, efficient interactive tools including financial ratios, business plans, fraud protection, and hiring policies and procedures.

**Bplans.com: www.bplans.com (Accessed Fall 2005).

This well-established, frequently updated site, sponsored by Palo Alto Software, Inc., is the best for help in writing your business plan but also contains articles on a wide range of small business topics. Fully searchable, users can quickly find topics that they need, such as business structure, SWOT analysis, cash flow, starting costs, and business plan legalities. Other sections include Finance and Capital, Marketing & Advertising, Buying a Business, Market Research, and a monthly Newsletter. The section titled Write a Business Plan contains articles, calculators on cash flow, starting costs, breakeven, and more, a business plan template, and executive summary and mission statement help plus access to Expert Advice. Bplans.com is a useful, practical site that also offers fee-based experts and assistance.

Edward Lowe PEERSPECTIVES: peerspectives.org (Accessed Fall 2005).

This nonprofit organization promotes entrepreneurship by providing information, research, and education. An outstanding article under the topic of Defining and Serving a Market, is on How to Conduct and Prepare a Competitive Analysis. It is an excellent place for new entrepreneurs to begin learning about how to monitor the competition. Similar to other articles on this site, resources are provided. Use this site to find practical articles on marketing, finances, human resources management, and legal issues and taxes. Networking possibilities include conferences and educational seminars listed here. Aimed at second-stage businesses, the Foundation provides good basic help too. The newsletter, *PeerSpectives*, is well worth subscribing to for inspiration.

Entrepreneur.com: www.entrepreneurmag.com (Accessed Fall 2005).

Maintained by *Entrepreneur Magazine*, this site supports new businesses and growing companies, and you are probably very familiar with it by now. Under First Steps, learn how to evaluate your idea and determine if there's a market for your business. Start Up Topics include location, naming your biz, and business structure. Another important topic here is Competitive Analysis—again discussing competitive analysis and advantage in relation to your business plan, this article explains that examining competitors' strengths and weaknesses can help you determine how to succeed and stay competitive. Find ready-made business forms here, too, in the FormNet section.

Online Women's Business Center: www.onlinewbc.gov (Accessed Fall 2005).

This site of the SBA's Office of Women's Business Ownership strives to help women business owners but provides a great deal of information free to all. Under Business Basics on the left side of the home page, you will find the Marketing Mall. Numerous topics on marketing, public relations, and advertising are covered in articles, both old and new. Learn more about a Competitor Analysis here. A wealth of information and links will help you develop your marketing strategy and develop your competitive advantage.

Society of Competitive Intelligence Professionals: www.scip.org (Accessed Fall 2005).

This international nonprofit organization, established in 1986, provides CI publications and annual conferences. You can also find names of CI consultants and CI training firms in your area on the website. The FAQs answer many questions about CI, how it makes a difference in your bottom line, how it is changing, plus tips on getting started collecting CI. Ethical and legal issues are covered as well.

**WebSite Marketing Plan: www.websitemarketingplan.com (Accessed Fall 2005).

This large website on online marketing contains a wealth of articles on a variety of articles relating to small business including Bobette Kyle's SWOT Analysis—Beyond the Text Book. Featured Directory Categories include articles grouped under Search Engine Marketing, Marketing Strategy, Marketing Plan, and Public Relations. Many commercial links but plenty of free help for the new entrepreneur, too. This site is especially helpful for those interested in e-commerce. Well organized and easy to navigate, the wealth of articles here will help you develop your competitive advantage through marketing.

GROWING YOUR BUSINESS AND MOVING ON

13

CHAPTER HIGHLIGHTS:

- Growing Your Small Business
- Exit Strategies to Consider
- Alternatives to Selling
- Selling Strategy for Your Business
- Mergers and Acquisitions
- Employee Stock Ownership Plans (ESOPs)
- Closing
- Initial Public Offering (IPO)
- Family Succession
- Retirement

When you first start your business, it may appear that expanding your business will be a terrific sign that you're a success. In the early days, things will be hectic, but you will still feel that the business is under your control. However, as you begin to juggle more tasks, decisions, and responsibilities and delegate some of these same items to your staff and still you don't have enough time to get everything done, you may decide it's time to expand your business. Be careful when planning this important step as success and expansion if done improperly can quickly bankrupt the entire business. Because business growth rarely occurs predictably and smoothly, fast growth can destabilize a successful business, providing a false sense of security while additional operating dollars quickly eat up any new revenues.

GROWING YOUR SMALL BUSINESS

Don't forget the main lessons from Chapter 3, Start-Up—plan for growth. Have a strategic reason to expand and pay careful attention to financial management.

Unplanned growth can result in loss of current customers if you and your staff are spread too thin. Also, remember from Chapter 8, Management, that good management is the root of business success and growth.

An excellent resource to help you identify when and how to expand your business is Jeffrey Hansen's *Mastering Business Growth and Change Made Easy* for the Entrepreneur Made Easy Series. This well-organized, clearly written guide includes self-assessment worksheets to help determine the state of your business as it matures while guiding you to solutions for challenges you will encounter.

> Hansen, Jeffrey. *Mastering Growth and Change Made Easy* (Entrepreneur Made Easy Series). Entrepreneur Press, 2005. 262p. ISBN 1-932531-64-5. $19.95.
>
> Hansen helps entrepreneurs understand change and how to control and plan for growth. He presents a view of a business's full growth cycle and provides self-assessment worksheets to determine the current stage of your company's development and to help strategize solutions to challenges that a growing business faces. Hansen also helps readers look at the environment in which they are doing business to determine how and when to expand. This outstanding resource helps small businesses plan and grow.

What are possible ways that your business could grow and expand? Consider these ideas:

- Add more products or services,

- Adapt your current products or services to meet the need of another niche market,

- Market your products or services to a new geographic area, or

- Compete with larger companies.

What are things you should consider when planning for expansion and growth? Remember that unplanned growth is destined to fail. The main rule to keep in mind is that you expand when there is an untapped opportunity such as a new niche you can fill or when a location is not being served. Other factors to consider include the financial ramifications of expansion; the logistics—especially if more than one location will be needed; and don't forget your emotional or personal readiness for the stress and additional work. Bluntly consider whether you can afford to expand and whether your cash flow can support the additional investment. Keep in mind that growth or expansion does not immediately result in more profit because when handling more volume or an added location there will be additional overhead as well. Keep your overhead as low as possible. Watch your profit margin.

Also be prepared to play a less hands-on role as your business grows. You may need more staff and even a manager for a new location. New players in your business mean new ideas, and you should be open to them. This loss of control can be an emotional issue for some entrepreneurs. An excellent resource for helping you plan for growth is *The Real World Entrepreneur Field Guide: Growing Your Own Business* by David H. Bangs and Linda Pinson. Bangs and Pinson will help you make a plan to start and grow your small business.

Bangs, David H. and Pinson, Linda. *The Real World Entrepreneur Field Guide: Growing Your Own Business*. Dearborn Financial Publishing, 1999. 652p. ISBN 1-57-41011-3-7. $59.95.

Learn how 10 successful entrepreneurs from all around the United States started and grew their small businesses. Discussed here are feasibility, business plans, cash management, websites, legalities, finding and keep good employees, planning and managing growth, and especially important are the real-life case studies. Learn how to select opportunities that your business should pursue and learn to develop sustainable competencies for your business. Bangs and Pinson discuss a planning model that includes an environmental analysis and an internal analysis to help select the best growth opportunities for your particular situation.

When considering expansion, you should also analyze the strategies of your competitors. Refer back to Chapter 12 and your competitive analysis. If your competitors are tapping into new opportunities, they may have stumbled onto a good idea, and you may consider waiting to see how it works for them or you may want to jump in to follow their lead. Maybe their new approach can stimulate your own thinking into how to fill a developing niche or provide a needed, new service or product related to your current business operation. You may want to complete another or carefully consider your SWOT analysis. As your business environment changes, you can use the SWOT analysis to analyze your business and its potential. Ask yourself how to prepare your business for change.

Hopefully you have been reading trade journals and newspapers and have joined a trade association to keep abreast of trends in your field. Becoming an authority on issues related to your business is necessary for the success and growth of your business. Look for trends and opportunities in your industry and your local business climate. Remember to keep focused on what brought you success in the first place. If you're the best at closing the sale, then hire staff for other support functions such as marketing, recordkeeping, etc., and keep doing what you're best at doing in the business.

Also, think about the reaction of your current customers. Timing is crucial in the decision to expand a business. Look at the overall outlook for the U.S. economy and your state's economic situation. Can your customers afford more services or products at this time? Keep in mind various alternatives and find the most appropriate vehicles for expansion for you and your business.

A terrific website to help you focus and plan the growth of your business is Business Know-How at (www.businessknowhow.com) under the section Growth and Leadership. Another good site is the U.S. government's Business.gov at (www.business.gov). This site will provide you with information you need to finance and grow a business. Under Growing, users will find many resources that will help you plan for expansion and growth in your business and industry. Learn how important it is to take calculated risks. The Managing section also will help you learn how to make good decisions, an essential part of business expansion.

Keep in mind that growth and expansion are not inherently good or desirable; remember your own definition of success. Be realistic and don't spread yourself too thin. If expansion takes you away from the passion and vision of your original dream and you lose control over your business and your life, it may make you richer but also unhappy.

EXIT STRATEGIES TO CONSIDER

Some entrepreneurs start a business believing that they will keep working in it "til death do us part," while others are "serial entrepreneurs." Most businesses do not last forever. In fact, research has shown that entrepreneurs who have a well-planned harvest option are more successful, because they have developed specific goals besides creating a job and a living for themselves. While your business is still growing you will want to begin planning how, if, and when you will move on.

There are many reasons why an entrepreneur decides to harvest the monetary value they have created in their enterprise. The reasons behind selling your business will determine how you approach the task and will also affect your expectations of the transaction. Ideally, you should plan to sell your business three to five years in advance of the actual sale.

Retirement is one reason for selling a business. If that is your reason, you can probably sell at any time over a range of years to choose the best offer available. If you have all your net worth tied up in the business and have become overly cautious, you might lose market share to more aggressive competitors. Then you may feel the need to diversify to prevent the loss of everything you've worked for to date. If you are in poor health, you might have to sell quickly. If you sense your business has reached its summit under your leadership, and needs an infusion of new ideas, skills, or resources to expand, you might decide to sell. Maybe the partner in your business wants to dissolve the partnership, and you need to buy out him or her. If a financial crisis arises, selling quickly at a low price may be the only way for you to avoid losing your entire investment. A death in your family or of a partner might also precipitate selling the business. Or, as stated earlier in the introduction, you may be a serial entrepreneur and feel the need to start a new venture.

ALTERNATIVES TO SELLING

If raising cash is your motive for selling your business, you may elect to sell only a portion of the business to raise some capital and use the cash to strengthen the part you keep. If you are experiencing financial problems, a partner might bring expertise and needed cash into the company.

How can you change the way you're doing business to cut expenses? Compare the costs of selling your business with the costs of keeping going. Even if you get an offer "too good to refuse," you probably want to take a long look at the value of your business and at what your life will be like after the sale. Selling a business is a major life-changing event and should not be rushed.

SELLING STRATEGY FOR YOUR BUSINESS

Just as you needed a plan to start your small business and a plan to grow your business, you need a plan for selling the business and reaping the rewards of your work. Once again you will probably want to put together a team of professionals that includes your attorney, banker, and accountant. You can sell your business yourself, but contracting with a business broker is also a good idea. Legal, tax, ethical, and accounting considerations are all involved in selling a business, plus a savvy broker knows how to reach the business buyer market. A good site to look at before you begin this process is the U.S. Government's Business.gov site at www.business.gov. The last tab on the home page is entitled Getting Out; here you will find articles about all the different ways you can sell your business, as well as an article on valuing your business, finding a buyer, and major issues to consider before deciding to sell your business.

Valuing Your Business

Selling your business will probably be one of the most important things you'll ever do, because unlike most other business decisions you've made, this one you'll only do once. One of the first considerations your new team will have to make is to value something that you have poured years of time, energy, and money into and that may feel like an extension of yourself. Most brokers will talk about "fair market value," which generally means "the highest price the property would bring free of any encumbrances at a fair and voluntary private sale for cash" (*Black's Law Dictionary*). Generally, there are four main methods of valuing a business: cash-flow-based, net assets, multiple earnings, and standard formulas. Cash-Flow-Based information and Net Assets can be found on the financial statements. The Multiple Earnings calculation is based on the price/earnings ratio or P/E ratio, which is more complicated to calculate for a privately held company. Standard formulas have been established for some industry sectors and can be investigated through trade and professional associations. Remember all of these methods are only as good as the information provided. Valuing an ongoing small business is not easy, nor is it an exact science. Entire books have been written on this subject, and one current good title is Wilbur M. Yegge's *A Basic Guide for Valuing a Company*. Yegge uses real-life examples and presents the information on valuing a business in an organized manner.

Yegge, Wilbur M. *A Basic Guide for Valuing a Company*. 2nd ed. John Wiley & Sons, 2002. 294p. ISBN 0-471-15047-9. $24.95.

This down-to-earth guide features an abundance of case studies from real companies, presents common valuation techniques, and describes tips for determining tangible and intangible values. Sample balance sheets and valuation exercises illustrate the author's thoughts about valuation for 10 different types of businesses including small retail stores, a small manufacturer, a wholesaler, and a restaurant. Besides brick-and-mortar companies, approaches to valuing start-up technology firms and dot-com businesses are also discussed. Yegge walks the reader through data collection to arrive at a saleable figure for many types of businesses, including both privately held and publicly traded.

Learn as much as you possibly can about this technical area before you put your business up for sale, and you will be able to make intelligent decisions when you work with a professional or your professional team. A few points to keep in mind when starting to value your business include:

1. Be realistic in setting your price, and don't forget that negotiations will be involved once you have an interested buyer(s).

2. Cash flow is usually more important than profits when valuing a small business.

3. Buyers will consider values other than financial considerations or psychological value versus dollar value.

4. The ownership of a trade secret, proprietary process, or patent may increase the value of a business. License agreements and long-term contracts are also sometimes considered.

5. Sometimes physical location can be an important component of value. High-traffic spots, tourist destinations, and other proximity factors may affect the business value.

6. An intangible known as goodwill is sometimes a key consideration. Reputation or a long-established customer base can be considered part of goodwill. Often the amount paid above the net asset value of a small business is called "goodwill."

The price you settle upon is extremely important, and with so many things to consider in valuing your small business, you may want to find a trained, certified expert. The National Association of Certified Valuation Analysts (NACVA) at www.nacva.com will help you find an expert. The Directory where you can enter a zip code and find an analyst is found under the Resources tab. The website also provides some very basic information on valuation.

■ Present and Prepare Your Business for Sale

Another thing that most small business owners do to present their business for sale is prepare a comprehensive documentation package, sometimes referred to as the "selling prospectus." The selling prospectus allows you to highlight the important features of your business and document its value and your reasons for selling. Included here are the business history, location, operations, employees, financial statements, and competition. Also include in your package a confidentiality statement, justification for your price, and terms of sale.

Because many small business owners operate their business in a way calculated to minimize taxes, you may have taken perks and benefits and plowed profits back into capital improvements in order to keep your profits low. Now you must consider maximizing the company's value. Your accountant can adjust or recast your past income statements to reflect what would have happened if you removed your perks and your family members' salaries, removed non-operating expenses, and removed interest payments on business loans. Your accountant can also adjust your balance sheets to remove assets that won't be sold with the company, value current inventory at current replacement cost, value assets at current fair market value, write off any loans the company made to you, and remove any debt that will not be assumed by the buyer. These changes should be documented on the face of the financial statements so the buyer knows you aren't covering anything up but just clarifying how the financial statements would look with a new owner. Your accountant should then prepare projected financial statements for the next five years with reasonable assumptions about future growth or decline in income, expenses, etc. using trends established in the past several years. For articles and information on selling your business and working with an accountant, try the StartupJournal.com published by the *Wall Street Journal* at www.startupjournal.com/runbusiness/selling. Covering most of the exit strategies, articles are updated continually and the Running a Business section is easily searchable.

Besides the documentation package, you should also prepare your business for sale. Reduce discretionary expenditures such as travel and entertainment; maintain your property and business assets including machinery, office equipment, etc.; improve your cash flow if possible; and maintain good relations with suppliers and customers.

MERGERS AND ACQUISITIONS

If you can't or don't want to sell your business to another small business owner, sometimes you can transfer ownership to another business in a merger or acquisition. Mergers usually involve two similar-sized firms, while acquisitions involve larger firms taking over smaller businesses. Another business might buy your business in order to reduce their cost per unit, increase their market share,

Figure 13.1 Screenshot of Startup Journal: Selling Your Business (www.startup journal.com/runbusiness/selling)

decrease competition, acquire new technology or new customers, acquire a unique distribution channel, or increase their presence in your location. When two companies combine or merge, sometimes current management is allowed to stay on to help run the new company either permanently or for a limited amount of time; but mergers involve new partners or bosses, and the former owner may have less control.

Mergers and acquisitions are very complex transactions. If you have no experience with them, enlist experienced legal and financial professionals to help you with this type of transaction. If neither of the two companies is publicly held, the complexity is further complicated. Be particularly aware of what method is used to value your business, how payment is to be structured, and what your relationship will be to the new company.

For excellent articles and advice on mergers and business valuation, check out the Small Business Notes website at www.smallbusinessnotes.com.

EMPLOYEE STOCK OWNERSHIP PLANS (ESOPs)

ESOPs are a vehicle for owners to realize some liquidity through sale of their stock to the plan and employees. Because an ESOP creates ownership of stock among employees, it can be seen as a positive motivational device for the company, too. The owner may or may not exit the company but in either case he or she is able to obtain a considerable amount of money. ESOPs were originally created to provide retirement benefits for employees, but many are now used to help current owners harvest capital or increase their cash flow.

ESOPs are designed to allow employees invest in their company's stock. The U.S. government encourages this by providing significant tax advantages for ESOPs. An ESOP covers all employees, and the company needs to disclose a great deal of confidential information. Because of the many legal and tax implications, be sure to seek legal and financial professional advice when considering an ESOP. For more information on ESOPs, check out the website of the National Center for Employee Ownership at www.nceo.org.

CLOSING

Under some circumstances, it is best to simply sell your inventory and fixtures, pay your creditors and any employees, close the door, and walk away. If your business is failing, isn't valuable enough to invite a merger or acquisition, or depends on you personally for success, closing may be the best choice. Depending on your financial circumstances, filing for voluntary liquidation or declaring bankruptcy is also an option. Bankruptcy is supposed to give you a second chance, but it may result in the end of your business. Read the Schollanders's book before you take any steps toward bankruptcy.

Schollander, Wendell and Schollander, Wes. *The Small Business Owner's Guide to Bankruptcy: Know Your Legal Rights, Recover from Mistakes, and Start Over Successfully.* 226p. ISBN 1-57248-219-2. $21.95.

These two bankruptcy lawyers want to help small business owners avoid the mistakes that can cost them their business and other property. Learn how to use the system to solve your money problems and help you to recover financially. Read about the myths of debt and bankruptcy and what mistakes to avoid in operating your business in bad times. Discover the ins and outs of a financial inventory, the alternatives to bankruptcy, and how to create a personal and business budget. One section also covers rebuilding your credit. Read this book before your business is in serious financial trouble.

Legislation passed by Congress in 2005 has changed the rules of filing for bankruptcy so be sure to get current information from a lawyer or counseling service.

INITIAL PUBLIC OFFERING (IPO)

Few small firms ever qualify for an IPO, because they are too small, too limited in their potential, or in an industry that doesn't attract investor interest. An IPO is also expensive and involves close public scrutiny of all the firm's operations. The advantage of an IPO is the higher price the entrepreneur will obtain for the business through this means. Opportunities to reap large harvests for a small business through an IPO occur very infrequently.

FAMILY SUCCESSION

When the small business is the main component of family wealth, the desire to perpetuate it in one form or another is strong. However, the paramount management challenge may be an orderly succession to family members. Issues involved include business legalities, family dynamics, tax considerations, and estate issues. If you perceive the succession of ownership as a process, not an event, it will ease the course of the change. This process requires planning, teamwork and compromise, and constant re-evaluation. If you don't plan the succession, it may be done in a crisis with many unintended consequences. The following book, *Family Business Succession*, can help you plan and implement a successful family succession, passing assets and power on smoothly and efficiently.

Aronoff, Craig E. and Ward, John L. *Family Business Succession: The Final Test of Greatness*. 2nd ed. Business Owner Resources, 2003. 74p. ISBN 1-891-65209-5. $18.95.

Learn how good succession management is like good strategic planning, and how to divide succession planning into manageable pieces. The authors identify different types of leadership transitions, how to prepare the family for a successful transition, how to develop outstanding successors, and how to implement succession. Post-succession mistakes and problems are also discussed. Real-life case studies and practical tips are also provided. If you're planning to have a family member succeed you in your small business, this book will help you work through the process smoothly.

RETIREMENT

The most important keys to a happy retirement are financial security, good health, and physical and mental activities that interest you. You'll have more time to do the things you enjoy most. Before you decide how to spend your retirement, it must be funded. As in every other step of business, retirement should be planned. The earlier you start planning and saving money, the better off you'll be when the time to retire comes. And, of course, the best way to accumulate funds is through a steady process of saving that starts early. *Ernst & Young's Retirement Planning Guide* is a classic source often used to help small business owners put together a thoughtful, practical plan as well as finding a suitable investment vehicle.

> Kavouras, Freida, Nissenbaum, Martin, Pape, Glenn N., Ratner, Charles L., Rouse, Kenneth R., Voss, David C., Wiley, Patricia A., and Arnone, William J. *Ernst & Young's Retirement Planning Guide.* 3rd ed. John Wiley & Sons, Inc., 2001. 320p. ISBN 0-471-08338-0. $19.95.

> Though slightly dated, this classic is still a good guide to planning your retirement no matter what stage of life you are in currently. Use the Economic Growth and Tax Relief Reconciliation Act of 2001 to your advantage in retirement planning. Highlighted here are important financial and personal issues you should consider during your pre-retirement and retirement years. Worksheets, tips, and action items as well as additional resources including websites are provided. Easy-to-understand charts and tables present practical ideas clearly. Remember that failure to plan often means planning to fail.

In sum, a well-thought-out plan for exiting a business is just as important as the planning required when starting a business. Save time, money, and frustration by putting together a good exit strategy. The resources below will help you prepare and develop different contingency plans for whatever stage of your business life you are in today.

REFERENCES

(Starred titles discussed in the chapter)

▦ Print Resources

American Bar Association. *Legal Guide for Small Business.* Three Rivers Press, 2000. 523p. ISBN 0-8129-3015-0. $17.00.

This handy guide will help small businesses understand their legal responsibilities and options. It thoroughly covers the legal aspects of topics such as employees, franchising, contracts, taxes, and start-up basics. One section covers Various Endings and financial difficulties, selling a business, retirement planning, and family succession. Getting help and choosing a lawyer are also useful chapters. Contract law is covered as well as protecting your intellectual property rights.

**Aronoff, Craig E. and Ward, John L. *Family Business Succession: The Final Test of Greatness.* 2nd ed. Business Owner Resources, 2003. 74p. ISBN 1-891-65209-5. $18.95.

Learn how good succession management is like good strategic planning, and how to divide succession planning into manageable pieces. The authors identify different types of leadership transitions, how to prepare the family for a successful transition, how to develop outstanding successors, and how to implement succession. Post-succession mistakes and problems are discussed. Real-life case studies and practical tips are also provided. If you're planning to have a family member succeed you in your small business, this book will help you work through the process smoothly.

**Bangs, David H. and Pinson, Linda. *The Real World Entrepreneur Field Guide: Growing Your Own Business*. Dearborn Financial Publishing, 1999. 652p. ISBN 1-57-41011-3-7. $59.95.

Learn how 10 successful entrepreneurs from all around the United States started and grew their small businesses. Discussed here are feasibility, business plans, cash management, websites, legalities, finding and keep good employees, planning and managing growth, and especially important the real-life case studies. Learn how to select opportunities that your business should pursue and learn to develop sustainable competencies for your business. Bangs and Pinson discuss a planning model that includes an environmental analysis and an internal analysis to help select the best growth opportunities for your particular situation.

Bromage, Neil. *100 Ways to Business Success: A Resource Book for Small Business Managers*. 2nd ed. How to Books, 2005. 222p. ISBN 1-84528-017-2. $19.00.

This slim volume covers the basics of running and growing a small business. Learn how to manage yourself as well as your employees, to promote yourself and the business, to use the Internet, and to succeed in managing a growing enterprise. Get advice to help you face and master the challenges of every day in the business world. Discover how to manage effectively and efficiently.

Cohn, Mike and Pearl, Jayne. *Keep or Sell Your Business: How to Make the Decision Every Private Company Faces*. Dearborn Trade, 2000. 320p. ISBN 1-57410-139-0. $22.95.

Understand all your options as well as the practical and personal repercussions of your decision when considering whether to sell your business. Walk through the detailed steps in analyzing the status of your company, examine the opportunities to sell, and consider the benefits of keeping your company. Identify your company's strengths and weaknesses and its resources. Tips on preparing a business for sale and negotiating the deal are also given. Learn how to manage your wealth after the business is sold too.

Crosier, Louis P. *Selling Your Business: The Transition from Entrepreneur to Investor*. John Wiley & Sons, Inc., 2004. 336p. ISBN 0-471-67426-5. $39.95.

Crosier and his contributors describe the issues a business owner should consider prior to an IPO or sale. Written concisely and in layman's language, this handbook will help you avoid costly mistakes. Topics discussed cover the psychology of wealth, selecting investment managers, asset allocation, global investing, and philanthropy.

Feldman, Stanley J., Sullivan, Timothy G. and Winsby, Roger M. *What Every Business Owner Should Know about Valuing Their Business*. McGraw-Hill, 2002. 272p. ISBN 0-071-40992-0. $21.95.

A collection of case studies demonstrate valuations for a variety of industries, variables, and situations. Specific types of businesses used as illustrations include an insurance agency, an environmental consulting business, and a metal fabrication company. Each case study includes a current tax return for the business involved. Explanations of valuation basics, cost of valuation, and legal and accounting aspects necessary to a fair valuation are provided. An excellent discussion of the implications of different business structures including C corporations, S corporations, and partnerships is included.

Frisch, Robert A. *ESOP: The Ultimate Instrument in Succession Planning.* 2nd ed. 400p. John Wiley & Sons, Ltd., 2001. ISBN 0-471-43444-2. $69.56.

This comprehensive guide focuses on how ESOPs work, the rules that govern them, and in what situations they can be applied. Frisch explains how ESOPs can cost-effectively help small businesses meet their most basic financial and cash flow needs. Readers will find explanations of the latest IRS rules pertaining to ESOPs, strategies for using the ESOP as a tool in succession planning, and explanations on how to design an ESOP that motivates, retains, and recruits employees. Concisely and plainly written, readers will learn how to use ESOPs as a versatile financial tool to benefit their business and their employees.

Gabehart, Scott and Brinkley, Richard N. *The Business Valuation Book: Proven Strategies for Measuring a Company's Value.* AMACOM, 2002. 350p. ISBN 0-8144-0642-4. $39.95.

This volume helps demystify the business valuation process so that business persons can understand and use their practical approach to valuation. If you want to quickly estimate the fair market value of a small business or want to try to rigorously assess your own or another small business, this book will help. The accompanying CD-ROM contains several calculation tools, questionnaires, rules of thumb, and SBA guidelines.

Gabriell, Colin. *How to Sell Your Business—And Get What You Want!* Gwent Press, 1998. 256p. ISBN 0-965-6578-3-3. $24.95.

Learn when to get professional assistance, how to avoid mistakes, and what to be concerned about when you sell your business. Several of the 57 case studies concern sellers who stayed with their company after it was sold and if that is your situation, you will want to read this book. Individual chapters discuss different aspects of the sale process including preparation, valuation, brokers, negotiation, letters of intent, and more. An important section gives advice on how to react if the buyer wants a lower price.

Gottry, Steve. *Common Sense Business: Starting, Operating, and Growing Your Small Business—In Any Economy!* HarperBusiness, 2005. 368p. ISBN 0-06-077838-5. $19.95.

Gottry started and ran a large Minneapolis-based ad agency and video production firm, which failed after 22 years in business. You can learn from his mistakes. Well organized and clearly written, Gottry includes specific how-to's such as ways to prioritize bills for payment when cash flow is limited. He explains how to find solutions to the questions and challenges you're facing daily. Learn how to begin to understand yourself, your employees, your vendors, and your customers. Using humor, Gottry will help you successfully manage your business through good times and bad.

**Hansen, Jeffrey A. *Mastering Business Growth and Change Made Easy* (Entrepreneur Made Easy Series). Entrepreneur Press, 2005. 262p. ISBN 1-93-25316-45. $19.95.

Use this resource to learn how to grow your business at every stage, in any environment in which you find yourself. Hansen helps you look at the full life cycle of your business with self-assessment worksheets. Evaluate the different stages of your business as it grows. Learn how to strategize solutions to any challenge you and your business encounter.

Herman, Deborah Levine and Bodford, Robin L. *Fresh Start Bankruptcy: A Simplified Guide for Individuals and Entrepreneurs*. John Wiley & Sons, Ltd., 2003. 224p. ISBN 0-471-26313-3. $24.95.

This user-friendly guide leads you step-by-step through the bankruptcy filing process and supplies advice to help you survive the ordeal. Herman and Bodford, both attorneys, help you decide if you need legal counsel and provide guidance if you decide to go forward on your own. Learn how to protect your assets, deal with creditors, navigate bankruptcy court, and repair your credit. Millions of people have gone through this process and have come out with more financial savvy and learned how to start over.

Horn, Thomas W. *Unlocking the Value of Your Business: How to Increase It, Measure It, and Negotiate an Actual Sale Price—in Easy Step-by-Step Terms*. Charter Oak Press, 1999. 273p. ISBN 0-8752-1016-3. $39.95.

Often a good way to really examine how your business is doing is to analyze it as a potential buyer would. Horn explains in simple, everyday language how to calculate the value of your business and how to maximize its market value. Practical advice on negotiating the acquisition contract and how to prepare and present your business to potential buyers is included. Horn clearly presents "tried-and-true" formulas for valuing your business.

**Kavouras, Freida, Nissenbaum, Martin, Pape, Glenn N., Ratner, Charles L., Rouse, Kenneth R., Voss, David C., Wiley, Patricia A., and Arnone, William J. *Ernst & Young's Retirement Planning Guide*. 3rd ed. John Wiley & Sons, Inc., 2001. 320p. ISBN 0-471-08338-0. $19.95.

Though slightly dated, this classic is still a good guide to planning your retirement no matter what stage of life you are in currently. Use the Economic Growth and Tax Relief Reconciliation Act of 2001 to your advantage in retirement planning. Highlighted here are important financial and personal issues you should consider during your pre-retirement and retirement years. Worksheets, tips, and action items as well as additional resources including websites are provided. Easy-to-understand charts and tables present practical ideas clearly. If you're planning to retire early or if you're already retired, this handbook will help you enjoy your golden years.

Klueger, Robert F. *Buying and Selling a Business*. 2nd ed. John Wiley & Sons, Inc., 2004. 249p. ISBN 0-471-65702-6. $16.95.

Learn how to evaluate a business by analyzing financial statements. This step-by-step guide will help readers understand what buyers are looking for and what sellers need to tell prospective buyers and how to present it. Discover tips on negotiating for price, timing, stock and asset agreements, and noncompetitive agreements. The new chapter on LLCs is particularly informative. New tax law changes are also covered.

Little, Steven S. *The 7 Irrefutable Rules of Small Business Growth*. John Wiley & Sons, 2005. 256p. ISBN 0-471-70760-0. $18.95.

Find out Little's real and powerful principles for helping a small business expand and develop new business. Little acknowledges the difficulties small businesses have in today's global economy where competition comes from the Internet as well as the business down the street. Learn more about topics such as technology, planning, hiring and firing, and globalization as they relate to small business today. An entire chapter is devoted to each of his seven rules. For example, he explains why it is essential to have a thorough understanding of the marketplace, why processes must be customer-driven, and how to attract and keep the best and brightest. Practical solutions and strategies are presented to achieve and sustain a competitive advantage. Simply but effectively written, Little teaches entrepreneurs to have a realistic view of the marketplace and their place in it.

McKinney, Anne. *Real Business Plans and Marketing Tools: Including Samples to Use in Starting, Growing, Marketing, and Selling Your Business*. PREP Publishing, 2003. 224p. ISBN 1-885288-36-0. $24.95.

Designed to help entrepreneurs prepare paperwork relating to starting, growing, marketing, and selling a business, McKinney presents real business plans for 17 different types of businesses including a hair salon, brew pub, auto body shop, home-based wholesale company, and janitorial supply company, for example. Readers will also find samples of financial statements and other documents used to obtain bank loans and equity financing. This title will help new business owners in their strategic planning and guide them through the process of selling their business as well.

Minor, Ned. *Deciding to Sell Your Business*. Business Enterprise Press, 2003. 322p. ISBN 0-9655731-8-4. $17.95.

Minor walks entrepreneurs through the process of deciding to sell their business. Having worked with many business owners in his 25-year career, he synthesizes their mistakes and successes into this essential guide to help owners through the process with less stress and avoiding mistakes.

Nottonson, Ira N. *Ultimate Guide to Buying or Selling Your Business*. Entrepreneur Press, 2004. 304p. ISBN 1-932531-20-3. $23.95.

Successful negotiators understand the perspective and negotiating position of everyone at the table. In a straightforward manner, Nottonson shares the concerns of all parties including buyer, seller, accountant, lawyer, broker, and lender. Understanding the concerns of all parties will equal a negotiating advantage. The valuation concept presented is easy to understand and use. Worksheets to analyze and assess your talents and needs are included. Family succession planning issues are also discussed. Forms and sample contracts clarify business transfer concepts. Use this well-written, concise guide to help you sell your business.

Robb, Russell. *Selling Your Business: How to Attract Buyers and Achieve the Maximum Value for Your Business*. Adams Media Corp. 2002. 384p. ISBN 1-580-6260-2-5. $19.95.

No matter why you are selling your business, it is a complex often emotional decision. Robb explains how to determine the best time to sell, common and costly mistakes sellers make, assembling an advisory team, and dealing with contracts and sales and purchase agreements. The section on Understand the Financials is particularly well done, covering business valuation methods, unsatisfactory credit reports, setting the price for the business, and tax ramifications. Learn negotiating techniques, quick-close tactics, and ways to resolve impasses. This comprehensive work will help you sell your small business.

Rodrick, Scott S. and Rosen, Corey. *Leveraged ESOPs and Employee Buyouts*. 4th ed. National Center for Employee Ownership, 2001. 264p. ISBN 0-926902-75-X. $35.00.

The National Center for Employee Ownership (NCEO) is a nonprofit membership and research organization, serving as the leading source of accurate, unbiased information on ESOPs. This title is a guide to the complex issues involved in setting up and using an ESOP for a leveraged buyout. ESOPs provide new capital and a tax-advantaged employee benefit, which may help your company's cash flow and help you retain employees. Learn about contribution limits, valuation issues, and employee buyouts in plain English. Included are changes in ESOP rules brought about by the Economic Growth and Tax Relief Reconciliation Act of 2001.

Sampson, John E. *How to Sell Your Business: And Get the Best Price for It.* Beaver's Pond Press, 2003. 212p. ISBN 1-59298-000-7. $24.95.

This road map leads a business owner through the process of selling a business from preparing the business for sale through the negotiations and closing. Suggestions, insights, and techniques cover everything from when and how to tell employees about a forthcoming sale, through the related legal documents, and what the definitive sale agreement must include and why. Find out about legal representations and warranties, earn-outs, and how to handle the transition after the sale. Use this book to prepare you for the selling process.

**Schollander, Wendell and Schollander, Wes. *The Small Business Owner's Guide to Bankruptcy: Know Your Legal Rights, Recover from Mistakes, and Start Over Successfully.* 226p. ISBN 1-57248-219-2. $21.95.

These two bankruptcy lawyers want to help small business owners avoid the mistakes that can cost them their business and other property. Learn how to use the system to solve your money problems and help you to recover financially. Read about the myths of debt and bankruptcy, and what mistakes to avoid in operating your business in bad times. Discover the ins and outs of a financial inventory, how to analyze business debts and assets, the alternatives to bankruptcy, and how to create a personal and business budget. Understand the various types of bankruptcy and filing steps for Chapter 7, Chapter 11, and Chapter 13. If you have to file for bankruptcy, one section also covers post-filing issues and another rebuilding your credit. Read this book before your business is in serious financial trouble.

Simmons, Chad. *Business Valuation Bluebook: How Successful Entrepreneurs Price, Sell, and Trade Businesses.* 3rd ed. Corinth Press, 2005. 244p. ISBN 1-889150-47-9. $24.95.

Tools provided here include valuation techniques to determine a fair market value price, sellers' techniques to negotiate from strength, buyers' tactics to pay less, and more. A business valuation expert for over 20 years, Simmons presents the information on valuing a business in an organized, logical manner. Learn about trading businesses and how to defer capital gains taxes. Useful valuation models also included.

Sperry, Paul and Mitchell, Beatrice H. *The Complete Guide to Selling Your Business.* 2nd ed. Kogan Page, Ltd., 1999. 146p. ISBN 0-7494-2904-6. $24.95.

This guide to the complicated process of selling a business uses a case study to illustrate important concepts. Samples of a confidentiality agreement and a letter of intent are included. Learn how to determine when the time is right to sell from both a financial and personal point of view.

Steingold, Fred S. *Sell Your Business: Step-by-Step Legal Guide.* Nolo Press, 2004. 320p. ISBN 1-4133-0018-9. $49.99 with CD-ROM.

This overview of the sales process covers all the key concerns including price and payment terms, liability protection, restrictions on future competition, etc. Specific advice is presented on the tax consequences of selling a business, how to set a realistic price, how to create a marketing plan to attract buyers, how to investigate prospective buyers, and how to create sales agreements, consulting agreements, promissory notes, and confidentiality letters. Each chapter is complete with checklists and a list of tasks to accomplish. Forms and instructions are presented on the CD-ROM. Steingold, an attorney and prolific author, presents the material in a well-organized, concise manner.

Thaler, John. *The Elements of Small Business: A Lay Person's Guide to the Financial Terms, Marketing Concepts, and Legal Forms That Every Entrepreneur Needs*. Silver Lake Publishing, 2005. 354p. ISBN 1-56343-784-4. $24.95.

Specializing in small business law, this lawyer and small business owner presents tools, tips, and advice to help you get your business off to a smooth and legal start. Chapters are thorough and cover topics like Business Formation, Insurance, Computers and E-Commerce, Marriage and Divorce, Retirement Planning, and Exit Strategies. Each chapter concludes with a list of resources. Over 20 appendices provide forms and sample reports such as registration for a fictitious business name, operating agreement for an LLC, financial statements, etc. This well-written book will help more entrepreneurs.

Timmons, Jeffrey, Spinelli, Stephen and Zacharakis, Andrew. *How to Raise Capital: Techniques and Strategies for Financing and Valuing Your Small Business*. McGraw-Hill, 2005. 245p. ISBN 0-07-141288-3. $16.95.

The authors identify the financial life cycles of new ventures, provide entrepreneurs with a framework for financial strategies, and illustrate the investor's perspective when considering investing in a new venture. Entrepreneurs will learn how to find, contact, and work with funding sources from SBA lenders to venture capitalists. Besides learning the ins and outs of obtaining debt capital, entrepreneurs will learn how to manage debt. Also highlighted are key mistakes that defeat small businesses. Learn how to value your business throughout its history, and learn about harvesting options. The authors present many real-life examples of entrepreneurial success and failure. Learn how to finance your idea and create the financial foundations necessary for long-term success. This outstanding reference is useful for all new ventures needing financing.

Tuttle, Samuel S. *Small Business Primer: How to Buy, Sell and Evaluate a Business*. Streetsmartbooks LLC, 2002. 256p. ISBN 0-9709-4660-0. $95.00.

Written for the general reader, this valuable handbook teaches readers how to calculate and understand the value of any business. Tips, techniques, and strategies on improving your negotiating and decision-making skills and saving money are provided. Tuttle dispenses financial wisdom about assessment, acquisition, and profitable disposal of any business, no matter its size or complexity.

The Ultimate Small Business Guide: a Resource for Startups and Growing Businesses. Basic Books, 2004. 501p. ISBN 0-7382-0913-9. $19.95.

This large collection of how-to's, step-by-step objective lists, and enlightening FAQs covers all aspects of planning, launching, managing, and growing your small business. Sections cover Refining and Protecting Your Idea, Communicating with Your Customers,

Selling Online, and Managing Yourself and Others. Financing, pricing, cash flow, ratios, and assets are thoroughly and carefully covered in a section called Figuring It Out. An excellent section on Growing Your Business talks about SWOT analysis, understanding the effects of growth plus exporting and importing issues for expanding outside the country. The last section on Dignified Retreats will help you develop exit strategies that work for you and your business.

Van Horn, Mike. *How to Grow Your Business Without Driving Yourself Crazy: Tools to Tackle Barriers to Growth, Profitability, and Ease.* The Business Group, 2002. 279p. ISBN 0-9714114-2-5. $19.95.

In a very informal, natural style, Van Horn provides charts, tips, tables, and advice as well as humorous drawings designed to help entrepreneurs and small business managers avoid common mistakes and pitfalls. Learn how to solve problems, develop a plan of action, and stay on track. Practical, clear questions are asked that the small business owner/manager needs to ask himself or herself in order to grow and move ahead. Discover how to get more done efficiently and have time for a life outside the business.

Walters, Jamie S. *Big Vision, Small Business: 4 Keys to Success Without Growing Big.* Berrett-Koehler Pub., Inc., 2002. 200p. ISBN 1-57675-188-0. $17.95.

Walters demonstrates that a small business can stay small, remain healthy, and have a big vision. Entrepreneurs will learn here about principles of visioning, communication skills, expectations of customers and employees, and how to overcome obstacles involving money, risk, and competition. Each chapter builds on what you learn in the previous one to construct a total picture of your small business and where it is headed. If you want to create and maintain a small business with a social conscience and integrity, Walters will help you learn the basics.

Ward, John L. *Perpetuating the Family Business: 50 Lessons Learned from Long Lasting, Successful Families in Business.* Palgrave Macmillan, 2004. 256p. ISBN 1-4039-3397-9. $29.95.

Ward, an international expert on family business, draws the best practices from some of the most successful family businesses such as Ford Motors and Marriott Hotels. He has developed a framework of five insights and four principles in which to place his 50 "lessons learned" for business longevity. Tools and checklists are included to help readers apply these best practices to their own family businesses.

West, Tom. *The Business Reference Guide.* Business Brokerage Press, 2004. 14th ed. 767p. ISBN 0-97-4851-80-9. $92.00.

Loaded with information, this superb guide provides pricing guidelines, expanded industry trend information, and extensive benchmarking data for business expenses including rent, labor costs, sales per square foot, etc. The detailed table of contents and lengthy index enables users to find specific information quickly and easily. The Industry Expert Listing is a unique highlight of West's new edition.

**Yegge, Wilbur M. *A Basic Guide for Valuing a Company.* 2nd ed. John Wiley & Sons, Inc., 2002. 294p. ISBN 0-471-15047-9. $24.95.

This down-to-earth guide features an abundance of case studies from real companies, presents common valuation techniques, and describes tips for determining tangible and intangible values. Sample balance sheets and valuation exercises illustrate the author's thoughts about valuation for 10 different types of businesses including small retail stores, a small manufacturer, a wholesaler, and a restaurant. Besides brick-and-mortar companies, approaches to valuing start-up technology firms and dot-com businesses are also discussed. Yegge walks the reader through data collection to arrive at a saleable figure for many types of businesses, both privately held and publicly traded.

Online Resources

American Express Business: http://www133.americanexpress.com/osbn/Landing/ informyourdecisions.asp?us_nu=subtab (Accessed Fall 2005).

Small business owners will find help here on management, finding money, and marketing. This outstanding site has information on managing debt, business plans, fraud protection, and SBA loans. The article under Financial Management entitled Business Valuation Methods explains the various common methods used to come up with a value for a small business. The Starting a Business section also tells users about structuring their business as well as some information on types of insurance.

BizBuySell: www.bizbuysell.com (Accessed Fall 2005).

This very useful, practical website not only lets you list your business for sale on the Internet, but provides a wealth of articles on valuing and selling a business. The Common Questions and Answers covers items such as seller financing, how you can help your business sell, and what business brokers really do. Business brokers can be located from the site. Under Seller Resources, you'll find the fundamentals of selling a business as well as Valuation and Financing. Of course, you can search for a business to buy here as well.

BizQuest: www.bizquest.com (Accessed Fall 2005).

Billing itself as A Business For Sale Marketplace, this site lists businesses for sale and includes resources for buying or selling your business online. Users can search for businesses by industry or location or for a franchise for sale. A fee is charged for listing a business for sale. Under Tools and Resources, free information and links to free information are provided.

**Business.gov: www.business.gov (Accessed Fall 2005).

Another government site developed to help businesses find the information they need and want. Under Growing, users will find many resources that will help you plan for expansion and growth in your business and industry. Learn how important it is to take calculated risks. Under Getting Out, the entrepreneur will find guidance in the planning of how to get out of business; sections cover Transfer Ownership, Liquidate Assets, and File Bankruptcy. Links to information on major industries, population and demographic resources, plus Rural America Facts provide users with a multitude of useful resources. International trade connections are useful for global or Internet businesses, too. Major categories include Laws & Regulations, Buying & Selling, Financial Assistance, Taxes, etc. Also find workplace issue information on interviewing, working environments, training, hiring procedures, and employing minors. The Site Map works like a Table of Contents and gets you where you want to go quickly and easily.

BusinessKnow-How.com: www.businessknowhow.com (Accessed Fall 2005).

This large site has an abundance of articles on starting and managing a small business. A large department is titled Growth and Leadership, and it covers many issues involved in business growth and individual management skills development. Find advice on ways to expand your business incrementally and safely. Different areas cover incorporating online, business loans, human resources training and tools, and web design and tools. Users will find many articles on job descriptions, cash management and accounting, a breakeven calculator, and a job or product pricing system. Franchising and marketing strategies are also covered. Find basic business information here on a wide range of topics.

Business Owners Idea Café: www.businessownersideacafe.com (Accessed Fall 2005).

Developed by successful entrepreneurs and authors of published guides on starting a business, the large site presents short articles on all aspects of small business or entrepreneurial life. The main divisions include CyberSchmooz, Starting Your Biz, Running Your Biz, Take Out Info, Classifieds, The "You" in Your Biz, De-Stress and Have Fun, About Idea Café, and Join Idea Café. Here you can find experts to answer your questions or discuss your current business crisis. You'll find sample business plans, financing help, business forms, and business news. In the Running Your Biz section, you'll find the Managing part where there are articles about Business Services, Marketing and Sales, Running a Business, and Worldwide Business Information. Everything involved in growing and operating a growing business is discussed. A search engine takes you to relevant articles that may be of interest.

Business Owner's Toolkit: csi.toolkit.cch.com (Accessed Fall 2005).

Commerce Clearinghouse's Small Business Guide provides pages of information and tools to help individuals start, run, and grow a successful small business. Business Tools provided include sample letters, contracts, forms, and agreements ready for you to customize for your business and use. Several good articles on the fine points of selling your business including recasting your financial statements are included. An article called Valuation of Small Business is also quite thorough. Financial spreadsheet templates are available as well as checklists to help you stay organized in completing necessary tasks. IRS tax forms, state tax forms, employee management forms, and more are all linked to this site. Also find articles on how tax law changes could affect your business.

BusinessTown.com: www.businesstown.com (Accessed Fall 2005).

This large business information site has sections on Managing a Business, Home Businesses, Internet businesses, Accounting, Selling a Business, and more. The articles are not lengthy but quite thoroughly cover their subject. In the section Managing Fast Growth, you will find a variety of articles covering many areas of concern when a small business is growing and expanding, such as hiring good employees, finding new locations or larger facilities, and Adams Rules for Small Business Success, which present tried and true ways to run a profitable business. Under Selling a Business and Valuing a Business are several good articles about calculating the prices, getting the most value, finding buyers, and more. Log on to this useful and not too commercial site, to help you in any area where you need more information.

Entrepreneur's Guidebook Series: www.smbtn.com/businessplanguides/ (Accessed Fall 2005).

Defining real entrepreneurs as managers who adopt key behaviors developed by understanding key market concepts and theories and who are successful because of their planning and researching skills, this site covers a wide variety of subjects in its Small Business Plan Guides. Here you find a lengthy article on determining the proper valuation for a business; readers are walked through how financial statements are used to determine fair market value. Rule of thumb formulas are also presented for various specific types of businesses. Explore this website for more good ideas.

FindLaw for Small Business: smallbusiness.findlaw.com (Accessed Fall 2005).

Chock full of articles and guides on all aspects of business development, the Closing a Business section discusses the closing of businesses with all types of business structures. FAQs and forms involved in closing a business are provided. Articles discuss lawsuits after you close your business, options to closing, and more. Legal information on business structure, finance, and intellectual property is also covered thoroughly. Information on a wide variety of small business legal issues is covered including forms and contracts and starting a business. Tax issues are also covered including help in preparing for an audit. A directory of lawyers by zip code is also available. Links to relevant regulatory agencies are also provided.

MergerNetwork: www.mergernetwork.com (Accessed Fall 2005).

This large site helps facilitate the search for a business to buy. Users can search MergerNetwork's database of Businesses for Sale or create a Business Wanted ad. Basic membership is free at this time. You can browse businesses by location, size, relocation capability, franchises for sale, industry, and size. Their partner site, SellerWorks at www.sellerworks.com, provides listings for sellers of businesses. Business for Sale ads are free or a featured ad is available for $1.00 per day.

**National Association of Certified Valuation Analysts (NACVA): www.nacva.com (Accessed Fall 2005).

The NACVA will help you find a trained, credentialed expert to help you place a value on your business. Under the Resources tab, you will find a directory that you can search by industry and zip code or just zip code to locate a professional in your area. Some PDF forms and informational publications are available also, such as the IRS Business Valuation Guidelines.

**National Center for Employee Ownership (NCEO): www.nceo.org (Accessed Fall 2005).

The NCEO, a private, nonprofit membership and research organization, has a large site with many articles on Employee Stock Ownership Plans. Hot issues such as legislation and Securities and Exchange Commission decisions are presented and discussed. Articles cover steps to setting up, a history of the ESOP, selling a closely held business to an ESOP, and ESOP Distribution and Diversification Rules. Links to ESOP Books, ESOP Seminars and Webinars, and ESOP consulting are also provided. A Reference Desk provides basic information and statistics. Use this site to learn more about ESOPs.

PowerHomeBiz.com: www.powerhomebiz.com/financing (Accessed Fall 2005).

This large small business site has an outstanding Guide to Managing and Growing a Business. Featured articles include Growing Your Business, Developing Strategic Alliances, and Managing Customers. Must-Have Books are listed with some articles and Recommended Tools and Software as well. Recommended Magazines include several small business classics. This established, well-organized site will help new entrepreneurs with growing, financing, managing, and other parts of starting a new business or expanding one. Frequently updated, frequent visitors will identify trends in small and home-based businesses.

Small Business Administration: www.sba.gov (Accessed Fall 2005).

This official government site offers a wealth of resources and programs for starting and growing a small business. Under Growing and Managing Your Business, you will find advice and articles on managing for growth, forecasting the future, sharpening your management skills, and managing employees. Here you will also find Leadership Topics and a vital area for growing businesses is Leading Change. Financing Topics cover Capital for Growth and Borrowing Money. Strategic Planning articles explain how to match the strengths of your business to available new opportunities. Other major sections cover business planning, financing, managing, marketing, employees, taxes, legal aspects, and business opportunities. Find here online forms, business plans, loan information, and many publications. Some contents are available in Spanish.

Small Business Notes: www.smallbusinessnotes.com (Accessed Fall 2005).

Here you will find articles on starting or buying your first business as well as merging, planning, management, and legal issues. Explore articles on business incubators as well as marketing and choosing a business name. Basic articles contain links to fuller explanatory articles on a wide variety of topics like business models, recordkeeping, etc. The articles on Why Merge and Merge Wisely are enlightening and provide the owner with information and food for thought when considering a merger. Common business valuation methods are also discussed. A useful site for many topics related to small business and entrepreneurship come here for answers to basic and more complex questions.

**_Wall Street Journal_ Center for Entrepreneurs: www.startupjournal.com/ (Accessed Fall 2005).

WSJ's Startup Journal is an authoritative site that has a section entitled How-To and entrepreneurs will find there a great deal of help deciding if they are entrepreneurs, how to get started in business, and finally how to prepare for leaving your business. Collected here are many articles about different aspects of selling your business. Learn how to get top dollar when you sell, how to prepare for a death in the business, and how to prepare and approach retirement. Articles on important issues such as Should You Hire an Accountant will also get entrepreneurs off on the right foot and continue to use the financial statements an accountant prepares when you sell your business. Continually updated and well written, this site is useful to all entrepreneurs.

**Yahoo! Business and Economy: dir.yahoo.com/Business_and_Economy/ (Accessed Fall 2005).

Especially important categories are organizations, e-commerce, software, and use tax issues. This large site includes a wealth of information with good international coverage on a wide variety of topics. Besides articles, links to a wide range of sites covering issues and advice on finances, interactive tools and services, industry trends, tips on managing a growing business, and how to obtain new products or services. Under organizations, users will find listings for trade associations in nearly every industry. Under its small business site (smallbusiness.yahoo.com/) the e-commerce section covers online shopping centers, privacy seal programs, and digital money. For industries it covers manufacturing as well as the retail industry. Check this site for current, accurate business information.

GLOSSARY

The glossary lists only terms used in this book that may be new or used in a new way to readers. A larger and more complete small business dictionary is available on the web at www.small-business-dictionary.org.

Advertising: paid communication about a product or service through various media.

Angel investor: high-net-worth individual who provides early-stage or start-up business capital in the form of debt, ownership capital, or both.

Assets: balance sheet items in which a business invests in order to conduct business.

Balance sheet: summary or snapshot of all of a company's assets, liabilities, and equity as of a specific date.

Benchmarking: the process of identifying and learning about best business practices in a company, an industry, or the world.

Better Business Bureau (BBB): national organization dedicated to protecting consumers from unscrupulous business people.

Breakeven analysis: analysis that determines how much a company needs to sell in order to pay for the investment or the point at which a company's revenue will equal expenses.

Browser: software program that reads hypertext markup language (HTML) and allows web users to find and view information anywhere on the Internet.

Budgeting: process of developing financial plans that project inflows and outflows for a future specific time period.

Business incubator: facility that provides help for new businesses by providing a package of services, often affiliated with a college or university.

Business plan: detailed summary of a business including objectives and projects over a three- to five year period.

Business structure: legally recognized organizational framework for conducting business including but not limited to, a sole proprietorship, general or limited partnership, limited liability company, or corporation.

Capital: represents the investment in the company or business.

Cash flow statement: details the reasons for changes in cash during the accounting period.

Collateral: property that is promised by a borrower as security for a loan.

GLOSSARY

CI or competitive intelligence: also known as market intelligence and business intelligence, refers to the information a company is able to accumulate on another company gathered from public sources and effective interviewing skills.

Corporation: legal entity owned by stockholders that is authorized by law to act as a single person.

DBA or doing business as: fictitious business name or any name used to do business other than the owner's own name.

Demographics: population measures like age, race, income, gender, and occupation.

Domain name: name given to a specific computer and address on the Internet; the most common ones include .org, .com, .net, .gov at the end of the name.

Dot-coms: businesses that operate primarily or completely on the Internet.

Early stage: stage in business development in which a firm is usually expanding and already producing and delivering products or services but is less than five years old.

E-business: all the internal processes of a company or organization that become digitally based functions.

E-commerce: a company or organization that conducts business transactions via the Internet.

E-government: government initiatives to provide information and services electronically over the Internet through email and websites.

Economic indicators: statistical measures associated with business cycles.

EIN: Federal Employer Tax Identification Number, obtained from the IRS.

Employee: hired by a business to perform work under the control, direction, and supervision of the employer.

Entrepreneur: creative individual willing to risk investing time and money in a business activity that has the potential to make a profit or incur a loss.

Equity: value of a piece of property after deducting liens.

ERISA (Employee Retirement Income Security Act): imposes requirements on covered employers to manage employee pension funds for the benefit of their workers.

ESOP (Employee Stock Ownership Plan): a tax-qualified benefit plan designed to invest primarily in company stock.

Executive summary: part of a business plan that compellingly explains the opportunity, shows why it is timely, describes how the company plans to pursue it, outlines the entrepreneur's expectation of results, and includes a short sketch of the business.

Exit strategies: methods used by businesses to discontinue businesses, products, or relationships with customers or suppliers.

Ezine: electronic or email magazine.

226

FACNET: Federal Acquisition Computer Network; enables procurement process to be completed electronically from solicitation through award and payment.

FICA (Federal Insurance Contributions Act): which requires employers to withhold Social Security and Medicare taxes from employees' wages.

Fictitious business name (or doing business as [DBA]): any business name used for doing business other than the owner's own name.

Financial ratios: the result of dividing one financial statement item by another. Ratios help interpret financial statements by focusing on specific relationships and allow comparisons between companies and within the industry.

Financial statement: record of financial data needed to plan the future of your business.

Forecasting: analysis of past and current situations in order to anticipate the future.

Franchise: an agreement by which a person permits the distribution of goods or services under his trademark, service mark, or trade name, during which time the franchiser retains control over others or renders significant assistance to others (from the FTC rules).

Home equity loan: loan secured by an interest in the borrower's home, which creates a mortgage against the home.

Home page: default URL or beginning page of a website.

HR (Human Resources): a collection of related activities pertaining to the management of personnel within a company.

Hypertext: generic term describing any media format, such as graphics, sound, text, links to other documents, not limited to the Internet but used extensively there.

Income Statement or Profit and Loss Statement: compares revenues and expenses to illustrate how well a business is performing.

Independent contractor: hired to perform a specific task or project and paid on a per project basis.

Industry: group of businesses that produce a similar product or provide a similar service.

IPO (Initial Public Offering): the stock of a closely held corporation, proprietorship, or partnership is offered for sale to the public for the first time in hopes of raising cash for expansion and growth. Also known as "going public."

Internet: complex matrix of globally connected computer networks.

IRS (Internal Revenue Service): the national tax collection agency for the U.S. government, under the auspices of the Treasury Department.

Job description: describes functions of a job for your particular business, needed to hire and evaluate employees.

Limited liability company (LLC): business structure that allows business owner to limit personal liability without all the paperwork, expense, etc. of forming a corporation.

Line of credit: unsecured loan that allows you to use what you need and is replenished whenever you pay back into it.

Link: connection made between two websites.

Management: responsible for the accomplishment of the mission of an organization, using planning, organizing, leading, and controlling behaviors.

Market research: the development, interpretation, and communication of decision-oriented information for business owners or managers.

Market share: percentage of market sales a company controls.

Marketing: a plan or strategy designed to let current and potential customers know what you have to sell and why they should buy it from your business.

Mergers and acquisitions: joining together of two or more businesses.

Micro-loan: a small loan available to novice entrepreneurs with poor credit to enable them to start a small business.

NAICS: North American Industry Classification System developed by the United States, Canada, and Mexico to categorize businesses by the type of goods and services they provide in their principal activity using a six-digit coding system.

Networking: the art of making connections with other business people to help you generate new business, find working capital and new employees, and keep an eye on your competitors.

Partnership: two or more persons associated for the purpose of conducting business, with each contributing money, property, skill, or labor and with all expecting to share in profits or losses.

Patent: protective rights given to inventors by the federal government.

Performance review: structured, formal interview between a supervisor and employee in which the employee's work is evaluated and discussed, held at least annually.

Positioning: a company uses its marketing strategy to create and maintain a unique image in the minds of consumers.

Press release: news about your business, products, or services sent to reporters or editors as source of material for news articles.

Profit and Loss Statement: see Income Statement.

Publicity: technique aimed at raising public awareness of your business, product, or service.

Public relations (PR): process of influencing your image in the media.

Record keeping: organizing and tracking information that helps you understand how and if your business is growing.

Retirement plan: provides income to an employee after retiring or results in a deferral of income by employees during their employment.

Return on investment (ROI): the simple ratio of net profits to total assets.

RFP (request for proposal): asks for offers from suppliers for products or services needed by an organization.

Revolving credit: set amount of credit from a financial institution.

Search engine: database of website addresses and page contents that you can use to search for information on a particular topic.

Seed money: the amount of capital you need to get your business up and running.

Sexual harassment: form of employment discrimination in the workplace; this form of sex discrimination violates Title VII of the Civil Rights Act of 1964, which applies to employers with 15 or more employees, including federal, state, and local governments and includes any behavior that affects an individual's employment or work performance or that creates an intimidating, hostile, or offensive work environment.

Software: program that a computer runs to control the functioning of the hardware and direct its operations.

Sole proprietorship: individual engaged in a trade or business without any protection against legal liability.

Start-up: a new business of any size but usually small.

Statistics: the classification, tabulation, and study of numerical data.

SWOT (Strengths, Weaknesses, Opportunities, and Threats) analysis: a marketing/management tool used to evaluate a company's competitive position.

Target market: group of buyers toward whom a business or company directs its marketing efforts.

Temporary workers: hired through another company, which is responsible for making payroll deductions, hiring, firing, and paying, and generally not considered your employees.

Time management: controlling the use of one's most valuable asset, time.

Trade associations: industry group used for networking and valuable business contacts.

Trade publication: carries articles and advertising targeted at the specific needs of businesses in a certain industry.

Trademark: a name, symbol, or other device identifying a product, officially registered and legally restricted to the use of the owner or manufacturer.

GLOSSARY

Uniform Offering Circular (UFOC): disclosure document containing required information supplied by the franchiser to the franchisee.

URL (Universal Resource Locator): the identifier of a web page or file on the Internet.

Valuation: entire perceived worth of a company's assets.

Venture capital: money invested in your business by professional investors, often with the expectation of high risk and high return.

INDEX

INDEX

marketing and advertising, 122
  raising capital, 99
Powerhouse Marketing Plans (Johnson), 115
Practice What You Preach (Maister), 153
Pratt's Guide to Private Equity Sources, 95
Pratt, Stanley E., 95
Prepared Foods Magazine, 34
Prescott, John E., 197
price/earnings (P/E) ratio, 205
Prichinello, Michael, 115
pricing, marketing and, 102
print resources, 5-7
probability, 17-18
probationary employment, 149
Procurement Classification Codes, 178
Procurement Technical Assistance Center
  (PTAC), 179
Product and Trade-Name Franchise, 72
product liability insurance, 44
Profitability and Operating Ratios, 16
projections, 18-19
promotion, 103, 108-109
PRO-Net online system, 178
proposals, writing, 181-183
Proposal Writer website, 186
Proquest database, 34
Proven Strategies in Competitive Intelligence
  (Prescott and Miller), 197
PTAC (Procurement Technical Assistance
  Center), 179
publications. *See* trade publications
public relations, 107-108
publishers, commercial, 15-17
purchasing agents, 181, 183
purchasing power, franchises, 71
Purple Cow (Godin), 113-114

raising capital. *See* financing
Raising Entrepreneurial Capital (Vinturella),
  96-97
Rasberry, Salli, 117-118
Raskin, Oliver, 114
Ratner, Charles L., 211, 214
Rea, Kathryn P., 47
Real Business Plans and Marketing Tools
  (McKinney), 61, 64, 78, 116-117, 215
The Real World Entrepreneur Field Guide (Bangs
  and Pinson), 203, 212
ReferenceUSA database, 162
"Registering your Business Name" (Laurence),
  39
regulations. *See* legal considerations
Reiss, Bob, 6, 95-96
Request for Proposal (Porter-Roth and Young),
  182, 184
Request for Proposals (RFPs), 181-183

researching
  businesses, 16-17, 19-26, 29-30
  industries, 16-17, 19-26, 29-30, 32-34
  markets, 16-17, 19-26, 29-30, 57, 101, 102-106
  SWOT analysis, 193-195
Retail Industry Benchmarks, 16
retirement, 86, 204, 210-211
revolving credit, 88
RFPs (Request for Proposals), 181-183
RMA Annual Statement Studies, 15, 21
RMA Universe, 15, 25
Robb, Russell, 215
Robert Morris and Associates, 15, 21
Robinson, Robert J., 90, 96
Rodrick, Scott S., 215-216
Rogak, Lisa, 2-3, 6, 48-49, 65
Rosenberg, Eva, 170
Rosen, Corey, 215-216
Rothbert, Helen, 197-198
Rouse, Kenneth R., 211, 214
royalty fees, franchises, 71
Rule, Roger, 65, 78
Rule's Book of Business Plans for Startups, 65

salaries, 148
Sales and Marketing Management magazine, 106,
  118
sales per foot, 16
sales target (marketing plan), 106
sales tax, collecting, 163
sampling, 17-18
Sampson, John E., 216
Sant, Tom, 184
Savvy Savings Guide for Home and Business
  (Carter), 166-167
SBA. *See* Small Business Administration
The SBA Loan Book (Green), 93
SBA Loans (O'Hara), 95, 117
SBDC (Small Business Development Center),
  178, 179, 186
SBDCNET
  business plans, 55, 68
  management, 142
  researching resources, 25
  starting up, 30
SBICs (Small Business Investment Companies),
  89
sbtv.com, 127
Scarborough, Norman M., 139
Schedule C (Form 1040), 163
Schedule K-1 (Form 1065), 164
Schedule SE (Form 1040), 163-164
Schell, Jim, 50
Schenck, Barbara, 118
Schollander, Wendell, 209-210, 216
Schollander, Wes, 209-210, 216

INDEX

INDEX

ABOUT THE AUTHOR

SUSAN C. AWE is an Associate Professor and Director of Parish Memorial Library, University of New Mexico, Albuquerque. A frequent contributor to such professional publications as *Library Journal* and *Booklist/Reference Books Bulletin*, and regular reviewer for *American Reference Books Annual*; she also edited the *ARBA Guide to Subject Encyclopedias and Dictionaries*, 2nd ed. (Libraries Unlimited, 1997); contributed the "Business and Careers" chapter to *Reference Sources for Small and Medium-sized Libraries* (1999); and the "Current Events" chapter to *Topical Reference Books* (1991).